# The Boys' Life Book of Outdoor Skills

Lyons Press is an imprint of Globe Pequot Press.

Library of Congress Cataloging-in-Publication Data is available on file.

ISBN 978-0-7627-8014-3

Printed in China

10 9 8 7 6 5 4 3 2 1

Staff Credits:

Text: J. D. Owen
Executive Editor: Jennifer Barr
Studio Manager: Stephen Cary
Cover design: Emily Clarke and James Pople
Production: Maria Petalidou

With special thanks to the staff of *Boys' Life*,
including Adryn Shackleford and Lenore Bonno

# The Boys' Life Book of Outdoor Skills

The essential practical
guide for all Boy Scouts

LYONS PRESS
Guilford, Connecticut
*An imprint of Globe Pequot Press*

# CONTENTS

# INTRODUCTION

Scouting is about adventures—exploring the great outdoors through hiking, camping, backpacking, paddling, fishing, skiing, and an almost endless list of other possibilities. *Boys' Life* brings these adventures to life, showing readers the excitement of following a mountain trail, floating down a river, or wandering along the seashore. Through award-winning writing and photography, the magazine displays all the opportunities Scouting has to offer.

To enjoy these adventures to the fullest, Scouts must possess a comprehensive set of skills. In addition to being physical fit, they must know how to tie knots and lashings, administer first aid, use a map and compass, identify plants and animals, swim and paddle a canoe, plan and pack for trips, pitch a tent, build a fire and use a backpacking stove, shop for food and cook it, use a pocketknife and woods tools, and understand and practice the principles of Leave No Trace (walking lightly on the land).

Scouts must be prepared for many challenges and adventures, and *Boys' Life* fills its pages every month with tips and articles on how to learn and hone the skills they need to benefit from the Scouting program. This book is a sampling of the variety of stories that the magazine has published since 1911, giving Scouts pointers, reminders, and examples of the basic skills they have to know, whether going on an overnight camp or an extended trek in the backcountry.

Almost as important as the knowledge a Scout possesses is the equipment that he takes when on an outing or other activity. *Boys' Life* offers advice on what to buy, how to use it, how to take care of it, and how to pack it. Many Scouts get satisfaction from making their own stuff. This compendium includes instructions for simple projects like spinning lures and camp beds, as well as for essential items such as a life buoy, a charcoal grill and boiler, and a solar oven, and even tells you how to make more ambitious objects like an air rifle range, a ski rocket, a motor scooter, and even a house.

With knowledge and skill comes confidence, and Scouts test their outdoor prowess by rolling out their sleeping bags in all climates—snowy forests, mountains, deserts, marshes, and beaches. These wide-ranging campouts are covered in the pages of *Boys' Life,* along with tips on how to prevent and treat conditions like hypothermia and heat exhaustion. The magazine provides advice on how to survive—and thrive—in extreme conditions.

Scouting skills are truly put to the test when a Scout comes to the aid of people in trouble. "A True Story of Scouts in Action" illustrates the heroic deeds of Scouts who, sometimes at the risk of their own lives, assist others in peril. The Scouts depicted in the stories have been awarded medals by the Boy Scouts of America for bravery or for the use of Scout skills.

Outdoor skills are essential in Scouting. Watching the sun rise on a mountain peak or the moon glisten on drifts of snow, canoeing through the surf as it rolls toward the beach, walking with pack horses as they kick up dust on the trail, cooking a fresh-caught fish over an open fire—these are experiences that Scouting—and the pages of *Boys' Life*—have been providing for more than a century.

# BOYS' LIFE
# EQUIPMENT

When Scouts go to the outdoors, they must take the right equipment to ensure an enjoyable and safe experience—cooking gear, shelter, map and compass, first aid kit, etc. And, of course, they must know how to use the equipment properly. As the *Official Handbook for Boys*, published in 1911, stated: "One of the chief characteristics of a Scout is to be able to live in the open, know how to put up tents, build huts, throw up a lean-to for shelter, or make a dugout in the ground, how to build a fire, how to procure and cook food, how to bind logs together so as to construct bridges and rafts, and how to find his way by night as well as by day in a strange country."

These skills are still the hallmark of a Scout (though hut building obviously is no longer emphasized). To support these competencies, *Boys' Life* publishes pieces demonstrating how to select, use, care for, and even make the equipment Scouts will need to have successful outdoor adventures. Most of these articles pertain to camping—cooking with aluminum foil, taking care of a pocketknife, selecting the right backpack, and so on. But occasionally the magazine tosses in a fun project that a boy can make, such as a motor scooter or ski rocket, even a house. The magazine reviews and rates gear but also advises Scouts to make or improvise their own if necessary.

Being a Scout means being prepared for any contingency. The magazine covers how to set up an emergency communications system and how to pack emergency equipment. Pesky insects shouldn't bother you while camping—the magazine illustrates setting up a mosquito bar—and "How to make a camp bed" demonstrates that camping doesn't have to be uncomfortable.

For more than a century, the Boy Scouts of America has been a leader in teaching responsible stewardship of the land. The Conservation merit badge was one of the original badges introduced in 1910. As Scouts pushed further into the backcountry in the decades that followed, they realized their potential impact on wilderness areas and increased their efforts to protect trails and campgrounds. In 1948, the BSA introduced the Outdoor Code: "As an American, I will do my best to be clean in my outdoor manners, be careful with fire, be considerate in the outdoors and be conservation-minded."And in the 1990s, the BSA joined with federal land-management agencies in espousing the principles of Leave No Trace:

(1) Plan ahead and prepare.
(2) Travel and camp on durable surfaces.
(3) Dispose of waste properly.
(4) Leave what you find.
(5) Minimize campfire impacts.
(6) Respect wildlife.
(7) Be considerate of other visitors.

As the consciousness of demands on the land evolves, *Boys'Life* carries the message to its readers. Pioneering projects, such as making a rope bridge, are now usually done in a camp setting that provides the poles (rather than chopping off tree limbs) and rope. Projects are disassembled after completion for the next group to use. However, the point of going outdoors is to have fun and practice skills, and what better way to do that than to catch a fish on a homemade lure or to bake a cobbler in a homemade solar oven. Readers of *Boys' Life* learn how to do both.

# EMERGENCY COMMUNICATIONS

IN AN EMERGENCY, COMMUNICATION IS IMPORTANT AND COMMUNICATIONS PREPAREDNESS SHOULD BE A PART OF YOUR "FAMILY ALERT" PLAN.

IF ELECTRIC POWER IS OUT—A CRYSTAL SET MAY BE THE ONLY WAY TO KEEP IN TOUCH WITH LATEST NEWS, DISASTER REPORTS AND EMERGENCY INSTRUCTIONS BECAUSE IT NEEDS NO BATTERIES OR ELECTRICITY.

THE SIMPLEST RADIO—THE CRYSTAL SET IS COMPOSED OF FEW PARTS AND CAN BE WIRED IN MANY WAYS. THE SET SHOWN ON THIS PAGE WAS MADE FROM:

1. A MAILING TUBE (SHELLACKED) 2½" IN DIAMETER BY 7" LONG, WRAPPED WITH #22 ENAMELED WIRE FOR THE TUNING COIL.

2. A STRIP OF COPPER OR BRASS AS THE TUNING SLIDER.

3. A PIECE OF ½ INCH COPPER TUBING TO HOLD THE GALENA CRYSTAL DETECTOR.

4. A BENT SAFETY PIN AND RUBBER ERASER...OR A PIECE OF COILED WIRE AS A CATWHISKER DETECTOR.

OR IN PLACE OF THE GALENA CRYSTAL...USE A GERMANIUM DIODE AS A DETECTOR. BUT THIS ISN'T AS MUCH FUN BECAUSE ONE OF THE THRILLS OF BUILDING A CRYSTAL SET IS FINDING A SENSITIVE SPOT ON THE CRYSTAL THAT WILL BRING IN A RADIO SIGNAL.

5. A .01 MFD. (MICROFARAD) CONDENSER (OR CAPACITOR WHICH MEANS THE SAME).

6. 6 NUTS AND 9 SCREWS TO HOLD CONNECTING WIRES AND PARTS IN PLACE ON THE 6" BY 8" PINE MOUNTING BOARD.

7. BRASS OR COPPER CLIPS TO HOLD EXTRA SETS OF EARPHONES.

8. AN EARPHONE (ONE FOR EACH LISTENER)...CAN BE FROM A TRANSISTOR RADIO IN SOME CASES.

9. AN ANTENNA—USE A 100-FT. PIECE OF BELL CORD WIRE OR USE YOUR TV ANTENNA. IF YOU USE AN OUTDOOR ANTENNA, BE SURE TO ATTACH INSULATORS AT EACH END AND A LIGHTNING ARRESTOR BETWEEN ANTENNA AND SET. MOUNT ANTENNA AS HIGH AS POSSIBLE AND AVOID CONTACT WITH ANY OTHER WIRES.

10. A GROUND—USE A WATER PIPE.

THE ONLY VARIATION IN THIS SET IS IN USING A GERMANIUM DIODE IN PLACE OF THE GALENA CRYSTAL. WHEN SOLDERING WIRES TO A GERMANIUM DIODE, DON'T HEAT TOO LONG OR YOU'LL DAMAGE THE DIODE. HOLD WIRES WITH LONG-NOSED PLIERS WHICH WILL DRAW OFF HEAT.

DON'T GIVE UP IF THE SET DOESN'T WORK AT FIRST—CHECK YOUR DIAGRAM, ANTENNA, GROUND AND CONNECTIONS. USUALLY THE SET'S O.K., BUT IT'S EASY TO MAKE A SMALL MISTAKE.

---

# How To Make Rope Bridges

## Instructions Which Scouts in Camps or on Hikes Will Find Most Helpful

IN the Indies, the natives make bridges with three ropes tied across stream. Scouts might well adopt the idea.

One of the ropes, after having been well tested for strength and quality, plays the part of the road and the two others are hand rails at right and left. These will dance a bit, but you can pass over just the same without difficulty.

If you desire to establish a bridge which will serve for several days, it is worth while to consolidate the system by lacing the ropes together with another, making a triangular structure. We give a series of diagrams which explain the manner of procedure. The weight is divided along the three main ropes and the little bridge, besides being more secure, can hold up a much greater weight.

The description seems rather complicated, but it is really easy to carry out.

First string up your three ropes, the most solid at the bottom. A and B show the manner of knotting the lower rope E. and F show how to place the two upper ropes. Of course, one Scout must have in some way crossed the stream to make the ropes firm there.

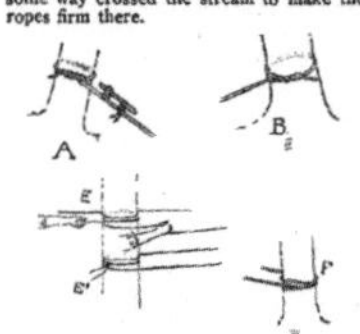

A Scout now stands on the bridge, and going forward, pushes the knots a b along with his hands on the upper rope, and with his feet pushes the lower ones. These loops, put in place, will take the formation shown in D. When he arrives at the other end of the bridge the Scout Master makes fast the ends of the ropes with which the lacework was made.

The Eclaireur de France for January shows a scheme something like this, in which two ropes are enough. The drawing explains this system clearly.

It is necessary to use ropes of the very highest quality, and to prove them carefully before starting to build the bridge.—Le Scout.

then repeat, passing the rope under 3 each time.

All these knots on ropes 1 and 2 are bunched up together and the loops under cord 3 should hang freely for two yards or so, in order to permit spreading them out later.

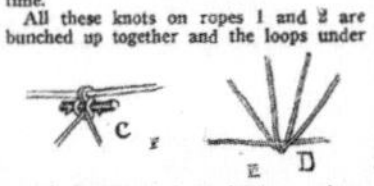

As we have made this first series of loops,

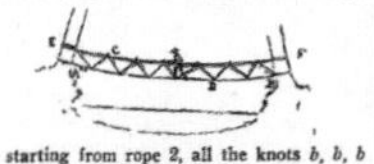

starting from rope 2, all the knots b, b, b are between the knots a, a, a.

## How To Make A Raft

### Fifth Requirement for Camper's Merit Badge

### By DILLON WALLACE

(Instructions on the other requirements for this Merit badge were given by Mr. Wallace in the July Boys' Life.)

We are required to know how to make a raft. The Scout's necessity to use a raft usually occurs in cross-country traveling when he possesses no other tools than his axe or hatchet and his knife. He must therefore know how to make a serviceable raft without the assistance of saws, augers or nails.

The size of the raft will depend in each case upon the amount of load it will be called upon to carry, therefore it will be necessary for us here to go into dimensions and measurements. We are simply required to construct a staunch raft.

The logs which are to be used must be as nearly alike in size as possible. Of course, they will all be cut the same length, but they must also be of nearly similar diameter at the butt, and also of nearly the same diameter at the smaller end.

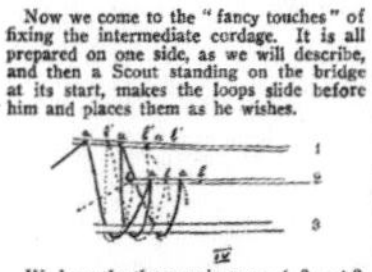

We have the three main ropes, 1, 2 and 3, stretched. Take a few rope, the end of which is fixed at the knot of the lower rope 3. Carry it up to rope 1 and make a knot as indicated in diagram C, then pass the rope under 3 and bring up to rope 2, where another knot of the same sort is made, and

On one side of each log, and fifteen or eighteen inches from each end, cut a notch.

Now in order to make crosspieces cut four stiff poles a foot or so longer than the width of the proposed raft. Roll the logs into the water and arrange them side by side, butts all one way, and notched side up. Fit one of the cross poles into the notches at one end of the logs, pass another of the poles under the logs opposite the pole resting in the notches, and lash securely the end of the two poles together where they protrude at each side of the raft. Fit the two remaining poles in place and lash them in the same manner at the other end of the raft. It will be seen that the notches must be an equal distance apart on each log, else the second set of poles cannot be fitted into place.

This raft will hold and serve very well on smooth water, but if the water to be navigated is at all rough, it might sag and go to pieces unless braced by diagonal poles. These poles should be lashed firmly to the side log at each end, with the ends of the poles fitting snugly against the crosspieces. One of the braces will of course have to be sprung down over the other at the intersection in the middle, unless very thick poles are used which may be notched at the point of intersection without weakening them too much. Where the braces cross each other they should be lashed firmly together with a line which also passes under and around one of the logs of the raft. Still greater stability may be given the raft by notching the logs for the under as well as the upper crosspieces.

## Are You Sure Now?

During last summer, for instance, I found it necessary when in the Labrador wilderness to put into practice all of these tests except two—building a latrine and building a fire without matches. Any scout who is a Scout will always have matches with him when he goes into the woods, though it is, nevertheless, a mighty good stunt to know how to make a fire without them. Last summer I even found it necessary to build a raft, after my canoe was wrecked, to transport my outfit across a wide river.

## Biggest Man-Made Waterfall

THE world's record for the height to which water has been elevated by a single pump was broken recently when fire underwriters and the New York Fire Department made a test of the standpipes and protective apparatus of the Woolworth Building in New York City. Water was forced up fifty-seven stories to the roof of the tower and expelled from pipes, 780 feet from the street. The former record was 767 feet, says the Technical World.

The building is 791 feet high, from the lowest point of its ground floor to the point of its tower. A pump in the basement, capable of exerting a pressure of 385 pounds, was started, forcing 800 gallons every minute up the nearly 800 feet of pipe.

On the fifty-seventh floor a 26-pound stream of water was shot from a ¾-inch nozzle to the four points of the compass. On the fifty-fourth floor some more pipes were at work on the outside of the building, and 12- and 15-pound streams were shot from similar nozzles down to the thirtieth floor. This made the liveliest kind of a water-fall, 1,000 gallons of water a minute flowing into the street.

The regular city supply of water was used for the test. With the ordinary pressure for hydrant and general household use, this does not go much above the fourth or sixth floor. The pumping engines, three floors below the surface of the street, were in good working order and registered the capacity mark.

---

# Make Your Own Spinning Lures!

### by DON RAY

BASS, TROUT, PIKE, PICKEREL, PERCH AND SEVERAL KINDS OF SALT WATER FISH ARE CAUGHT REGULARLY ON PLUGS, SPOONS, SPINNERS, POPPERS AND BUGS CAST WITH SPINNING TACKLE. YOU CAN MAKE THESE LURES YOURSELF FROM RAW MATERIALS OR FROM ASSEMBLY KITS AVAILABLE IN MOST SPORTING GOODS STORES. IT'S FUN TO MAKE YOUR OWN LURES—SAVES YOU MONEY— AND YOU GET MORE SATISFACTION OUT OF FOOLING FISH WITH HOMEMADE LURES.

PIKE — TROUT — PERCH — LARGE MOUTH BASS

**SURFACE PLUGS** FOR BASS, PIKE, SNOOK OR SMALL TARPON CAN BE MADE FROM BROOM HANDLES, DOWEL STICKS OR THIN SQUARE BLOCKS. SHAPE WITH KNIFE, SANDPAPER, PAINT WITH GOOD ENAMEL, AND ATTACH HARDWARE.

**POPPING BUGS** FOR BASS ARE CARVED SO THAT THE HEAD IS CONCAVE AND SLANTS UPWARD FROM THE WATER. AS THIS LURE FLOATS, YOU TWITCH YOUR ROD SHARPLY TO MAKE IT "POP."

**UNDERWATER PLUGS** FOR THESE GAME FISH ARE SIMILAR TO SURFACE PLUGS EXCEPT THAT THEY ARE WEIGHTED SO THEY SINK SLOWLY. EXPERIMENT WITH DIFFERENT DEGREES OF "WEIGHT" UNTIL YOUR LURE SINKS TO ABOUT TEN FEET IN TEN SECONDS.

**SPOONS** FOR CASTING OR TROLLING FOR TROUT, PIKE OR PICKEREL MAY BE MADE FROM DIME STORE STAINLESS STEEL TABLESPOONS, SOUP SPOONS OR TEASPOONS. SPLIT RING AND TREBLE HOOK COME FROM KIT OR MAY BE BOUGHT SEPARATELY AT TACKLE SHOPS.

**HAIR BUGS, FROGS, MICE** TAKE CONSIDERABLE SKILL, BUT OFTEN ARE VERY EFFECTIVE LURES FOR BASS OR TROUT. LOOK AT A GOOD FLY TYING BOOK IN YOUR LIBRARY OR CONSULT AN EXPERIENCED FISHERMAN FOR COMPLETE DETAILS ON HOW TO DO IT. TRY MAKING THIS SPINNING LURE MOUSE...

**SPINNER** FOR PANFISH OR TROUT AND **SPOON** FOR TROUT, BASS OR PIKE, ARE EXAMPLES OF ASSEMBLY-KIT LURES. BUY THE KIT AND ASSEMBLE THE LURES FROM PRE-FAB PARTS.

---

### Scout Program:
### KNOW KNOTS

# EMERGENCY ESCAPE

### BY DICK PRYCE
### PHOTOGRAPHS BY GENE DANIELS

On location photos shot at Crow Wing Scout Reservation, the Gamehaven Council's summer camp near Nevis, Minn.

Start prussick by passing ends of rope (top left) through bight. Repeat process (top right). Finished prussick (above and right) slides easily but holds under pressure (below and opposite page).

Imagine you're standing in a creekbed flanked by 50-foot walls. Because of heavy rain, a flash flood is roaring down the canyon. Your only way out is to climb a rope that drops straight down from a big overhanging rock at the top of the cliff.

Could you escape? Sure you could—if you had the strength and experience to climb straight up on a rope for 50 feet.

But if you had two 1/4-inch lines about five feet long, you could escape with prussick knots.

The prussick—it's a hitch, really—may be slid up and down a climbing rope by hand. And yet when pressure is applied, it will not slip.

Using prussicks with step-in loops tied in the free end of the line, you can climb straight up a rope or a pole. All you do is alternately move one prussick up, step in the loop, move the second prussick up, step in the loop, and so on.

Rock climbers use prussicks frequently when they want to remove weight from waist loops. So do rappelers, for anyone who dangles for 20 minutes from a waist loop will probably suffocate.

Learning to tie and use prussicks may save your life some day. And if anyone ever offers you $1000 to paint a flagpole, you'll be ready to do the job. ✦

# EMERGENCY COMMUNICATIONS

IN AN EMERGENCY, COMMUNICATION IS IMPORTANT AND COMMUNICATIONS PREPAREDNESS SHOULD BE A PART OF YOUR "FAMILY ALERT" PLAN.

IF ELECTRIC POWER IS OUT—A **CRYSTAL SET** MAY BE THE **ONLY** WAY TO KEEP IN TOUCH WITH LATEST NEWS, DISASTER REPORTS AND EMERGENCY INSTRUCTIONS BECAUSE IT NEEDS NO BATTERIES OR ELECTRICITY.

THE SIMPLEST RADIO—THE **CRYSTAL SET** IS COMPOSED OF FEW PARTS AND CAN BE WIRED IN MANY WAYS. THE SET SHOWN ON THIS PAGE WAS MADE FROM:

SCREW TO BASE
TO ANTENNA
TO GROUND
TUNING COIL
TO CONDENSER
TUNING SLIDER
SAFETY PIN AND ERASER
CONDENSER
SCREW TO BASE
Ⓐ-Ⓑ HEADPHONE JACKS (NOTE ADDITIONAL HOLE FOR SECOND HEADPHONE)
HEADPHONE
PIVOTS HERE
GALENA CRYSTAL

① A MAILING TUBE (SHELLACKED) 2½" IN DIAMETER BY 7" LONG, WRAPPED WITH #22 ENAMELED WIRE FOR THE **TUNING COIL.**

② A STRIP OF COPPER OR BRASS AS THE **TUNING SLIDER.**

③ A PIECE OF ½ INCH COPPER TUBING TO HOLD THE **GALENA CRYSTAL DETECTOR.**

GALENA CRYSTAL DETECTOR
METAL SCREW TO HOLD CRYSTAL TIGHTLY IN TUBE
CUT COPPER TUBE BEND UP— DRILL SCREW HOLES

ERASER
CUT OFF SAFETY PIN HEAD
DRILL HOLE FOR SCREW
GERMANIUM DIODE

④ A BENT SAFETY PIN AND RUBBER ERASER...OR A PIECE OF COILED WIRE AS A **CATWHISKER DETECTOR.**

OR IN PLACE OF THE GALENA CRYSTAL...USE A **GERMANIUM DIODE** AS A DETECTOR. BUT THIS ISN'T AS MUCH FUN BECAUSE ONE OF THE THRILLS OF BUILDING A CRYSTAL SET IS FINDING A SENSITIVE SPOT ON THE CRYSTAL THAT WILL BRING IN A RADIO SIGNAL.

TUNER SLIDER
GALENA CRYSTAL
CONDENSER
COILED WIRE CATWHISKER
PHONE JACK

THE ONLY VARIATION IN THIS SET IS IN USING A GERMANIUM DIODE IN PLACE OF THE GALENA CRYSTAL. WHEN SOLDERING WIRES TO A GERMANIUM DIODE DON'T HEAT TOO LONG OR YOU'LL DAMAGE THE DIODE. HOLD WIRES WITH LONG-NOSED PLIERS WHICH WILL DRAW OFF HEAT.

⑤ A **.01 MFD.** (MICROFARAD) **CONDENSER** (OR **CAPACITOR** WHICH MEANS THE SAME).

⑥ 8 NUTS AND 9 SCREWS TO HOLD CONNECTING WIRES AND PARTS IN PLACE ON THE 6" BY 8" PINE **MOUNTING BOARD.**

⑦ BRASS OR COPPER CLIPS TO HOLD EXTRA SETS OF EARPHONES.

⑧ AN **EARPHONE** (ONE FOR EACH LISTENER)...CAN BE FROM A TRANSISTOR RADIO IN SOME CASES.

⑨ AN **ANTENNA**—USE A 100-FT. PIECE OF BELL CORD WIRE OR USE YOUR TV ANTENNA. IF YOU USE AN OUTDOOR ANTENNA, BE SURE TO ATTACH INSULATORS AT EACH END AND A LIGHTNING ARRESTOR BETWEEN ANTENNA AND SET. MOUNT ANTENNA AS HIGH AS POSSIBLE AND AVOID CONTACT WITH ANY OTHER WIRES.

⑩ A **GROUND**—USE A WATER PIPE.

TUNER SLIDER
CONDENSER
GERMANIUM DIODE
PHONE JACK

DON'T GIVE UP IF THE SET DOESN'T WORK AT FIRST. CHECK YOUR DIAGRAM, ANTENNA, GROUND AND CONNECTIONS. USUALLY THE SET'S O K, BUT IT'S EASY TO MAKE A SMALL MISTAKE.

64532

SCOUT PROGRAM

# SCOUT KNIFE KNOWHOW

**BY NORMAN STRUNG**

A Scout knife is like a piece of rope or a wheel; simple in appearance but complex in the many jobs it can do. As a survival tool it can save your life. It can whittle a simple block of wood into an artistic sculpture, and repair tools and machinery. When you add these to the dozens of cutting jobs it does during a day, a Scout knife becomes more than pocket stuff. It becomes a valuable friend.

Like any friend, it deserves your care. Its weakest point is where the blade joins the handle. This is called the "bolster"—a metal hinge that functions as a pivot, holding the blades tightly, in place. Bolsters will not withstand severe pressure from the side. Never use a Scout knife like a crowbar—the blades will loosen and the knife eventually will come apart.

Throwing the knife is another sure way to ruin a good friendship. The constant, jarring impact loosens rivets, and weakens the bolster. (Besides, pocketknives make terrible throwing knives. They are not properly balanced).

Your knife will last longer if you keep it clean. The bolsters and interior of the handle are bound to pick up dust, gunk, and dirt. Once a month, clean these insides by immersing the knife in hot, soapy water. If the dirt won't float away, scrub the inside with an old toothbrush. When the knife is clean, rinse it in hot water, and let it dry with all the blades open. Before you pocket it, squeeze one drop of oil on each bolster. Clean and properly oiled, all blades should pop open and close with a solid-sounding snap.

If you live in a humid climate, or use the knife for fishing or hunting, protect the blades with a light coating of oil or silicone spray to deter rust. The salt in sea water and blood rusts steel in a matter of hours.

In order for your knife to function properly, it must be sharp. It's also safer that way; a dull knife will slip. Getting a knife blade truly sharp—

*Other than the corundum (dark) and novaculite (light) sharpening stones, you should have most knife-care items at home: oil, soap, brush, water, leather.*

*The most practical way to clean the inside of your pocket knife is with an old toothbrush, and hot, soapy water. Then rinse with hot water and let dry open.*

*Sharpening is a two-step process. Use two pennies braced against the back of the blade as a guide for the proper angle during both the beveling and polishing.*

*Stropping is the last step. Move the blade away from the cutting edge on a leather belt or barber's strop. This step gives the knife blade a final polish, and restropping will keep it sharp for weeks.*

sharp enough to shave with—is a two-step process.

*Beveling* is first. Select a coarse-grit sharpening stone like corundum, and lay the blade flat. Raise the blade's back the height of two pennies, and move the blade *into* the stone. At the end of the stroke, flip the blade over, raise the knife to the same height, and bring it back.

After a while, you'll get the feel of the right height. Even the dullest knife should bevel out after 25 strokes to a side. Rinse the stone with water when a powdery residue builds up. A good way to make sure you have created a bevel is to run your thumb—carefully—across the blade. It should feel sharp. Next, *lightly* draw the edge across your thumbnail. You should feel a definite drag.

*Polishing* is the second step. It is accomplished by honing the blade against successively finer grits. Maintaining the same bevel angle, move the blade into a fine-grit stone like the Arkansas white (novaculite) for about 15 strokes to a side.

Your local Scout distributor has a double grit (No. 1314) or single grit (No. 1326) sharpening stone.

Next, strop the blade on leather. A leather belt or razor strop is best; a leather boot or knife sheath also will work. Pull the blade *away* from the edge, the way a barber strops a razor. About 15 strokes to a side should polish the blade until it's sharp enough to shave the wetted hair on your arm.

As you use the knife, the edge gradually will dull. This will happen to any knife; they don't stay sharp forever. To re-sharpen the knife, all you need do is strop it on leather at first. Eventually, though, you'll have to touch up the edge on the Arkansas white stone, and strop it. When the Arkansas stone no longer produces a shaving edge, it's time to re-bevel the blade and go through the entire polishing process. Even with heavy use, however, you shouldn't have to re-bevel your master blade more than once a month. ❖

**Kurt Weisbrod, designer and builder of motor scooter, bowls happily along a country road.**

# MOTOR SCOOTER

## You will get as much pleasure out of building this lively little vehicle as in riding it

### By HI SIBLEY

HERE IS A MOTOR scooter which can easily be built by the average sixteen-year-old. That is the age at which one is eligible for a driver's license in most states. If your state has a higher age minimum, you will just have to wait, for *you are not permitted on the roads without a license.* A power scooter is considered subject to the same state vehicle regulations as any other motor vehicle. The operator is allowed on highways, and it is assumed he will prefer the more quiet side streets. Most freeways do not permit motor scooters to operate on them.

The machine must have a brake, headlight and tail light. In some states, a rear-view mirror is also required. To earn a license, a "tag along" system is sometimes used, in which the motor scooter follows a test car of the motor vehicle department around a prescribed course.

This model was designed and built by Kurt Weisbrod of Riverside, California. The first step is to build the frame of one-inch thin-wall electrical conduit. The bending is done with a hand bending tool and the joints are welded by an auto mechanic. The boiler-plate floor piece is also cut to shape and welded to the frame by him.

You can obtain the dimensions of all parts by counting the one-inch squares in the plan and profile shown in Figure 1. It also gives

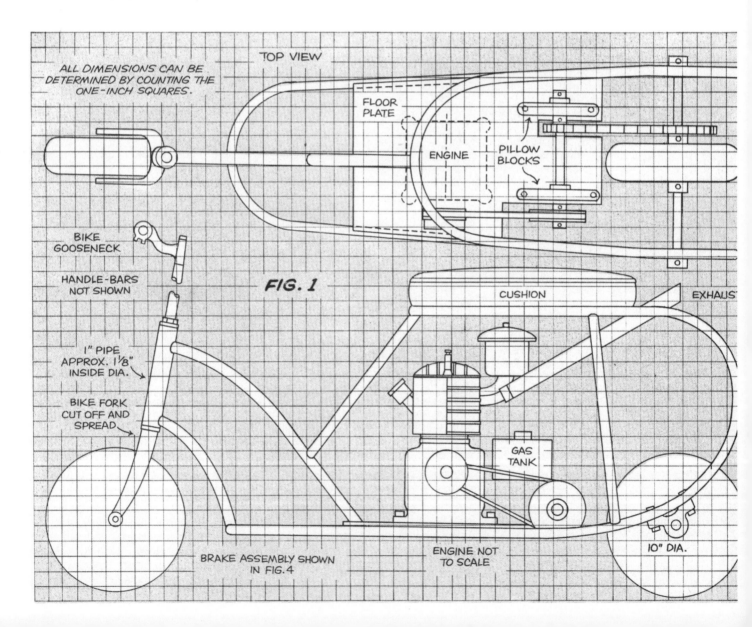

ALL DIMENSIONS CAN BE DETERMINED BY COUNTING THE ONE-INCH SQUARES.

TOP VIEW

FLOOR PLATE

ENGINE

PILLOW BLOCKS

BIKE GOOSENECK

HANDLE-BARS NOT SHOWN

FIG. 1

CUSHION

EXHAUST

1" PIPE APPROX. 1⅛" INSIDE DIA.

BIKE FORK CUT OFF AND SPREAD

GAS TANK

BRAKE ASSEMBLY SHOWN IN FIG. 4

ENGINE NOT TO SCALE

10" DIA.

the relative locations of the crankshaft, jack-shaft, and rear axle.

More detailed assembly plans are illustrated in Figure 2, which gives locations of bearings, or pillow blocks. These are stock items, which are available at some hardware stores, or at machine supply dealers. Bolt them into place as indicated. The bicycle fork has been shortened and widened to accommodate the 2½-inch tires of the wheels (obtained from Sears-Roebuck).

For the drive plan, study Figure 3. The small jackshaft sprocket is locked on the shaft with a set screw; the axle sprocket, from a bicycle, is welded to the hub of the wheel. They turn on a fixed axle. Both pulleys on the jackshaft are secured with set screws, as are the collars on each end of the axle. A centrifugal clutch from a power mower simplifies operation. On this engine, Kurt Weisbrod uses a rope starter, but it could be adapted to a kick starter.

Operating on the jackshaft, the brake is more powerful than it would be on the axle because of greater r.p.m. ratio. The foot pedal gives strong leverage and draws the V-belt snugly around the pulley. A tension spring keeps the belt loose when not in use and a stop-pin (cotter) prevents it from becoming

Three views of the motor scooter to show its trim design and compact driving unit assembly. Note (lower right) how foot brake is applied.

too slack. See Figure 4 (below) for details.

On this scooter, the engine is a 1½ H.P. Briggs-Stratton, but any other engine is acceptable if it fits in the available space. Current for the lights is provided by a small generator running by friction on the rear wheel. The generator is clamped to the upright just above the rear wheel.

Smooth any roughness on the welded edges with a file, before painting your frame to suit your taste.

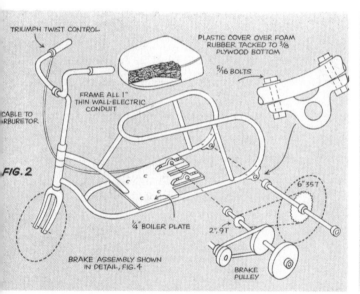

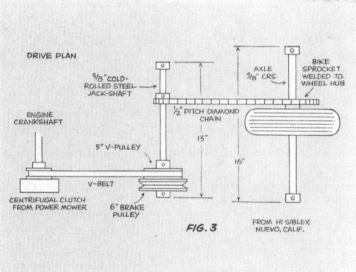

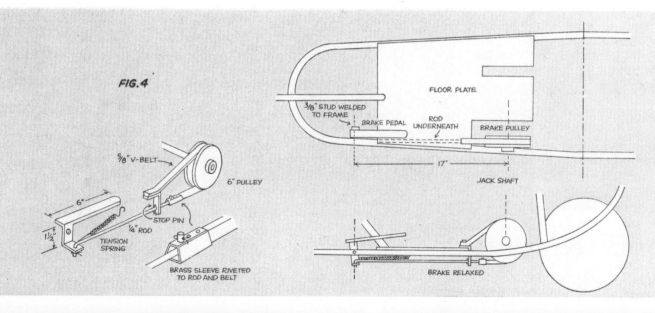

# How To Make Rope Bridges

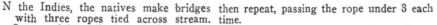

## Instructions Which Scouts In Camps or on Hikes Will Find Most Helpful

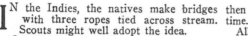

IN the Indies, the natives make bridges with three ropes tied across stream. Scouts might well adopt the idea.

One of the ropes, after having been well tested for strength and quality, plays the part of the road and the two others are hand rails at right and left. These will dance a bit, but you can pass over just the same without difficulty.

If you desire to establish a bridge which will serve for several days, it is worth while to consolidate the system by lacing the ropes together with another, making a triangular structure. We give a series of diagrams which explain the manner of procedure. The weight is divided along the three main ropes and the little bridge, besides being more secure, can hold up a much greater weight.

The description seems rather complicated, but it is really easy to carry out.

First string up your three ropes, the most solid at the bottom. A and B show the manner of knotting the lower rope E. E and F show how to place the two upper ropes. Of course, one Scout must have in some way crossed the stream to make the ropes firm there.

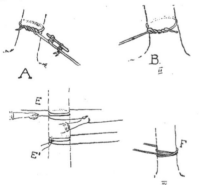

Now we come to the "fancy touches" of fixing the intermediate cordage. It is all prepared on one side, as we will describe, and then a Scout standing on the bridge at its start, makes the loops slide before him and places them as he wishes.

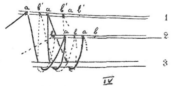

We have the three main ropes, 1, 2 and 3, stretched. Take a new rope, the end of which is fixed at the knot of the lower rope 3. Carry it up to rope 1 and make a knot as indicated in diagram C, then pass the rope under 3 and bring up to rope 2, where another knot of the same sort is made, and

then repeat, passing the rope under 3 each time.

All these knots on ropes 1 and 2 are bunched up together and the loops under

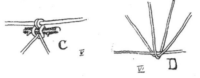

cord 3 should hang freely for two yards or so, in order to permit spreading them out later.

As we have made this first series of loops,

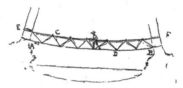

starting from rope 2, all the knots *b, b, b* are between the knots *a, a, a*.

A Scout now stands on the bridge, and going forward, pushes the knots *a b* along with his hands on the upper rope, and with his feet pushes the lower ones. These loops, put in place, will take the formation shown in D. When he arrives at the other end of the bridge the Scout Master makes fast the ends of the ropes with which the lacework was made.

The *Eclaireur de France* for January shows a scheme something like this, in which two ropes are enough. The drawing explains this system clearly.

It is necessary to use ropes of the very highest quality, and to prove them carefully before starting to build the bridge.—*Le Scout.*

## How To Make A Raft

### Fifth Requirement for Camper's Merit Badge

### By DILLON WALLACE

*(Instructions on the other requirements for this Merit badge were given by Mr. Wallace in the July* BOYS' LIFE.*)*

We are required to know how to make a raft. The Scout's necessity to use a raft usually occurs in cross-country traveling when he possesses no other tools than his axe or hatchet and his knife. He must therefore know how to make a serviceable raft without the assistance of saws, augers or nails.

The size of the raft will depend in each case upon the amount of load it will be called upon to carry, therefore it will not be necessary for us here to go into dimensions and measurements. We are simply required to construct a staunch raft.

The logs which are to be used must be as nearly alike in size as possible. Of course, they will all be cut the same length, but they must also be of nearly similar diameter at the butt, and also of nearly the same diameter at the smaller end.

On one side of each log, and fifteen or eighteen inches from each end, cut a notch.

Now in order to make crosspieces cut four stiff poles a foot or so longer than the width of the proposed raft. Roll the logs into the water and arrange them side by side, butts all one way, and notched side up. Fit one of the cross poles into the notches at one end of the logs, pass another of the poles under the logs opposite the pole resting in the notches, and lash securely the ends of the two poles together where they protrude at each side of the raft. Fit the two remaining poles into place and lash them in the same manner at the other end of the raft. It will be seen that the notches must be an equal distance apart on each log, else the second set of poles cannot be fitted into place.

This raft will hold and serve very well on smooth water, but if the water to be navigated is at all rough, it might sag and go to pieces unless braced by diagonal poles. These poles should be lashed firmly to the side log at each end, with the ends of the poles fitting snugly against the crosspieces. One of the braces will of course have to be sprung down over the other at the intersection in the middle, unless very thick poles are used which may be notched at the point of intersection without weakening them too much. Where the braces cross each other they should be lashed firmly together with a line which also passes under and around one of the logs of the raft. Still greater stability may be given the raft by notching the logs for the under as well as the upper crosspieces.

### ARE YOU SURE NOW?

During last summer, for instance, I found it necessary when in the Labrador wilderness to put into practice all of these tests except two—building a latrine and building a fire without matches. Any scout who is a Scout will always have matches with him when he goes into the woods, though it is, nevertheless, a mighty good stunt to know how to make a fire without them. Last summer I even found it necessary to build a raft, after my canoe was wrecked, to transport my outfit across a wide river.

## Biggest Man-Made Waterfall

THE world's record for the height to which water has been elevated by a single pump was broken recently when fire underwriters and the New York Fire Department made a test of the standpipes and protective apparatus of the Woolworth Building in New York City. Water was forced up fifty-seven stories to the roof of the tower and expelled from four pipes, 780 feet from the street. The former record was 767 feet, says the *Technical World.*

The building is 791 feet high, from the lowest point of its ground floor to the point of its tower. A pump in the basement, capable of exerting a pressure of 395 pounds, was started, forcing 500 gallons every minute up the nearly 800 feet of pipe.

On the fifty-seventh floor a 20-pound stream of water was shot from a ⅞-inch nozzle to the four points of the compass. On the fifty-fourth floor some more pipes were at work on the outside of the building, and 12- and 15-pound streams were shot from similar nozzles down to the thirtieth floor. This made the liveliest kind of a water-fall, 1,000 gallons of water a minute flowing into the street.

The regular city supply of water was used for the test. With the ordinary pressure for hydrant and general household use, this does not go much above the fourth or sixth floor. The pumping engines, three floors below the surface of the street, were in good working order and registered the capacity mark.

# MAKE A CORACLE!

When the ancient britons came to a stream too deep to ford they would make a coracle and, with their hands, paddle themselves across. They used brushwood made into a large wreath for the frame, then covered the whole thing with a hide.

Make your own coracle from twigs and branches, lashing them with binder twine and using a waterproof tarpaulin instead of a hide.

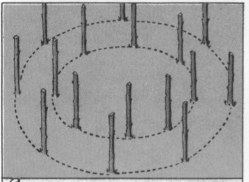

Cut sixteen two-foot stakes. Pound eight of them into the ground in a five-foot circle, the remaining eight in a six-foot circle.

Fill the space between the two circles of stakes with twigs and flexible branches about a foot high.

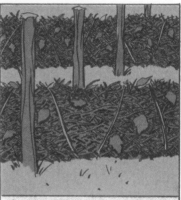

Lash this brush into a crude wreath with binder twine.

Pull up the stakes. Lash a spider-like web of rope around the wreath. Wrap the tarpaulin around the wreath...

Cross section view of tarpaulin wrapped around wreath.

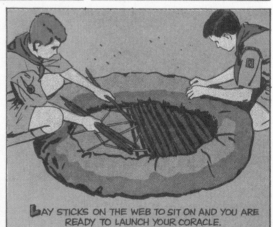

Lay sticks on the web to sit on and you are ready to launch your coracle.

Mandan indians made coracles of willow covered with buffalo hide. Pitch was used to make them watertight.

A coracle is tricky to paddle because of its circular shape. If you are alone, paddle evenly with both hands. Two fellows must strike an even rhythm to keep from turning in circles.

IMPORTANT: DO NOT PUT OUT IN A CORACLE YOU'VE MADE YOURSELF UNLESS YOU CAN SWIM WELL!

# Equipment for

BY GEORGE LAYCOCK

ILLUSTRATIONS BY ALLEN WELKIS

Saving up to buy a fine piece of outdoor equipment makes real sense. It is going to cost less in the long run than cheaper equipment, replaced several times. And, the longer you own a favorite rod, tent, or backpack, the more you come to appreciate the job it does for you. Each time you pick it up, it brings back pleasant memories. Here are some of the items that can last and last, providing you choose good ones in the beginning.

## Sleeping Bag

Your sleeping bag makes a fine camp bed, but remember that it does not *provide* heat. It only *holds in* your body heat, and some sleeping bags are better at this than others. Goose down is the best lightweight insulation for a sleeping bag. It is also the most costly. Whether you choose goose down or a synthetic filler depends partly on how you will go camping. If you expect to backpack where every ounce counts, you need a down-filled bag.

But down has disadvantages if it gets wet. Down is hard to dry, and while wet, it gives very little insulation. Synthetics give some insulation even when wet.

Pick a sleeping bag to match your size. A bag too small means a cramped, miserable night's sleep, and one too big will not keep you warm on cold nights. The zipper should be heavy-duty and should have a wind strip inside it to keep the breezes from blowing through.

## Tent

Match the choice of tent to the way you will camp. If you camp by automobile, weight is not much of a problem. But for backpacking or canoeing, where you may have to portage, you need a lightweight tent. Backpackers want tents that weigh no more than six or seven pounds for a two-person

# a Lifetime

shelter. The modern material for lightweight tents is nylon, the kind that "breathes," so moisture doesn't condense on the inside. Tubular aluminum frames are strong and lightweight. If you can, set up the tent before making your purchase, and see if it is easy to set up and take down. Check to see that it has heavy zippers, a stitched-in waterproof floor, and screened windows for cross ventilation. The material should be folded together and double-stitched at the seams. Remember, light colors reflect more sunlight and are cooler.

## Canoes

Canoes should last a lifetime. The most popular is a 17-footer with a standard stern. The choice of materials includes aluminum, plastic, fiberglass, wood, and wood and canvas. If you will canoe mostly on large, open waters, the regular keel can make paddling easier. But for white water, you want a shoe keel, or perhaps no keel at all. If you will run rough water, you want to consider a canoe with more ribs for greater strength. As with buying any kind of costly outdoor equipment, take time to study the choices. Talk with people who have used various kinds of canoes, then pick the one that promises to fit your kind of trips best.

## Backpacks

Your new backpack should be lightweight, strong, roomy, and adjustable. Today's lightweight materials let us choose a backpack with frame made either of tubular aluminum or tough, light plastics. Metal parts used in backpacks should be welded together, and the manufacturer should guarantee his welds. The backpack should be equipped with shoulder pads and a padded hip belt, and a ventilated back band that fits the load to the contours of your back.

Select a backpack with small outside pockets so you can reach cameras or lunch without unloading the pack. The pack should close tight enough to protect its contents from rain and dust.

## Camp Knife

Most of all, a good knife must have a blade of quality steel. One way to tell if the steel is high quality is to pick a well-known brand name. Some outdoorsmen carry only a pocketknife. But if you will be hunting and fishing, as well as camping, a belt knife carried in a good sheath may be a better choice. But remember, a big knife does not make a good outdoorsman. A smaller knife, with a blade 4½ or 5 inches long, will do all the jobs any of us is likely to ask of it. The handle should be just heavy enough to give the knife balance.

**When it comes to acquiring outdoor equipment, you'll find that buying the best pays off in the long run. Arm yourself with lots of facts, and be sure to choose gear that matches your own special outdoor needs. You'll be rewarded with years of solid service and a batch of warm memories.**

## Binoculars

A good pair of binoculars can help you with a lifetime of bird watching, football games, backpacking in the mountains, or all of the above. The most popular binoculars are either 7 x 35 or 8 x 40. The first figure tells the magnification. More powerful ones are harder to hold steady. It is a sound idea to invest in the best binoculars you can afford. The quality ones have fine lenses, and the lens elements are not so easily jarred out of line as in cheap ones. Check the literature packed with the binoculars to see that all lens surfaces are coated.

# Equipment for a Lifetime

**To assure peak performance from all of your outdoor gear, you'll need to keep it in top condition. That means treating it gently, keeping it clean and repaired, and checking it carefully after each use.**

### Fishing Tackle

There are enough rods and reels on the market to confuse you, but here are some basic guidelines to help you pick the good ones. First, consider the manufacturer, and choose a well-known name so you will know where to send it if it needs repairs. Pick a spinning or casting rod with ceramic guides. Single-piece rods give the best action. If you need a rod that breaks down into sections for travel, look at the ferrules that hold the sections together. These should be made of fiber, not metal, for the best rod action.

Reels, including the line pickup on spinning reels, should be quiet, smooth-running machines. The drag is best equipped with multiple, leather washers. Some better, close-face, spin-casting reels now have a ceramic ring lining the hole through which the line flows. Ask also if parts are readily available for the reel you choose.

Whatever your outdoor equipment, from canoes to pocketknife, it is going to last longer, and do a better job, if you give it proper care. Banging any kind of equipment around does nothing to improve it. Neither do dirt and excess moisture. Parts need to be kept secure and well-adjusted. This calls for a few minutes of care at the end of a trip, and an inspection before storing equipment at the end of the season. But good care has its rewards. Treat your outdoor equipment right, and it is going to last for years, maybe a lifetime. ♣

# A Mosquito Bar

## By GLENN WAGNER

WE certainly enjoyed camping out in the open last summer with our sleeping bags, but we found the mosquitoes liked it too—especially eating! So we decided to make a mosquito bar to cover our heads. We designed it with a box pleat in the front to give free space over our chests. Then we set it up in the attic to be sure everything fitted. The material used was 1⅔ yards of green mosquito netting—it comes 60" wide (actually 58") and 10 yards of ⅝" white awning braid. We have to admit we had some feminine help with the sewing.

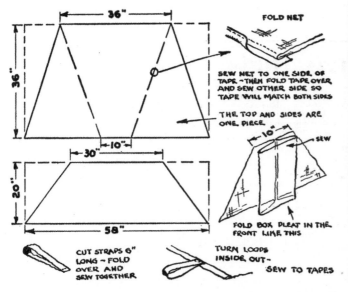

CAMP BEDS

FOR SLEEPING IN TENTS OR SHELTERS.

How much you enjoy your camping depends on how much you enjoy your night's sleep. For only a night or two, you can put up with almost anything, but for a longer period you had better pay as much attention to your bed as to your food.

Because cotton attracts moisture it is best to take loosely woven wool blankets for your bedding, even in the summer time. Hang them out to air every day. Don't just throw them on the ground, especially on green or wet grass.

For SOLID COMFORT dig a trench for hips and shoulders and lay your bedding over it. A 2" or 3" deep trench will suffice for hips.

In cold weather make your bed on the ground so no cold draft can get under you.

A SIMPLE MATTRESS can be made with a piece of canvas, ground cloth or a blanket folded over dry grass or leaves.

A BETTER ONE is a bag that can be filled with dry browse.

Roll your clothes in a neat bundle and chuck it in the mouth of the bag for a pillow.

ABOUT 6½ FT. BY 30 INCHES

Make beds about a foot longer than the occupant.

A LOG BED filled with soft dry browse and covered with a tarp or ground cloth, can be made for a more permanent camp.

Fluff up and rearrange the browse every day or perhaps add to it now and then.

Don't worry too much about your feet.

A COOL BED

Cut notch deep.

Sew with strong cord. 2" poles

A TEMPORARY WILLOW BED can easily be made of branches averaging ⅜ inches.

Fish line twisted around willows keeps them in place.

A waterproof ground cloth is a good thing to use at any time of the year.

Mattresses can be made of any light material such as muslin. You may want a hip trench even when using a mattress pad.

Be sure to have enough wool blankets. Two below and two to cover with in cold weather.

Don't forget blanket pins.

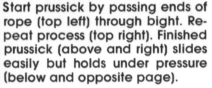

Start prussick by passing ends of rope (top left) through bight. Repeat process (top right). Finished prussick (above and right) slides easily but holds under pressure (below and opposite page).

# EMERGENCY ESCAPE

**BY DICK PRYCE**

PHOTOGRAPHS BY GENE DANIELS

On location photos shot at Crow Wing Scout Reservation, the Gamehaven Council's summer camp near Nevis, Minn.

Imagine you're standing in a creekbed flanked by 50-foot walls. Because of heavy rain, a flash flood is roaring down the canyon. Your only way out is to climb a rope that drops straight down from a big overhanging rock at the top of the cliff.

Could you escape? Sure you could—if you had the strength and experience to climb straight up on a rope for 50 feet.

But if you had two 1/4-inch lines about five feet long, you could escape with prussick knots.

The prussick—it's a hitch, really—may be slid up and down a climbing rope by hand. And yet when pressure is applied, it will not slip.

Using prussicks with step-in loops tied in the free end of the line, you can climb straight up a rope or a pole. All you do is alternately move one prussick up, step in the loop, move the second prussick up, step in the loop, and so on.

Rock climbers use prussicks frequently when they want to remove weight from waist loops. So do rappelers, for anyone who dangles for 20 minutes from a waist loop will probably suffocate.

Learning to tie and use prussicks may save your life some day. And if anyone ever offers you $1000 to paint a flagpole, you'll be ready to do the job. ♣

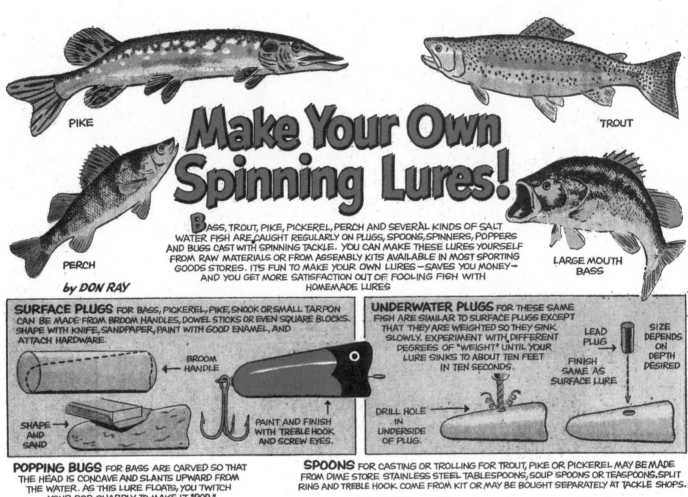

PIKE

TROUT

PERCH

LARGE MOUTH BASS

# Make Your Own Spinning Lures!

BASS, TROUT, PIKE, PICKEREL, PERCH AND SEVERAL KINDS OF SALT WATER FISH ARE CAUGHT REGULARLY ON PLUGS, SPOONS, SPINNERS, POPPERS AND BUGS CAST WITH SPINNING TACKLE. YOU CAN MAKE THESE LURES YOURSELF FROM RAW MATERIALS OR FROM ASSEMBLY KITS AVAILABLE IN MOST SPORTING GOODS STORES. IT'S FUN TO MAKE YOUR OWN LURES—SAVES YOU MONEY—AND YOU GET MORE SATISFACTION OUT OF FOOLING FISH WITH HOMEMADE LURES

by DON RAY

## SURFACE PLUGS
FOR BASS, PICKEREL, PIKE, SNOOK OR SMALL TARPON CAN BE MADE FROM BROOM HANDLES, DOWEL STICKS OR EVEN SQUARE BLOCKS. SHAPE WITH KNIFE, SANDPAPER, PAINT WITH GOOD ENAMEL, AND ATTACH HARDWARE.

BROOM HANDLE

SHAPE AND SAND

PAINT AND FINISH WITH TREBLE HOOK AND SCREW EYES.

## UNDERWATER PLUGS
FOR THESE SAME FISH ARE SIMILAR TO SURFACE PLUGS EXCEPT THAT THEY ARE WEIGHTED SO THEY SINK SLOWLY. EXPERIMENT WITH DIFFERENT DEGREES OF "WEIGHT" UNTIL YOUR LURE SINKS TO ABOUT TEN FEET IN TEN SECONDS.

LEAD PLUG

SIZE DEPENDS ON DEPTH DESIRED

FINISH SAME AS SURFACE LURE

DRILL HOLE IN UNDERSIDE OF PLUG.

## POPPING BUGS
FOR BASS ARE CARVED SO THAT THE HEAD IS CONCAVE AND SLANTS UPWARD FROM THE WATER. AS THIS LURE FLOATS, YOU TWITCH YOUR ROD SHARPLY TO MAKE IT "POP"

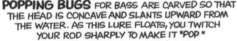

CORK OR BALSAM

CUT SLOT

INSERT HUMPBACK HOOK WOUND WITH TYING SILK— GLUE AND TAPE UNDER UNTIL DRY

HACKLE WOUND AROUND HOOK OVER TAIL FEATHERS

HACKLES TIED TO HOOK

SMALL WEIGHT

## SPOONS
FOR CASTING OR TROLLING FOR TROUT, PIKE OR PICKEREL MAY BE MADE FROM DIME STORE STAINLESS STEEL TABLESPOONS, SOUP SPOONS OR TEASPOONS. SPLIT RING AND TREBLE HOOK COME FROM KIT OR MAY BE BOUGHT SEPARATELY AT TACKLE SHOPS.

DRILL HOLES

CUT

FILE SMOOTH AND POLISH

SPLIT RING AND TREBLE HOOK

LEADER

SPLIT RING WITH SWIVEL

## SPINNER
FOR PANFISH OR TROUT AND **SPOON** FOR TROUT, BASS OR PIKE, ARE EXAMPLES OF ASSEMBLY-KIT LURES. BUY THE KIT AND ASSEMBLE THE LURES FROM PRE-FAB PARTS.

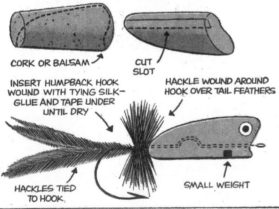

TREBLE HOOK

WIRE

BEAD

LEAD BODY WITH CORE

BEAD

SPINNER BLADE

BEAD

SWIVEL

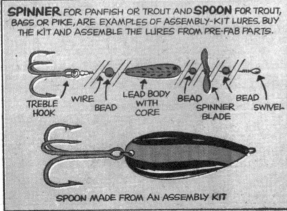

SPOON MADE FROM AN ASSEMBLY KIT

## HAIR BUGS, FROGS, MICE
TAKE CONSIDERABLE SKILL, BUT OFTEN ARE VERY EFFECTIVE LURES FOR BASS OR TROUT. LOOK AT A GOOD FLY TYING BOOK IN YOUR LIBRARY OR CONSULT AN EXPERIENCED FISHERMAN FOR COMPLETE DETAILS ON HOW TO DO IT. TRY MAKING THIS SPINNING LURE MOUSE...

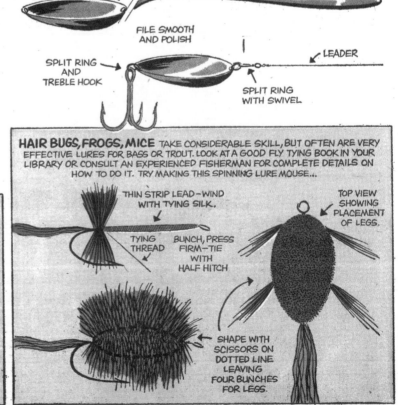

THIN STRIP LEAD—WIND WITH TYING SILK.

TYING THREAD

BUNCH, PRESS FIRM—TIE WITH HALF HITCH

TOP VIEW SHOWING PLACEMENT OF LEGS.

SHAPE WITH SCISSORS ON DOTTED LINE LEAVING FOUR BUNCHES FOR LEGS.

# How a Boy Built a House

*YOU KNOW, Fellow Scouts, that I have a deep-seated belief that the education of the fingers is the education of the brain. Also that the education of the fingers makes a fellow self-reliant. Just to show you how I am succeeding with some of the boys, I here give you a letter and diagrams made by one of them in Buffalo, N. Y., whom I only know through correspondence. I have never seen the lad but he will make a splendid Scout.*                                DAN BEARD.

### BY VICTOR AURES

I AM sending drawing and descriptions for making a house out of two piano boxes.

The top and back of both boxes are removed as shown in Fig. 1.

Next a doorway is cut in the boxes. This can easily be done by sawing out half of the doorway in each box as indicated by dotted lines in Fig. 1. A window can also be put in, in the same manner at the other end.

Before anything more is done to the house, a foundation must be made on which to build the house.

A simple foundation can be made by driving small boards into the ground, in the shape of a box, with cross pieces to keep them together. Large stones are next placed in the box until they form a pile even with the top of the box as shown in Fig. 2.

If a complete foundation is to be built as shown in Fig. 3, only four of these boxed foundations will be necessary; but if just the boxed stones are to be used, five of them will be needed—one at each corner and one in the center to hold up the flooring where the two boxes meet.

After this has been done the boxes are placed together upon the foundation, back to back.

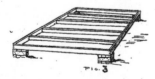

The two boxes should be held together by two boards at each end, being nailed from side to side one at the bottom and one just below the gables; at each end of the house BB Fig. 4.

A number of two-by-fours must now be procured to build the gable. Four or five rafters should be nailed from each side of the house, beginning at C Fig. 4, and terminating at the ridge.

After the rafters have been put up, the boarding may be nailed on. It will be

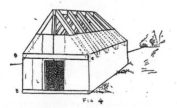

found that sufficient wood for this purpose will be on hand from the tops and backs taken from the boxes. The boarding for the roof will of course be the proper length if the tops and backs are used.

Fig. 5 shows how to cut the boarding at the front and back of the house.

Fig. 6 shows the house completed.

## From a Scout's Mother

TWO or three years ago there were a great many boys in our neighborhood. There were seven on our block, between the ages of ten and fourteen. It was considered a good neighborhood and the boys were as good as they generally are. But there was not much for amusement, so after school and on holidays they wandered around, sometimes as many as twelve or more in a group, looking for something to do.

Often they built "shacks" out of old boards and a hole in the ground; or in a near-by woodyard, where they would stow themselves away, and no one knew what was going on. It was quite certain that there was one who could teach them something they did not know of mischief or worse, so that the mothers were rather anxious about those meeting places.

Other times they just ran around through the yards and alleys, bothering people who had no boys, climbing telephone poles, etc. Whatever they did usually ended in a fight, so that people fairly dreaded the time for school to close.

These were not the bad boys of the city, but just the ordinary boys living in a good neighborhood.

Then came the Boy Scouts Movement, and what a change! All of the boys are good friends now; there is no more fighting, or very seldom any. They are all trying to live up to the Scout rules and doing "at least one good act a day," etc. There have been hikes into the country on Saturdays and holidays to look forward to. And what relief to the mothers to know their boys were out having such a good time, and in the care of some good man.

Besides all this they are learning so much that will help them as they grow up. In fact, it is a fine start to make them good men, for a good Scout is sure to become a good man.                         MRS. C. H. JACQUOT.

## For the Bats.

Bats eat mosquitoes. In Texas houses are built for these leather-winged creatures. Tin shields guard the foundation posts so that no rats may creep up, and the bats take kindly to the superior quarters given them, and they are doing a great deal to combat yellow fever and malaria.

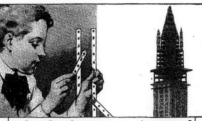

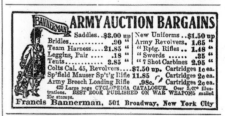

# Orange Crate Canoe

## By BEN HUNT

We say you'll need 30 orange crates because you won't be able to use all of each. Throw out all split and knotty slats and those that are noticeably thicker than the rest. Otherwise, such irregularities will show through the covering of the finished canoe.

The base plank is spliced for easy removal. If it isn't spliced you'll have to saw it in two to remove it. Be sure your base is rigid and does not sag in the middle. Slats should be laid one-eighth inch apart so when they become water soaked they'll spread rather than buckle. Start all planking at the center and work toward the ends. Do *not* remove the screws as you go along. Finish both sides (leaving out slats where the screws are), and let the glue set before you remove the screws and

place the last slats. Allow the ends to project over the gunnel until the canoe is taken off the base plank. Then insert the thwarts before you remove the forms. The slats are left until the ends have been built up, and should project about three inches. Sawing and trimming along the gunnel is done when the canoe is right side up.

Give the entire canoe a good coat of spar varnish and turpentine. A 50-50 mixture should do the trick. This will soak well into the slats.

For covering, use light canvas, drill or unbleached muslin. We used two 16 foot strips of drill sewed together along the keelson. This material is light weight and strong. You will note that drill has a right and a wrong side. Put the ribbed surface to the inside. The drill or other material will cover your entire canoe without a fold or wrinkle if tacked along the keel first, then carefully worked toward the ends, and finally held fast by one inch outwale strips. Any fold marks in the

cloth can be removed by sponging with water. The dope will do the rest.

We used six coats of clear airplane wing dope and two coats of colored dope for finishing. This dries very fast and is quite easy to apply. Use thinner with it for easy brushing. Follow instructions that your dealer will furnish with the dope. After the last coat has dried for about 24 hours, give the inside of the canoe a good coat of spar or marine varnish, getting it in *every* nook and corner. Give the keel and outwales two coats.

Now just a word more about the forms and base. Much of your success will depend on the rigidity of the form you build the canoe over. Any "give" in the form will result in a warped, unsymmetrical canoe. We also suggest you lay two duck boards on the bottom on each side of the keelson. These can be of one-half by four inch or five inch pine or one-quarter inch waterproof plywood. Be sure to use enough waterproof Weldwood glue and nails.

**1** Make full drawings of stems and forms. Saw out the stem segments and glue them together. Nail forms together and saw out the notches.

**2** Nail plank to rigid supports and carefully nail forms to it. Center and align them. Fasten keelson first, then stems, chines and gunnels.

**3** Now use clamps and rope to hold chines and the gunnels until they are screwed to the forms. Bead both the side strips at the same time.

**7** Now you're ready for the planking which is glued and nailed with three-quarter inch rosin coated nails. Use plenty of both nails and glue.

**8** Use only the good slats. Ends can be sawed off later. This does away with a lot of fitting. Be sure to saw off the slats flush with the chines.

**9** Notice how curve changes. First, nail along keel, and then along the chines. Press the slats to fit in place. No steaming is necessary.

**13** This method will prevent splitting of slats. Saw off excess at stem but allow slats to project about 3" beyond the gunnels at ends.

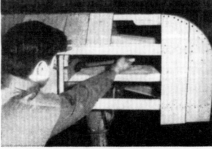

**14** Take out blocks which hold number three forms since you are now about to close up ends and may not be able to loosen them later.

**15** Finish planking. Loosen blocks, open splice and remove base plank. Lift canoe off. Put in thwarts, remove forms, work ends. See drawing.

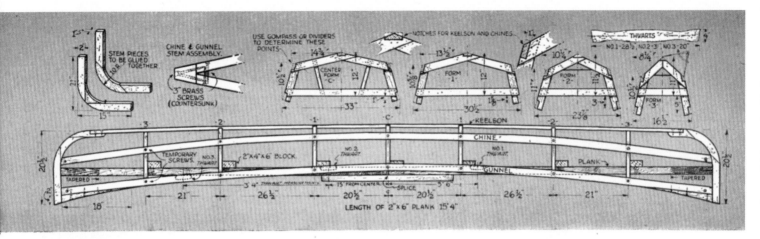

## List of Materials

About 30 orange crates.

3—1" x 2" x 16'—white pine for chines and keelson.
2—¾" x 2" x 16'—white pine for gunnels.
2—¾" x 1¼" x 16'—white pine for fenders on outwales.
1—1" x 1¼" x 14'—oak for keel.
1—1" x 4" x 8'—thwarts (pine).
1—2" x 6" x 16' plank to nail forms to, (forms and base plank are temporary).
¾"-pine for ends.
⅛" x 1" x 60" brass, aluminum or copper for ends.
1½ lbs. ¾", 17 gauge wire nails.
3 doz. 3" No. 12 F.H. brass screws.
7 doz. 1¾" No. 10 F.H. brass screws.
½ lb. ⅜" copper tacks.
2 lbs. Weldwood glue.
1½ gals. Aeroplane wing dope (clear).
½ gal. Thinner.
1 gal. Marine or Spar Varnish. 1 gal. Turpentine.
11 yds. of 30" drill, or 5½ yds. of 54" cover material.

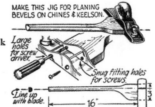

Here's a handy gimmick for you to use when you get ready to plane the chines and the keel.

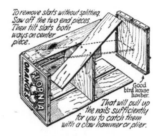

When you get ready to take apart your orange crates, do it this way (see cut).

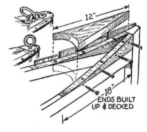

Build up the ends inside of the projecting planking and next nail the planking to it.

**4** Glue and fasten stems with brass screws. Cut the chines to fit inside of the stems and then screw them securely in place using 3" F.H. brass.

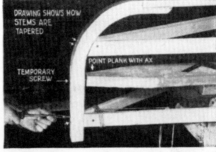

**5** The screws are used to fasten the chines and the gunnels together and against the stems. Be sure to use glue where two pieces are fastened.

**6** Next, you bevel and plane the keelson and chines. This step is an important one since it forms the flat surface for your slat planking.

**10** Plank only this far and then start on sides. Leave out front pieces where chines and the gunnels have been already screwed to the forms.

**11** Note pieces saved for screwed places not yet covered. When rest of the sides are planked, remove screws and then plank these gaps last.

**12** Now for the ends. The first two strips on each side go on as shown. Nail along gunnel first, then bend slowly by using a piece of wood.

**16** Now trim off all projecting ends along gunnels. Rough sandpaper inside and outside. Give entire canoe a coat of thinned spar varnish.

**17** Sew two 16' strips of 30" drill together. Stretch seam over keelson, tack every 1½". Start at center. Split at ends. Overlap at stems.

**18** Sew up surplus material over top. Be certain to leave it until after the dope has been applied. This will keep material stretched.

# Charcoal Grill and Broiler

**By GLENN A. WAGNER**

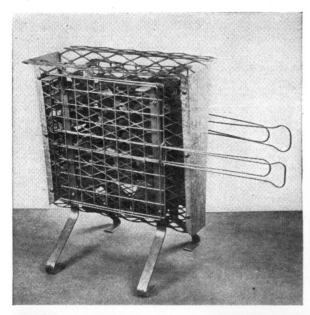

THERE'S nothing quite like steak broiled over a charcoal fire, or even hamburgers, for that matter. Here's a portable charcoal grill that not only will broil steak, but will cook your whole meal. Just hang one 10" wire toaster on each side, then put your pans on top.

The materials you'll need are 1 pc. 1" x 2" mesh expanded steel sheet 12" x 30" for the grill (we got a scrap piece at an iron and steel supply house); 2 pcs. 4½" x 12" galvanized or black iron for the ends; and 4 pcs. ⅛" x ⅞" x 20" band iron for the legs. You'll also need 20—³⁄₁₆" x ½" round head stove bolts and washers.

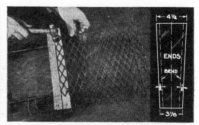

Bend edges of the sheet metal and the ends of the expanded metal over two inches as shown above. To do this, nail or clamp two wood slats together.

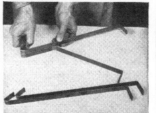

Make a paper pattern for the sheet metal ends and cut them. Next, scribe lines on each side for bending. Now bend the end edges as shown above.

Using a vise and hammer, bend legs to shape. Be sure they're all alike. Drill 3/16" bolt holes in the ends and legs to match diamonds in grill.

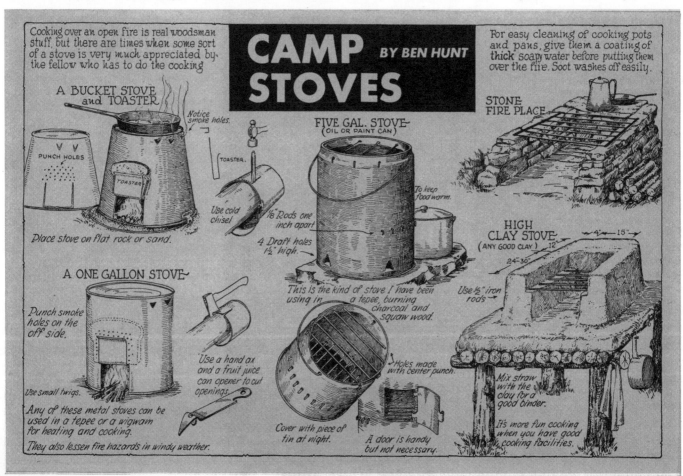

# CAMP STOVES
## BY BEN HUNT

Cooking over an open fire is real woodsman stuff, but there are times when some sort of a stove is very much appreciated by the fellow who has to do the cooking

For easy cleaning of cooking pots and pans, give them a coating of thick soapy water before putting them over the fire. Soot washes off easily.

A BUCKET STOVE and TOASTER
Notice smoke holes.
PUNCH HOLES
TOASTER
Place stove on flat rock or sand.
Toaster.
Use cold chisel
⅛" Rods one inch apart

FIVE GAL. STOVE
(OIL OR PAINT CAN)
To keep food warm.
4 Draft holes 1½" high.
This is the kind of stove I have been using in a tepee, burning charcoal and squaw wood.
Holes made with center punch.
Cover with piece of tin at night.
A door is handy but not necessary.

STONE FIRE PLACE

HIGH CLAY STOVE
(ANY GOOD CLAY)
Use ½" iron rods
Mix straw with the clay for a good binder.
It's more fun cooking when you have good cooking facilities.

A ONE GALLON STOVE
Punch smoke holes on the off side.
Use small twigs.
Use a hand ax and a fruit juice can opener to cut openings.
Any of these metal stoves can be used in a tepee or a wigwam for heating and cooking.
They also lessen fire hazards in windy weather.

# HOME RIFLE RANGE

By TED COLLINS

THE $CO_2$ PELLET-SHOOTING rifle has changed the whole concept of target shooting. Powered by a replaceable $CO_2$ gas cartridge, the rifle makes possible safe, powderless shooting indoors with soft lead pellets that flatten upon impact without danger of ricochet. No longer do you have to wait for warm weather or a suitable outdoor firing range to enjoy target practice. Now you can have year-'round shootin' fun right in your home. All you need to set up an indoor firing range is 15' to 25' of unobstructed floor space that can be protected against entry ahead of the firing line. Official shooting distance is 25' but you can vary this to suit your shooting pleasure. Set up your target against a blank wall with a plywood backstop behind it. Establish the firing line with a chalk line, a piece of colored Scotch tape, a row of chairs, or a table or bench. You can make your own target or rig up one of the commercial models available. The photos show you three types of targets and mounting suggestions so they may be interchanged. Target should be at eye level. For safety, block off all doorways between firing line and target with tables or suitable obstructions. **Keep everybody behind the shooter.**

Set up in a basement, an indoor range gives year-'round shootin' fun and keeps you in practice.

Available in sets, fun targets add to the thrill of group competition as well as fun in game shooting.

A simple and very effective backstop can be made with a cardboard carton filled with newspapers; set on box.

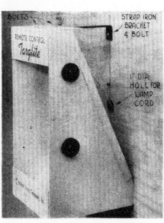

The ultimate in remote control targets—a sheet metal box bolted to the plywood backstop; note bracket.

Every time you hit the bulls-eye, this target rings out the good news. Paper insert is 25' official target.

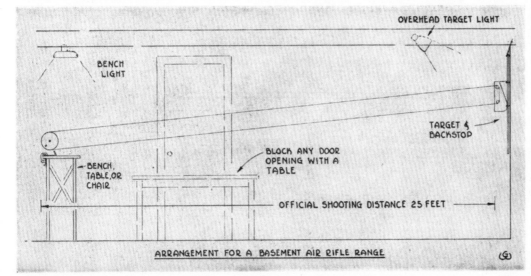

ARRANGEMENT FOR A BASEMENT AIR RIFLE RANGE

Hung by chains from above, a ½" x 3' x 4' sheet of plywood makes a good backstop. Move board with the chains to prevent wear in one spot.

ALL you have to do is strap them on and start walking. Snowshoeing is that easy providing you follow the rules and don't immediately tackle the more difficult maneuvers such as side-stepping, herringboning, the up hill notch climb and others which require more than a little skill.

A week or two of practice, however, should soon make you as able a snow footer as our American Indians who are the originators of snowshoes of many varieties. Wet or dry, crusted or loose—no matter what snow condition you have, the long narrow snow shoe called the standard Maine enables you to crunch your way easily across rugged terrain, up and down hills, in and out of wooded areas.

When you or your Troop plans a first snowshoe expedition you'll find that no matter how deep the snow is you will sink down only a few inches—with or without a pack—as you start out on that hike. When your day's tramping is halted and you're ready to sack in, make sure your snowshoes are away from the reach of field mice, rabbits and other rodents. They like to chew on the leather straps because of the salts used in the tanning process.

But let's go back to the beginning and find out a little more about the snowshoes themselves and how you can learn to use them correctly.

# Snow Feat

*. . . can become either two left feet or an invitation to danger if you don't know when to use proper techniques.*

## By EMIL BRODBECK

The normal stride taken in correct snowshoeing is here represented by the imprints in the snow. Notice that the chap's legs are eased only slightly farther apart than during regular walking. This is important, for if the novice or even the veteran straddles while snowshoeing, his first mile will end in near exhaustion. So take it easy at first.

The frames of each snowshoe nearly touch each other. With your weight on the right foot you now advance the left, raising it about an inch above the snow's surface.

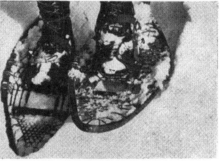

Here is the step at a midpoint position. Notice that the inside edge of the snowshoe nearly touches the boot of the right foot, three inches from the left.

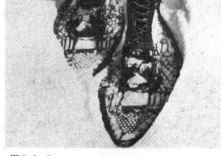

With the first step completed and your weight forward you are ready to check off miles and try your skill at climbing some of those hills and rocky areas ahead.

Here, the boy at the left is side stepping up hill while the chap on the right is herringboning down. The overlapping of snowshoes should be avoided.

Notice the soft boots which should be worn and how the toe is dug into the crusty surface for another climb step.

Right and left are two types of the Maine class snowshoe. Center is a bearpaw variety.

Shown here are the differences in angles of the Maine senior, junior and bearpaw varieties.

# Outdoors

## YOUR FRIEND THE POCKETKNIFE

### By Robert Birkby

**A well-cared-for pocketknife can last for decades. Here's how to keep yours in prime condition.**

A NEIGHBOR OF MINE was a Scout 50 years ago. In his pocket he still carries the knife he had as a boy. The Scout emblem was long ago worn smooth, and the metal casing is polished bright from decades of use. But the blades are sharp, the joints clean and oiled. He still uses the knife nearly every day.

A pocketknife is the most useful tool a Scout can own, a helpful friend for many occasions. For campers, the most useful models are those with one or two blades, a can opener, a bottle opener and an awl.

As my neighbor's knife proves, good pocketknives don't wear out. But they can die of neglect.

New Scout pocketknives are forged from hard steel alloys and have sides made of plastic. They're strong, and their blades aren't likely to rust. But normal use will dull cutting edges, and even a pocketknife that rarely leaves the pocket will get clogged with dust and lint. Regular care, cleaning and sharpening are a must.

*To clean your knife*: Open all the blades, handling the knife carefully so you won't cut your fingers. Twirl some cotton onto the end of a toothpick, moisten it with light oil and then swab out the inside of the knife. Take special care to clean the joints around which the blades rotate. After you've removed the grime, use a clean swab to wipe out excess oil.

*To sharpen cutting edges*: Moisten a whetstone with a few drops of oil. As you sharpen your knife, tiny bits of grit will float in the oil, honing the blade much the same way sandpaper smooths wood.

Hold the blade against the oiled stone at an angle of about 30 degrees. That means the back of the blade is tilted up off the whetstone about one-third of the way to vertical. Now you can start sharpening.

Move the blade in small circles, lightly pressing the cutting edge against the stone. Not all of the edge will touch the stone at once, so move the knife forward and backward as well as in circles until the entire edge has gotten equal grinding.

Turn the blade over and repeat for the other side. Wipe the blade with a clean cloth, then turn the edge toward the light. The edge of a dull blade is shiny, and nicks show clearly. A sharp edge is so thin that it's hard to see.

A knife's cutting blades and openers should be worked only up and down, *not* sideways. Only the awl and the screwdriver tip of the bottle opener are designed to be twisted.

If your knife has two blades, you may want to use one for heavy work, like cutting rope and opening cardboard cartons, and save the other blade for jobs needing an extra sharp edge, such as whittling.

About the worst thing that happens to pocketknives is that they get lost. They have a way of slipping out of pockets. Here's how to keep track of yours:

Attach it to one end of a three-foot length of cord. Tie the other end to a belt loop of your Scout pants. The cord is long enough so you can use the knife without untying it—a surefire way to keep it within arm's reach.

Keep track of your knife, keep it clean and sharp, and it could last 50 years or more. Just ask my neighbor. ♣

# Build a Solar Oven

## BY JESSE SLOME

Open the family car door on a sunny summer day and you feel a blast of escaping hot air. Heat from sunlight striking the car has been stored inside. Like an oven, isn't it?

With the same principle, you can build a solar oven using the sun's energy to prepare an entire dinner.

A solar oven, like a car or a greenhouse, allows light to enter easily through glass windows. Once inside, the sun's rays strike a dark surface and become heat. They cannot easily bounce back through the glass. Thick walls help to hold the heat inside.

Contruct two plywood boxes so that one fits inside the other leaving a 1½″ space between the two on all sides and bottoms (see diagram). The inner box (¼″ plywood) should be large enough (10″ x 18″) to hold one or two medium-sized baking dishes.

Cover the floor of the outer box (½″ plywood) and the space between the side walls of both boxes with fiberglass insulation material. Seal the opening between the two boxes with strips of plywood, in such a way that a sheet of window glass will fit snugly in place as a cover. Fill all cracks where hot air might escape. Paint the interior walls with a non-lead, flat, black paint.

If you use four shiny aluminum reflector panels, you will help direct heat into the oven. To increase the amount of heat produced and stored, use a double sheet of glass with an air space in between.

To check the temperature, attach a thermometer against one of the inside walls. Your oven should reach over 200° F. (93° C)—hot enough to cook a meat loaf or bake breads in several hours.

To cook, place your pots inside and set the oven where the most sunlight will strike the floor. If you raise one side slightly with a rock, be sure your foods don't spill. As the sun changes, rearrange your oven every so often to keep getting the most heat. When the food is cooked, cover the glass with the aluminum reflectors. Your dinner will stay warm until chow time.

For instructions for a more advanced solar oven which can reach 350° F., check your local library or bookstore for *Experiments with Solar Energy* (Grosset & Dunlap) by D. S. Halacy, Jr. ♣

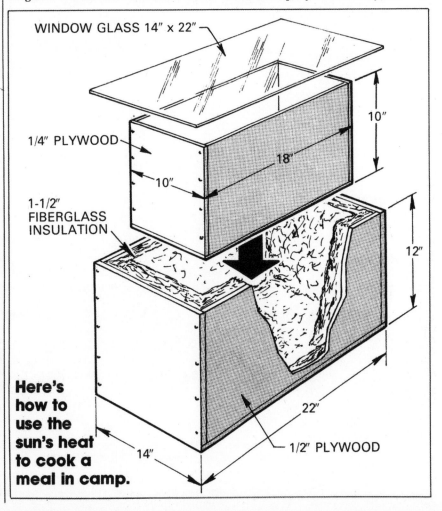

WINDOW GLASS 14″ x 22″

1/4″ PLYWOOD

1-1/2″ FIBERGLASS INSULATION

10″

18″

10″

12″

22″

14″

1/2″ PLYWOOD

**Here's how to use the sun's heat to cook a meal in camp.**

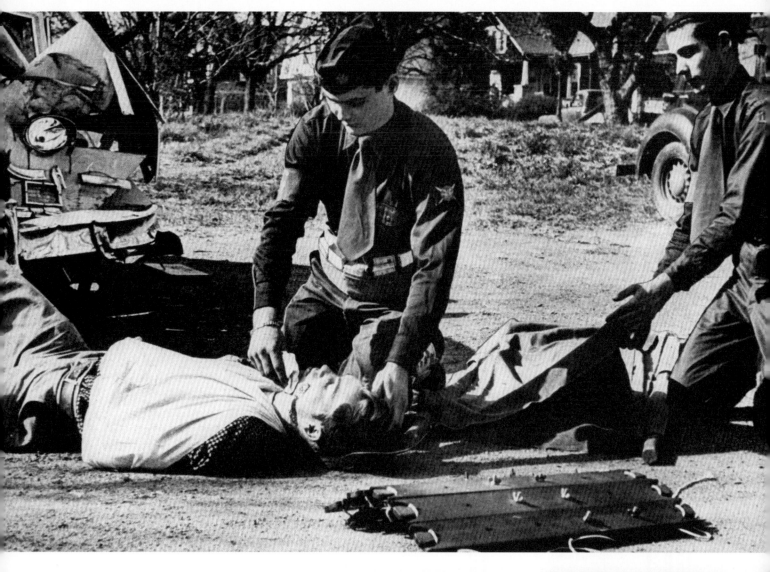

**Be Prepared**

**For Anything**

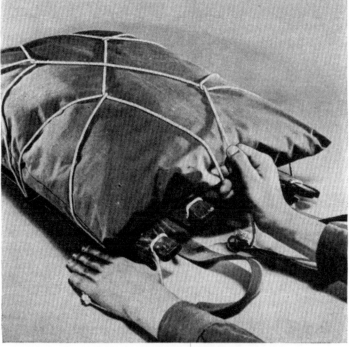

PACK FRAME EMERGENCY UNIT is assembled by first lashing splints to frame. Then fold up two blankets and place on stretcher canvas. Fold canvas over blankets to protect against rain, attach to frame with modified diamond hitch.

Make two STRETCHER POLES of 1¾" x 1¾" spruce 7' long. Plane corners octagonal. Round 6" off each end to form handle. Sand. Varnish.

FIRST AID BELT KIT. Use canvas, 16" x 28½". Hem edges. Sew ⅛" ridges parallel with long edge, 4", 5¾", 10½", 12¼" from front edge.

# Your Emergency Equipment

**By WILLIAM HILLCOURT**
**National Director of Scoutcraft**

EVERY SCOUT TROOP and Explorer Post in the country is going in for first aid—training for advancement, and, more important, *training for preparedness.*

But even the best-trained first aider will be stumped at times if he doesn't have the equipment he needs.

So here's Emergency Equipment in portable form, for the quick mobilization of your gang. It's designed for the use of a Patrol or a Crew, to be carried by two of the members. It consists of a stretcher for transportation, splints for fractures, blankets for shock treatment, first aid belt kit, canteen. The splints, blankets and stretcher cover are carried on a pack frame. You'll have little difficulty in making your own Emergency Equipment if you follow the photographs, the working drawings for the belt kit (below), and the instructions for the pack frame on page ooo.

The belt kit shown contains 4 triangular bandages (cut from two 40" squares of muslin) each with a couple of safety pins attached, 1 blunt scissors, 1 forceps, 4 flat paper cups, 1 oz. dropper bottle of antiseptic, and the following first aid kit units: 4"x6 yds. sterilized gauze bandage, 3"x3" gauze pads, 4" bandage compresses, 2" bandage compresses, 1" adhesive compresses, ammonia inhalants, iodine swabs, burn ointment tubes. If it proves difficult for you to get the regular kit units, make up your own collection of equivalent items before sewing the pockets of the belt kit. Then you can measure and make the pockets to fit size and shape of the items you have.

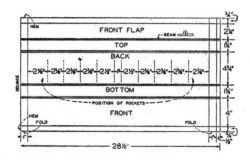

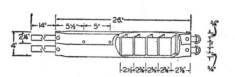

***Making this Emergency Equipment will prove an interesting handicraft activity for your Patrol or Crew.***

STRETCHER takes 3'x6'2" heavy duck. Hem ends. Sew 5" pockets along sides. Semi-circular opening has 4" radius.

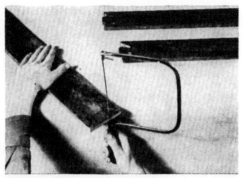

Make five SPLINTS from white pine, ½"x3", 26" long. Notch the two ends with double notches, 1¾" deep, for traction bandages. Plane edges. Varnish.

Drill ¼" holes 4½" apart for ¼" wing nut bolts, 1¼" long. Single splint makes ordinary rigid splint; two make traction splint for arm, three for leg.

Hem 4¼"x40¼" piece of canvas. Sew to back of kit to form pockets for first aid units and bandages. Fold kit flaps over.

Rivet two 1" web straps to one end of belt kit, closing end. To other end, rivet strap loops, each with two 1" rings. Add snap fasteners to flap and front.

Kit is designed to hold four triangular bandages and eight standard first aid units, small bottle of antiseptic, scissors, forceps, safety pins, paper cups.

# FOOD CACHES

By BEN HUNT

You'll not starve to death if something steals your grub while on an overnight hike, but it will certainly be a hungry hike back home. You'll probably say "Aw, what's going to swipe our grub around here?" Well, it may be a farmer's prowling dog, or a 'coon that you'd never expect so close to a city, or a porcupine, or a fox. Then there are mischievous squirrels and any number of field mice. They're all hungry all the time, and anything salty or greasy is fair prey to them. Have you ever had ants get at your food pack? They sure can mess up your grub. Play it safe and eat hearty.

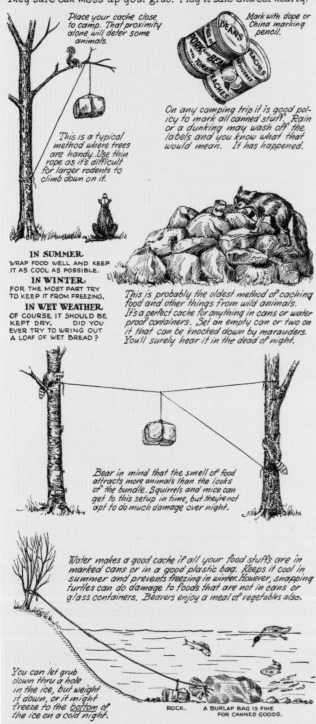

Place your cache close to camp. That proximity alone will deter some animals.

This is a typical method where trees are handy. Use thin rope as it's difficult for larger rodents to climb down on it.

Mark with dope or China marking pencil.

On any camping trip it is good policy to mark all canned stuff. Rain or a dunking may wash off the labels and you know what that would mean. It has happened.

**IN SUMMER** WRAP FOOD WELL AND KEEP IT AS COOL AS POSSIBLE.

**IN WINTER** FOR THE MOST PART TRY TO KEEP IT FROM FREEZING.

**IN WET WEATHER** OF COURSE IT SHOULD BE KEPT DRY. DID YOU EVER TRY TO WRING OUT A LOAF OF WET BREAD?

This is probably the oldest method of caching food and other things from wild animals. It's a perfect cache for anything in cans or water proof containers. Set an empty can or two on it that can be knocked down by marauders. You'll surely hear it in the dead of night.

Bear in mind that the smell of food attracts more animals than the looks of the bundle. Squirrels and mice can get to this setup in time, but they're not apt to do much damage over night.

Water makes a good cache if all your food stuffs are in marked cans or in a good plastic bag. Keeps it cool in summer and prevents freezing in winter. However, snapping turtles can do damage to foods that are not in cans or glass containers. Beavers enjoy a meal of vegetables also.

You can let grub down thru a hole in the ice, but weight it down, or it might freeze to the bottom of the ice on a cold night.

ROCK.      A BURLAP BAG IS FINE FOR CANNED GOODS.

---

## FIVE KEYS TO A
# CAMP SITE

By ERNEST F. SCHMIDT

**Director of Camping, Schiff Scout Reservation**

THE RIGHT CAMP SITE can spell the difference between comfort and misery on a camping trip. So it pays you to judge a site carefully before deciding to stop over for the night. Check out the site you are considering against the five keys to a good location.

You want an open, well-drained spot, which has all five of the qualities shown in the pictures below. Help anchor these qualities in your memory by remembering them as a handful of points—one for each finger.

Safety is one of the most important site signals. In addition to the points given under the pictures, make sure that the spot has not already been staked out by insects (check nearby for any swamp, stagnant water, or high grass). Look around for poison ivy. The area should be fireproof enough to prevent your campfire from spreading. And, for easy sanitation, make sure the site is one which can easily be kept clean.

**TERRAIN·** Open (not too much brush); elevated (for drainage); level (for comfort), not in low area such as valley (to avoid floods, cold winds).

**SAFETY:** Don't pitch camp directly under trees—danger from deadfalls, annoyance from dripping rain. For other safety checkpoints, see text.

**EXPOSURE:** Site should have eastern exposure for morning sun to dry and warm camp. Protection from prevailing winds is also important.

**FIREWOOD:** Is it fairly close by? For boiling, use quick-burning wood (pine, fir, spruce). For grilling, choose hickory, oak, birch, locust.

**WATER:** Is it near? Is it safe? If there is least doubt about safety, stir in charred wood, boil 5 minutes, aerate before drinking.

# HOW TO MAKE IT...

# A LIFE BUOY
## FROM A POTATO SACK AND AN INNER TUBE

GET A POTATO SACK...A 100-POUND ONE AND AN INNER TUBE...BE SURE THE INNER TUBE DOES NOT LEAK...TEST IT WELL, AND SEE THAT IT HAS A VALVE CAP.

RUN A ROPE AROUND THE SACK. SEW TO SACK EVERY SIX INCHES WITH HEAVY TWINE FOR HAND GRIPS.

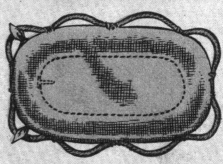

INSERT THE INNER TUBE. PARTLY CLOSE THE OPEN END OF THE POTATO SACK WITH HEAVY CORD SEWED CRISS CROSS...THEN INFLATE THE INNER TUBE, AFTER WHICH YOU CLOSE THE END OF THE SACK COMPLETELY, TYING THE ENDS OF THE HEAVY CORD TOGETHER...AND YOU'VE GOT A ONE-MAN LIFE FLOAT WITH HAND GRIPS THAT WILL KEEP AT LEAST FIVE PEOPLE AFLOAT.

## HERE ARE THREE GOOD WATER SPORTS
PLAY THEM IN THE SHALLOW END OF THE POOL.

### SPLASH!
PLAYERS LINE UP IN TWO ROWS ABOUT SIX FEET APART. SPLASH THE WATER WITH PALM OF HAND. THE LINE THAT STICKS LONGEST WINS.

### TAKE AWAY
SWIMMERS CHOOSE SIDES...TOSS BALL IN CENTER. OBJECT OF THE GAME IS FOR ONE SIDE TO TAKE THE BALL AWAY FROM THE OTHER.

### BULL IN THE RING
BULL TRIES TO BREAK THROUGH THE CIRCLE.

FOR A NEW WINTER SPORT, MAKE A JET-AGE

# SKI ROCKET

By JOHN TAYLOR

**G**ET SET FOR THE thrill of a lifetime the first time you board your SKI ROCKET and start down a snow-covered hill! Hang on to your seat, for you're in for a fast, exciting ride. Balancing and turning on a single runner takes real skill, but once learned, you can't beat it for thrills.

Long before skiing became a popular winter sport, boys in the country devised a rig of their own for sliding down hill—a T-frame made of pieces of 2 x 4's and a wood barrel stave. Known as "Jack Jumps," these crude craft could go like the wind. The sport is being revived today at some ski areas.

The SKI ROCKET is a modern, streamlined design for one of these craft using an odd ski for the runner; the ski should be cut 48" to 50" long, measuring from the forward end. The design given shows the oak cleats extending forward to the tip as applied to a solid wood ski to prevent the ski from snapping if it hits a bump. If you have a laminated or metal ski, the forward ends of these cleats may be omitted, allowing more flexibility (see drawing). All joints are reinforced with Weldwood Glue and ¼" bolts; here are the various sizes used: ski to oak cleats, four 2½" and two 3" stove bolts; oak cleats to stabilizer, four 3" carriage bolts; seat cleats to stabilizer, two 4" carriage bolts; seat to cleats, four 2½" stove bolts. Finish: apply plywood sealer, then paint.

**Modern as a jet—sleek as an arrow—all set to go!**

Assemble cleats temporarily with bolts and scrap plywood spacers to locate and drill bolt holes in ski.

Clamp seat blocks in position while drilling holes through stabilizer so parts align, then bolt together.

Glue and nail half-round molding at each end of seat to make non-slip hand grips. You'll need 'em!

After you have finished making your ski rocket, apply a plywood sealer, then paint and decorate.

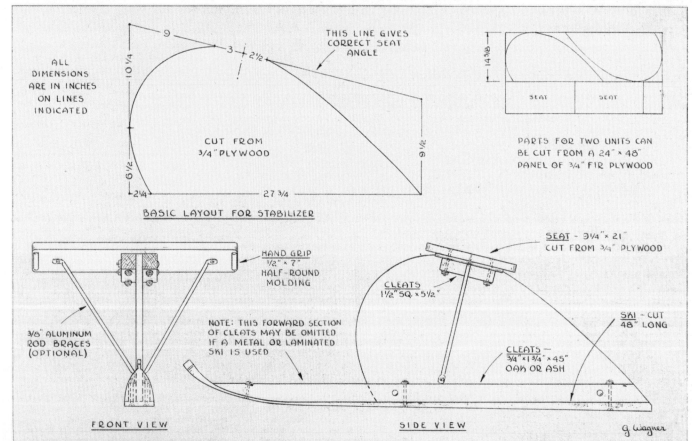

ALL DIMENSIONS ARE IN INCHES ON LINES INDICATED

THIS LINE GIVES CORRECT SEAT ANGLE

CUT FROM ¾" PLYWOOD

BASIC LAYOUT FOR STABILIZER

PARTS FOR TWO UNITS CAN BE CUT FROM A 24" x 48" PANEL OF ¾" FIR PLYWOOD

SEAT

HAND GRIP ½" x 7" HALF-ROUND MOLDING

⅜" ALUMINUM ROD BRACES (OPTIONAL)

NOTE: THIS FORWARD SECTION OF CLEATS MAY BE OMITTED IF A METAL OR LAMINATED SKI IS USED

SEAT - ¾" x 21" CUT FROM ¾" PLYWOOD

CLEATS 1½" SQ. x 5½"

SKI - CUT 48" LONG

CLEATS — ¾" x 1¾" x 45" OAK OR ASH

FRONT VIEW

SIDE VIEW

G. Wagner

### THE
### SKI PACK,
OR NORWEGIAN-STYLE PACK IS MADE FOR ROUGH HIKING AND CLIMBING. RIDES PERFECTLY ON YOUR BACK.

### THE
### GREEN BAR BILL PACK—
YOU CAN MAKE THIS PACK YOURSELF. WRITE TO GREEN BAR BILL, % BOYS' LIFE FOR PATTERN.

### THE
### PACK BASKET—
THIS WAS THE KIND MADE BY THE NORTHWOODS INDIANS. IT'S MADE OF ASH STRIPS PEELED OFF A GREEN LOG.

### THE
### YUCCA PACK,
A VERY POPULAR OVERNIGHT PACK. SEE PICTURES BELOW FOR INSTRUCTIONS HOW TO PACK IT.

### THE
### PACK FRAME—
THIS IS AN IMPROVEMENT ON THE EARLY TRAPPERS' PACKBOARD. IT'S VERY POPULAR TODAY IN THE WEST.

# THE
# PACK ON YOUR BACK

EVER HIKE WITH A PACK THAT WASN'T WELL BALANCED OR SOMETHING YOU'D PUT IN WAS DIGGING INTO YOU... OR THE STRAPS WERE CUTTING INTO YOUR SHOULDERS? TAKES ALL THE FUN OUT OF HIKING, DOESN'T IT? WITH A LITTLE FORETHOUGHT, YOU CAN AVOID ALL THAT. PROPERLY PACKED WITH GOOD, WIDE SHOULDER STRAPS, YOUR PACK CAN BE SO COMFORTABLE YOU'LL HARDLY KNOW YOU'RE TOTING IT. HERE'S HOW TO PACK IT RIGHT...

LAY PACK ON BED, TABLE OR OTHER FLAT SURFACE, THE SHOULDER STRAPS DOWN.

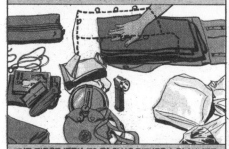

THE FIRST ITEM TO PACK IS EITHER A BLANKET, TENT, OR OTHER UNIFORMLY SOFT ITEM WHICH IS FOLDED TO COVER THE ENTIRE BACK OF THE PACK. (THIS IS TO HAVE SOMETHING SOFT AGAINST YOUR SHOULDERS).

THE NEXT LAYER WOULD CONTAIN PLASTIC OR OTHER TYPE OF BAGS WITH VARIOUS SPARE UNIFORM PARTS—UNDERWEAR, EXTRA SOCKS, AND SHOES. ALSO SWEAT SHIRT AND/OR PAJAMAS.

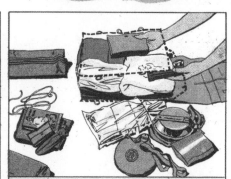

THE TOP LAYER WOULD CONTAIN TOILET KIT, CANTEEN, COOK KIT, WASH BASIN. ON EACH SIDE OF THE PACK, DEPENDING ON TYPE OF TRIP TAKEN, A FLASHLIGHT NEAR THE TOP ON ONE SIDE, AND A PACK AXE ON THE OTHER SIDE.

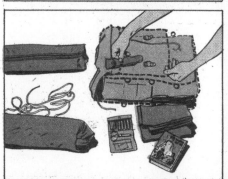

IN THE POCKET ON THE FLAP PLACE READY-TO-USE ITEMS SUCH AS SEWING OR REPAIRING KIT, EATING SET, INDIVIDUAL FIRST AID KIT, BOY SCOUT HANDBOOK, AND PONCHO. THESE ARE IN THIS POSITION FOR QUICK AND EASY ACCESS.

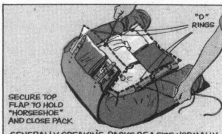

"D" RINGS

SECURE TOP FLAP TO HOLD "HORSESHOE" AND CLOSE PACK

GENERALLY SPEAKING, PACKS OF A SIZE NORMALLY USED BY SCOUTS ARE NOT LARGE ENOUGH TO HOLD A SLEEPING BAG ALONG WITH ALL OTHER REQUIRED EQUIPMENT. SLEEPING BAGS OR BLANKETS CAN BE ROLLED LENGTHWISE FORMING A LONG SAUSAGE-TYPE CYLINDER APPROXIMATELY 6 INCHES IN DIAMETER AND 5 FOOT LONG. THIS CAN BE FOLDED HORSESHOE SHAPE ACROSS THE TOP OF THE PACK AND SECURED TO SIDES BY TYING TO THE "D" RINGS. THIS SHOULD GO UNDER THE TOP FLAP.

AND YOU'RE ALL SET FOR A COMFORTABLE HIKE WITH A PACK THAT RIDES WELL.

# TALKING TOOLS

**EVERYBODY NEEDS TO KNOW WHAT CERTAIN TOOLS ARE USED FOR AND HOW TO USE THEM RIGHT.**

**ADJUSTABLE WRENCH**

## WRENCHES
Wrenches are for tightening. Pliers will damage nuts or bolts, so use a wrench instead.

## HAMMER
To start a nail, hold the hammer midway up the handle and make close, light taps. You can use pliers instead of your fingers to hold the nail. When the nail is set well into the wood, take away your hand. Hold the hammer near the end of its handle and strike the nail.

Tip: If a hammer feels too heavy, don't choke up on its handle. Use a lighter hammer instead.

Tip: Stick a thin block of wood under the hammer to help pull out nails.

**COMBINATION WRENCHES**

FUN FACT: HOW MANY HITS DOES IT TAKE TO DRIVE A NAIL? BEGINNERS NEED 16 TO 30. EXPERTS USE 6 TO 8.

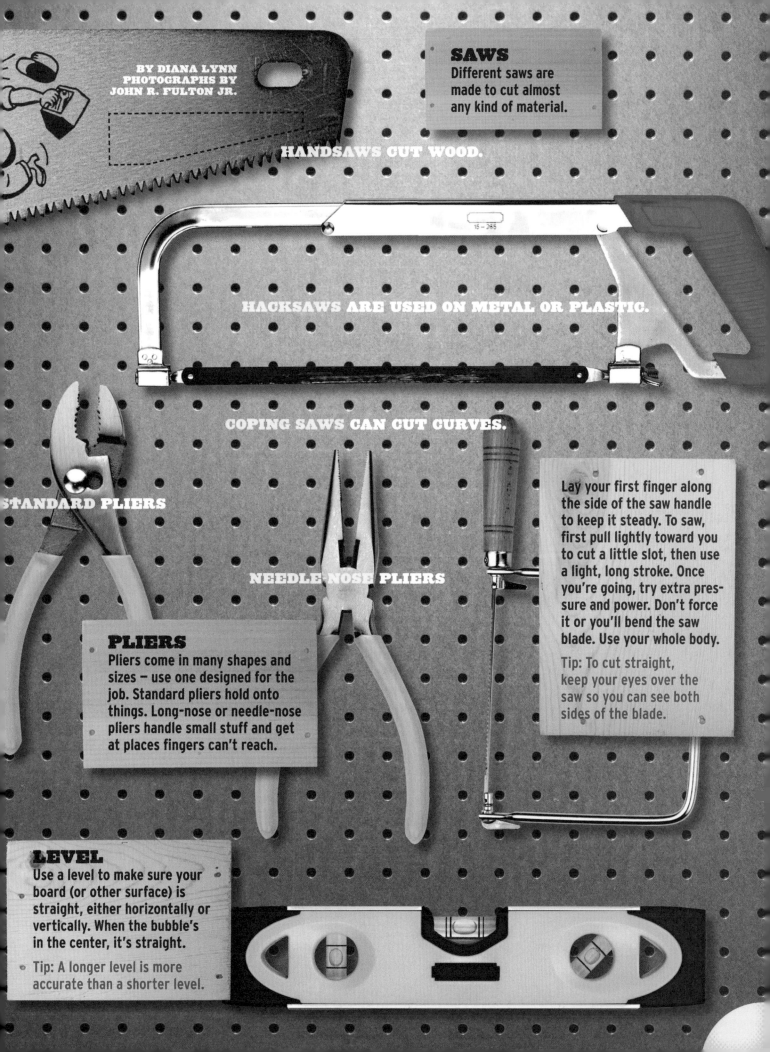

BY DIANA LYNN
PHOTOGRAPHS BY
JOHN R. FULTON JR.

## SAWS
Different saws are made to cut almost any kind of material.

**HANDSAWS CUT WOOD.**

**HACKSAWS ARE USED ON METAL OR PLASTIC.**

**COPING SAWS CAN CUT CURVES.**

**STANDARD PLIERS**

**NEEDLE-NOSE PLIERS**

Lay your first finger along the side of the saw handle to keep it steady. To saw, first pull lightly toward you to cut a little slot, then use a light, long stroke. Once you're going, try extra pressure and power. Don't force it or you'll bend the saw blade. Use your whole body.

Tip: To cut straight, keep your eyes over the saw so you can see both sides of the blade.

## PLIERS
Pliers come in many shapes and sizes — use one designed for the job. Standard pliers hold onto things. Long-nose or needle-nose pliers handle small stuff and get at places fingers can't reach.

## LEVEL
Use a level to make sure your board (or other surface) is straight, either horizontally or vertically. When the bubble's in the center, it's straight.

Tip: A longer level is more accurate than a shorter level.

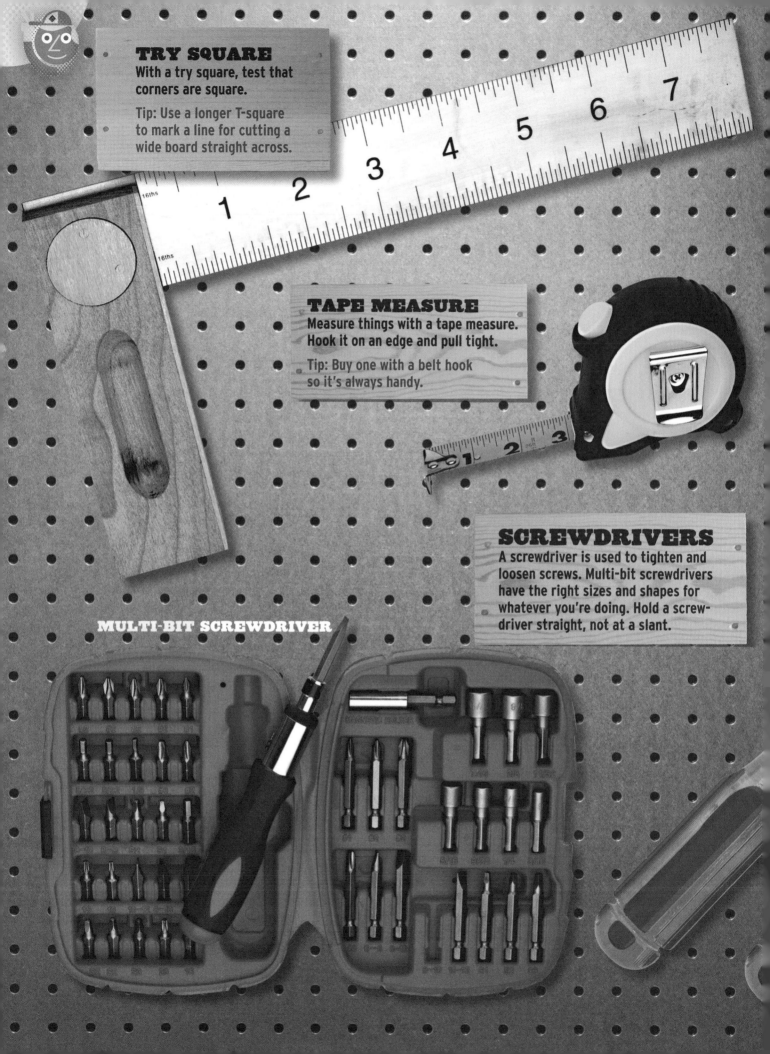

## TRY SQUARE

With a try square, test that corners are square.

Tip: Use a longer T-square to mark a line for cutting a wide board straight across.

## TAPE MEASURE

Measure things with a tape measure. Hook it on an edge and pull tight.

Tip: Buy one with a belt hook so it's always handy.

## SCREWDRIVERS

A screwdriver is used to tighten and loosen screws. Multi-bit screwdrivers have the right sizes and shapes for whatever you're doing. Hold a screwdriver straight, not at a slant.

MULTI-BIT SCREWDRIVER

## RULES FOR TOOLS
- Ask an adult to check you out on each tool before you try it yourself.
- Use the right tool for the right job. For example, don't use a pocketknife to open a paint can. If the tool looks like it's bending or otherwise being damaged, then it's probably the wrong tool.
- Concentrate. Don't let anybody distract you from your work.
- When someone is near you, be extra careful.
- Use goggles! Your eyes will thank you.
- Keep fingers out of the way! Use gloves as needed.

## POCKETKNIFE
Pocketknives are for cutting, carving and whittling soft materials, such as wood. Don't use them on metal.
- Always cut away from your body in case you slip.
- Get one with a locking blade so there's no chance it will suddenly fold up and catch a finger.
- Don't use for prying or poking holes.

**STANDARD SLOTTED SCREWDRIVER**

**PHILLIPS SCREWDRIVER**

**FILE**

**RASP**

## FILES
Use a file for smoothing metal or wood surfaces. Hold the point in one hand and the handle in the other. Use slow, even, steady strokes. Whatever it is that you're filing, hold it firmly.

Tip: File in the cutting direction and then lift it up before taking the next stroke. Dragging it backward dulls the file.

Tip: Use a rasp for rough work when lots of wood is to be removed. ✦

# BOYS' LIFE
## SURVIVAL STORIES

The ultimate tests for Scouting skills are outings in extreme conditions. Whether camping in the snow or in the desert heat, scaling mountain heights, or rafting down white-water rivers, Scouts must have the knowledge and equipment to bring them happily—and safely—through the experience.

*Boys' Life* features stories of Scouts meeting the tests of high-adventure outings—activities that have grown more challenging over the decades since Scouting's founding. Lighter-weight gear and rugged clothing have enabled Scouting to push further into wilderness areas. High-adventure outings are crowning events that match Scouts' training and stamina against the rigors of the backcountry. The pages of the magazine are full of these adventures, modeling for Scouts the variety of activities and locations available for pitting their knowledge against the elements.

Camping in cold-weather conditions requires the right clothing (in layers) and gear to have an enjoyable experience. The magazine offers tips on what to wear, what to bring, and what to do if you want to build a snow shelter or go snowshoeing, snowboarding, or skiing. In addition to equipment and activities, the magazine tells how to stay safe in the cold. Drinking plenty of liquids and eating energy-packed food for strenuous action keeps Scouts ready for the planned events, and knowing how to prevent and treat hypothermia keeps them protected from the dangers of cold weather. Wintertime is no time to stay indoors by the fire when there's so much fun to be had out in the snow.

Hiking and camping in warm weather requires its own set of gear and precautions. Sunscreen and insect repellent are necessary to have a comfortable experience. Drinking plenty of water and not overexerting yourself will help to prevent heat exhaustion. Light clothing and a cap with a brim or visor will keep you cool. Knowing how to take care of yourself on a trek is the outcome of the vast toolbox of information that Scouting imparts to a boy.

Encounters with wildlife are always a possibility when going into the backcountry, and knowing how to keep a respectful distance and stash food and other "smellables" properly keeps unwanted campsite visitors away (particularly bears). But animals are fun to track, and *Boys' Life* explains how to identify and follow tracks and other signs in the soil or snow. But don't get so absorbed in tracking that you get lost. Planning ahead and always knowing where you are will keep you on course. The magazine offers cautionary tales on losing your way—and what to do if you have trouble finding your way back.

The Boy Scouts of America offers premier activities at its high-adventure bases, and the magazine highlights the attractions of these diverse locales—from backpacking the mountains of northern New Mexico to snorkeling in the Florida Keys to wilderness canoeing in the lake country of Northern Minnesota and Canada. These bases provide Scouts the opportunities to try out their skills at first-rate facilities.

Survival stories are tales of well-prepared and well-trained Scouts taking on the challenges of the outdoors in all weathers and conditions, and emerging with the experiences that will mold them for a lifetime.

Use duel contests at your patrol meetings. For STICK FIGHT you need a staff, about five feet long. Two fellows grab hold of it. The winner is the one who first touches an end of the staff to the floor.

## MAKE THEM EAT BEAR MEAT

"EVERY PATROL HIKE should have an objective" they tell me. So who's disagreeing? Not I! That's what I've been preaching all along—although I haven't used such a highbrow word.

"So what's a hike objective, daddy?" Usually something in the line of general Second and First Class work, first aid, signaling, cooking, nature.

But how about making HIKING your hike objective this month? In other words—have a hike for the sake of hiking!

It's about time for all of us to re-discover hiking. It is one of the best exercises known. It strengthens the lungs and heart, straightens the back, develops the muscles, makes the blood run tingling through your veins.

The old vikings used to eat bear meat for strength—it was tough to chew and full of red blood. Well, there's another kind of "bear meat" that'll make you strong—our imaginary kind, the kind you "eat" the last couple of miles of a twenty-mile hike, the kind you "chew" when you fight your way through brambles and underbrush on an orienteering race, when you climb to the summit of a mountain.

Cook up a lot of that kind of "bear meat" in the form of real hiking and serve it red-hot to your patrol as often as possible.

As a patrol leader it is your responsibility to help your boys become "physically strong." Making them eat "bear meat" is one of the best ways of doing it.

After you're once in the swing of real hiking, keep it up! Go whole-hog and set your sights for the Hiking merit badge for every boy in the patrol.

What's involved in getting this He-man badge?

Check the requirements in your HANDBOOK FOR BOYS and you'll see that they amount to this:

● Five hikes of ten miles each over a six-month period. One hike of twenty miles. A written report of each of the six hikes. And finally, a demonstration before an examiner of proper hiking techniques and a written plan for a ten-mile hike.

● See what I mean now? In the first requirement you have the challenge of a definite schedule of real hiking. A regular patrol hike each month—and by the time six months are up, there'll be a Hiking merit badge on the uniform sleeve or sash of each of your boys.

So get tough! Get them out! Onward to the Hiking merit badge!

The outdoors is the best possible place for your toughening-up process. But bring fitness and fun into your patrol meetings as well.

How'll you do it? By using duel contests—they're absolutely the most for this purpose.

● Which will it be? Just take a look at the pictures on this page and take your pick. Then, on your next patrol date, imitate! Run each of the duel contests on

a championship basis: Pair the fellows against each other and let the winners fight it out until you've crowned a patrol champion.

● Or, even better, go in the opposite direction: Let the losers fight each other and find out who's the patrol "champ-nit." In this system, the weaker fellows get more practice and become better able to win the next time.

● Now don't stop with the four games on these pages. Use also other games from the Patrol Stunts chapter of your HANDBOOK FOR PATROL LEADERS as well as the physical fitness tricks we give you in the Duffel Bag section of every issue of BOYS' LIFE.

Still wondering how to get your fellows over the first aid hurdles for their Second and First Class badges? Nothing to it if you go about the job systematically.

● Get a large sheet of brown paper, a ruler, and a pencil. Draw as many horizontal columns as there are fellows in the patrol and put in their names. Next draw as many vertical columns as there are first aid items for Second and First Class and write in the items starting from the beginning; artificial respiration, shock, fainting, arterial bleeding of arm, arterial bleeding of leg, cuts, scratches, and so on and so forth. Now get the whole gang into the act.

● Demonstrate the first item yourself, then have the fellows perform. Watch to see that every boy does it right. When you're satisfied, check off that item on your chart for each fellow. Next item. You demonstrate, each fellow does it, you check him off. Next and next and next—until as you'd planned to do at that patrol meeting. Then more next time.

With this system you'll get your fellows through the first aid requirements in no man's time—and you'll have your patrol ready for the big first aid event that I have a suspicion your troop will spring on you in December (but don't tell anybody that I told you).

HAND WRESTLING—Two fellows place the outside of their right feet together, clasp right hands, try to throw each other off balance without moving their feet.

TRACTOR PULL—Two boys get down on all fours, facing away from each other. Two riders grasp hands. "Tractors" pull away from each other until a rider is unseated.

COCK FIGHT—Two opponents hop around on one leg, holding on to the other leg. Each of them tries to knock the other fellow off balance using his shoulders only.

---

Heat Exhaustion
Altitude Sickness
## Hypothermia
Frostbite

THE SILENT KILLERS

Losing body heat happens in all seasons, and it can kill. Know the symptoms and how to treat them.

Twelve-year-old Erick Cole was sick at heart, and scared.

Erick and his little brother, Andy, 4, had been sledding together out in the Nebraska snow. When it came time to go home, Erick decided to make another run; Andy said he'd wait for his big brother at the bottom of the hill. But as Erick reached the end of his final slide, he discovered Andy

---

# Scouting the salt marsh

In the apparent wasteland of a salt marsh, salt and fresh water meet land and sky to nourish a rich profusion of creatures.

By Nick Karas

*Scouts of Troop 92 netted tidal-zone wildlife (below), and gathered seashells from the beach (above).*

To casual eyes the place may seem to be a wasteland, but if any single type of land on the earth today could be called a cradle of life it would have to be a salt marsh. Along the grassy, muddy shores washed by the sea tides, life teems with great abundance and variety.

The salt marsh is a meeting place. It is the place where fresh water meets salt and where the oceans meet land and air as the tide changes and creates what scientists call the *inter-tidal biozone*.

This amazing world between land and sea is a very special place for the Scouts of Troop 92 from Smithtown, Long Island, N.Y. They spent a week-long summer camp living along its edge. The site was Cedar Point, on Long Island's south fork, next to Alewife Pond and Alewife Brook, both salty extensions of the sea into the surrounding land. As is often the case in nature, astonishing numbers of living creatures and plants exist unnoticed all about you until you learn how to see them. So it was with the Scouts, who spent the first few days fishing, sailing, rowing, and swimming in the outlet and along the surrounding beaches.

Then one morning, while the tide was low, they gathered at the mouth of the outlet, with collecting jars, seining net, and magnifying glasses, to learn how to see life in the "wasteland." Their object was to discover what life existed in the salt marsh and find as many forms as possible. Then they had to identify each and categorize them into phyla, or biological groups.

The Scouts quickly found that the secrets of a salt marsh lie hidden in great fields of grasses that provide home, food, and concealment for millions of animals.

---

Glacier National Park offers a little bit of everything. If you can bear it.

## "Hey, bear!" a kid calls. It echoes
across the rugged Rocky Mountains as Scouts continue their backpacking outing in Montana's Glacier National Park.

"Fresh meat!" another boy yells. "Come and get it!"

Naturally, the Scouts, from Troop 2, Madison, Wis., hope no grizzly takes them up on their offer. It's just that bears are more turned off by human voices than by the tinkling of bells tied to bootlaces. Glacier National Park is trying to minimize bear-human contact. Some bears have been trapped, moved and even destroyed.

And now a sign along the trail warns of mountain lion activity and advises hikers to stay in groups.

Scary? Sure. But it's all part of the backpacking experience in this sanctuary known for

# 'COME AND GET IT'

its glacier-carved valleys, rich forests and mountain scenery. Even bears.

### Back—and Up—to Nature

Troop 2 arrived at Glacier last August. While younger Scouts remained at base camp for day hikes or an overnight trip, four backpacking crews lit out into the wild for five-day, four-night excursions.

First, they had to get used to the thin mountain air. Although altitude sickness is usually not a problem at Glacier, spending a day or two in base camp to get used to low oxygen is wise. Glacier's trails can reach 8,100 feet above sea level. The average elevation back in Madison is 845.6 feet. ▶

*Left: Glacier's mountains began 170 million years ago along the Lewis Overthrust Fault. Right: Bear alert! Luckily, Carl Davis identifies a faraway visitor as a mountain sheep—maybe.*

TEXT BY JOHNNY D. BOGGS
PHOTOS BY GARTH DOWLING

OCTOBER 1989

BY BUCK TILTON * ILLUSTRATIONS BY JONATHAN CARLSON

 ## Heat Exhaustion

 ## Altitude Sickness

 ## Hypothermia

 ## Frostbite

Your body is more than half water. If you don't hydrate, you can cook your brain—and die. Know the symptoms and how to treat them.

John Musgrove was on his first backpacking trip, and he was not a happy hiker. "I'm tired, and I think I'm going to barf," he moaned.

The eighth grader and his Scout patrol were hiking a section of the Appalachian Trail in the Mark Trail Wilderness of north Georgia. John, 13, was a good student but he didn't exercise

When your body loses too much water and salt, trouble follows.

Heat cramps—muscle cramps caused by water and salt loss—aren't serious, but they do hurt a lot.

To get better, drinking water with a pinch of salt is very important. If you rest and gently stretch cramped muscles, and massage them a little bit, the pain goes away faster.

Your body loses water when you sweat; urinate or defecate; vomit or have diarrhea; and every time you breathe. Always drink before you're thirsty. If your urine isn't clear, you're not drinking enough.

E.Ottinger (2)

much and wasn't in very good shape. The summer heat was hammering him.

He sat beside the trail, slumped against his pack, pale as a ghost. Sweat poured down his face. His breathing was fast.

Pete Barnes, the Scoutmaster, helped John into a patch of shade. Mr. Barnes wet his bandanna from his water bottle, and draped it over the boy's head. He told John to drink the rest of the water in small sips. Over the next hour or so, John drained the bottle. By then, he seemed his same old self. Hiking slower and drinking more water, he was able to finish the trip.

## A Body of Water

You may look and feel pretty solid, but more than half of you is water—and you need it all. On a normal day you may lose a gallon or more (see sidebar) in various ways.

Usually you gain back the lost fluid by drinking and eating. But when you lose too much water, as John Musgrove did—a problem called dehydration—your health and maybe even your life are threatened.

## Sweat It

Sweat is mostly water, with some sodium chloride, also known as salt, in it. When sweat evaporates from your skin on hot days, that cools you inside. If you've lost too much water, or if it's too humid (moisture in the air) you may not be able to sweat enough, and you can begin to get sick from heat exhaustion.

Symptoms include headache, nausea, lightheadedness, pale skin and extreme fatigue. This is a serious health problem, but it's not life-threatening.

You can beat heat exhaustion by resting and drinking water the way John Musgrove did. It's a good idea to drink at least a quart of water, slowly, and to add just a pinch of salt to it. You can also nibble a few salty snacks while drinking.

Remember: Sip slowly so your body absorbs as much of the water and salt as possible.

## Too Hot, Too Dry

If you get too dehydrated, your skin becomes red and hot and you heat up inside. Your brain, which is very sensitive to rising temperatures, begins to cook. A hot brain can make you crazy, feel lost and want to argue or pick a fight.

Heat stroke has struck. You have only minutes to act!

A person with heat stroke should be cooled down as quickly as possible. Soak his skin with water and fan him to speed the cooling effect of evaporation. Massage his arms and legs to send the cooled blood near the skin back inside. If water is short, focus on cooling his head. And get medical help—immediately!

## Be Cool

You can prevent heat problems. Avoid hard exercise during the hottest part of the day. If you're not in shape, slow down and let your body adjust. Wear cotton clothes to help sweat evaporate. Eat snacks that contain a little salt. Drink water and keep drinking it.✤

## FURTHER READING

"Environmental Emergencies," by Charles E. Stewart, M.D. (Williams & Wilkins). "First Aid for Youths," by Buck Tilton, M.S., and Steve Griffin (Globe Pequot Press). "Wilderness Medicine," 5th edition, by William W. Forgey, M.D. (Globe Pequot Press).

## *A hot brain can make you crazy, feel lost and want to argue or pick a fight.*

# Scouting the salt marsh

*In the apparent wasteland of a salt marsh, salt and fresh water meet land and sky to nourish a rich profusion of creatures.*

By Nick Karas

To casual eyes the place may seem to be a wasteland, but if any single type of land on the earth today could be called a cradle of life it would have to be a salt marsh. Along the grassy, muddy shores washed by the sea tides, life teems with great abundance and variety.

The salt marsh is a meeting place. It is the place where fresh water meets salt and where the oceans meet land and air as the tide changes and creates what scientists call the *inter-tidal biozone*.

This amazing world between land and sea is a very special place for the Scouts of Troop 92 from Smithtown, Long Island, N.Y. They spent a week-long summer camp living along its edge. The site was Cedar Point, on Long Island's south fork, next to Alewife Pond and Alewife Brook, both salty extensions of the sea into the surrounding land. As is often the case in nature, astonishing numbers of living creatures and plants exist unnoticed all about you until you learn how to see them. So it was with the Scouts, who spent the first few days fishing, sailing, rowing, and swimming in the outlet and along the surrounding beaches.

Then one morning, while the tide was low, they gathered at the mouth of the outlet, with collecting jars, seining net, and magnifying glasses, to learn how to see life in the "wasteland." Their object was to discover what life existed in the salt marsh and find as many forms as possible. Then they had to identify each and categorize them into phyla, or biological groups.

The Scouts quickly found that the secrets of a salt marsh lie hidden in great fields of grasses that provide home, food, and concealment for millions of animals.

*Scouts of Troop 92 netted tidal-zone wildlife (below), and gathered seashells from the beach (above).*

Without the grasses life would not congregate nor multiply in the marsh. So what were the grasses? They learned to identify each. Three salt grasses make up the majority of those found in marshes on our three coasts. Salt meadow grass (*Spartina patens*) occupies the life zone at the edge of the high tide and above. Smooth cordgrass (*Spartina alternaflora*) occupies a saltier niche between low and high tide. Eel grass (*Zostera marina*) stays strictly in the salt water.

Among these grasses, the Scouts most frequently found creatures from four phyla of the animal kingdom. There were mollusks, crustaceans, annelids, and fishes. The mollusks were usually such easy-to-recognize creatures as snails, scallops, mussels, soft clams, and periwinkles. The crustaceans were most often fiddler, sand, and calico crabs, the ancient horseshoe crab, and grass and sand shrimp.

While the Scouts of Troop 92 found fish extremely plentiful in the marsh, they learned to seek them in the deeper, open parts as well as among the grasses. The quicksilver predators left the open water when they were hungry to feed on the killifish, spearing, and immature eels that take refuge in the grasses.

Other life forms were the annelids, or worms, which are closely related to the garden worm we all know on dry land. Salt-water relatives include sandworms that leave their burrows at night to hunt other worms and small fish. Bloodworms and long ribbon worms, which are often called tapeworms but are not even close cousins to them, also dwell in the marsh. The Scouts used shovels and forks to rout the worms from the sand and mud below the high-tide mark.

The Scout marsh detectives learned the best time to begin looking into the life of the salt marsh was on an ebbing tide, just before it was low. The moving water helped drifting forms move into the Scouts' seining net and allowed them to sweep in water that wasn't too deep. The falling tide exposed the beach and sod banks so the Scouts could trap or dig fiddler and hermit crabs. Low tide was also more likely to strand killifish and other fishes in small isolated pools, which made seining easier.

Some of the life forms were studied alive in a glass jar or a shallow tray filled with salt water. After a time, captured snails began to move. Crabs, less timid, were always moving, and fish containers had to be covered to prevent an escape. All the live specimens were returned to the marsh after they had been identified and studied. Some other creatures were preserved in alcohol or formaldehyde, and some were cured or dried. Formalin, a 40 percent solution of formaldehyde in water available at drugstores, was used for wet collections. Crabs, starfish, and shrimp were pinned and dried after they had been soaked for about 12 hours in a saturated solution of borax, which also is available at drugstores.

Some of the Scouts took notes and wrote the identifications of the animals as they were found. They also learned of the many books and other publications in local libraries that could be helpful when they wanted to work alone.

Most important, Troop 92 would never again look at a salt marsh as a wasteland or barren piece of the earth. Nor would they ever swim near one again without a sense of sharing the salty water with all its many creatures. ❖

Photographs by the author

*The Scouts' salt-marsh finds included, clockwise from top right, the pipefish, able to change color for camouflage; male fiddler crab, oversized left claw tucked under his chin like a violin; the hermit crab, whose lack of hard shell forces him to shelter in abandoned shells; pretty periwinkles; green crab; crab with camouflaging algal growth; the sandworm, a great bait; sand shrimp; rock barnacles, female crab with eggs visible on abdomen and legs; calico crab; striped killifish; a horseshoe-crab shell; a sand crab.*

# FROZEN ASSETS

The Scouts knew that building a snow shelter was a survival ski

ut what if the snow wouldn't stay stuck together?

By David DiBenedetto - Photographs by Vince Heptig

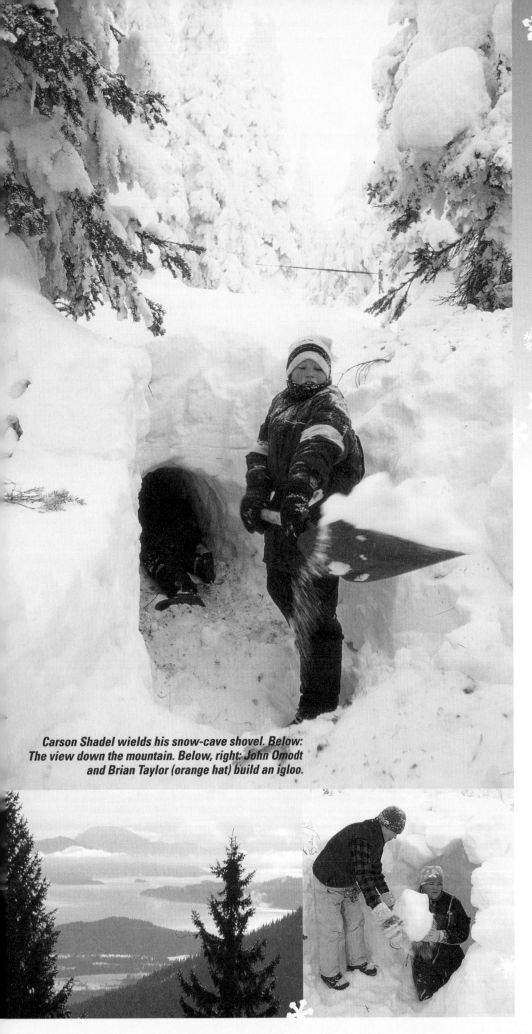

**Snow caves are fun to build.
They're even more fun to destroy.**

At least that's the way Daniel Schock sees it. Last winter, the 13-year-old Star Scout and his four buddies from Troop 111 in Sandpoint, Idaho, built such a sturdy shelter that when they tried to collapse it, the five guys had to repeatedly jump on top of it. "Even then," said Daniel, "we just made holes the size of our bodies and fell right through."

Not every Scout's cave was up to the task at the seventh annual Snow Cave Camporee on Idaho's Schweitzer Mountain last February. Because of mild temperatures, the boys weren't allowed to spend the night in their shelters for fear that they would collapse.

But that didn't stop the 200 campers from learning one of the best ways to stay warm when lost or stranded in winter conditions. It's a lesson that has saved Scouts before.

### A Survival Skill Comes in Handy

Two years ago, three young skiers, Aaron Peterson, Justin Haeger and Van Spear, all 15, got lost on Schweitzer. They spent about

## C-c-c-can'

24 hours in extremely cold weather while search parties scoured the mountain for them. Many assumed they had died in the harsh conditions, but the young men survived because they knew a survival skill— how to make a snow cave

No one at the camporee faced such dire straits, of course, but everyone took snow-cave building seriously. Afterward there would be plenty of time for fun.

They learned that location is everything when erecting a snow cave. The best place: a hillside or drift where the snow has gathered and will be easy to dig into. It also helps to have a good shovel.

"The best kind in the world is a square, metal shovel with the wooden shaft cut in half," said Richard Chapman, assistant Scoutmaster of

*Carson Shadel wields his snow-cave shovel. Below: The view down the mountain. Below, right: John Omodt and Brian Taylor (orange hat) build an igloo.*

Ben Gendro gets colder and colder as he hauls snow from his excavation. His mind is on his buddies out sliding down the mountainside.

# f-f-f-f-feel my lips...or my eyes...

## (but we're having some fun!)

Troop 497 in Spokane, Wash. Add a handle (from a hardware store, if one isn't already on the shaft) and your shovel will be compact yet strong, capable of moving large amounts of snow. "It works much better than those small shovels you normally see people using," said Mr. Chapman.

### Carving a Cave Home

The Scouts were told that, as they tunneled into the drift, they should dig an entranceway leading up to the enclosed area where they would sleep. This design helps trap body heat in the cave.

Daniel started digging, following that advice and adding a trick of his own that helped speed up the construction. "If you have a sled," he explained, "take it inside and load it with snow, then pull it out and dump it."

The Scouts dug snow and carved snow and scraped snow and dumped snow. They stopped digging when

### IN THE TRENCHES

The best snow for building a snow cave is the type that leaves boot prints just a few centimeters deep. Another option is a snow trench. Excavate a shallow depression slightly longer than your body and a couple of feet deep. Line the bottom with branches, lie down on top of them, and then cover yourself with another layer of pine boughs and leaf litter. Be sure to make a ventilation hole. Sweet dreams.

they started to see blue through the cave's roof. That signaled that the roof was about two feet thick. Next they carved shelves into the cave's inside wall for candles or other gear and, on the outside of the cave wall along the entrance tunnel, a shelf for a cook stove.

### Preventing Problems

The danger with digging snow is that the digger can start to sweat. And one of the last things a winter camper wants to be is wet. So building a snow shelter is slow work, and the Scouts took time to vent extra body heat before it turned to sweat that could freeze.

Then they continued the construction process, ventilating their snow caves by poking a few holes in the roof at 45-degree angles. The Scouts were told that it was a common safeguard for shovels to be kept in the cave. If the roof were to collapse during the night, the campers would need to shovel their way to the outside world.

# What if the

With most snow caves built by midmorning, the Scouts spent a little time relaxing. Which of course means that they spent it playing—zooming down the mountain on sleds and snowboards. The guys concentrated their need for speed on the backside of Schweitzer, where dodging trees was part of the game.

"It's tough to control a sled when you really get going fast," said Daniel, "I had four big wipeouts." Other Scouts on snowboards found plenty of drifts to launch themselves off of for some serious hang time, and a few campers tested their snowshoeing skills on serious mountain terrain.

### What Goes Up Must Come Down

By midafternoon, with many caves crumbling because of the warm temperatures, leaders decided to hold a demolition derby: All

*Michael Colby covers ground on his snowshoes. Below: Ben Gendro (left) and Nathan Simmet quaff some defrosted sports drink. Below, right: Ben fires up his campstove for breakfast.*

**TELL ME MORE**

For further information on building winter shelters, check out "Okpik: Cold-Weather Camping" ($9.95, BSA Supply No. 34040, phone 800-323-0732; www.scoutstuff.org).

*Yahoo!: Scouts demolish a snow cave.
Bottom: A sunken hole is all that's left.*

# snow won't stay stuck together?

## (you crush the structure—so it won't crush you)

Scouts would collapse their caves. It was a lot of fun, but the campers were soon busy with the task of setting up new shelters to keep warm. During the night temperatures would dip into the single digits, and snow was expected.

Luckily, many Scouts were able to build on the remains of their previous shelters. "We put a big tarp over the hole we had made for the snow cave," said Josh Berry, 16, Troop 111's senior patrol leader.

"It wasn't too cold because four of us stayed pretty close under the tarp," said Daniel, who also slept beneath a tarp and found a better way to stay warm. "I just slid to the bottom of my bag and went to sleep down there," he said.

And after a long day of digging caves, then collapsing them, it was a deep good sleep.

Don mixed the biscuit dough in the same bag we brought it in. We baked bread in globs on two layers of leaves over coals. We planked big fish, hung others over fire. Edible plants completed meal.

We each got a bedsheet from Mom—or used some other cloth—and waterproofed it with paraffin. We put pebbles in corners, in middle, tied them in to hold tent. Dead logs held leaves for beds.

We decided we'd do without matches. We struck sparks from a rock with the back of a closed knife. Caught sparks in charred cloth from waxed envelope we all carry. Also made fire by friction.

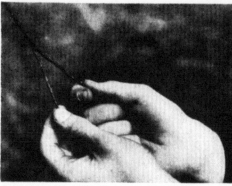
Food was plentiful—if you could catch it. Our Crew Leader twisted strands of Indian hemp into six feet of line. Mulberry root, tulip bark, or yucca would have worked. He made a briar hook.

Be Prepared 🛡 For Anything

# Survival Overnighter

### By DAVID DUNBAR  •  PHOTOGRAPHS BY BOB BROOKS

WE'RE THE PAUL BUNYON Crew of Post 333. At our first Post meeting last month, we challenged the other Crews to a "survival overnighter"—a camping trip where you live off the land. The idea is to take along next to nothing in gear and food—the only chow you pack is some salt and biscuit mix. You're going out to be on your own.

Once we got on the actual trip, it was pretty simple. All it took to find our own food was a little ingenuity and a yearn for making like Daniel Boone. What at first had looked like live-off-the-land-or-bust, turned out as one of our Crew's best trips.

Take a look at the way we did it, and you'll see how your Crew or Patrol can do the same—and get a big kick out of it, too. Also you'll be storing up some valuable know-how in taking care of yourself under survival conditions. That's mighty good insurance nowadays.

Here's all that each man took along: One bedsheet tent and 10 feet of cord for it. One blanket and one poncho. Some charred cloth in a waterproof envelope. Pocket knife, canteen, first aid gear. Biscuit mix, salt (and no more food!)

We started out right after breakfast one morning, and came back just before dark the next night. We foraged for four meals in all and ate well, as you can see.

Okay, that's how we took our "survival overnighter"—when's your gang go on one?

Worms and patience landed this big one. We surrounded and scooped in smaller fish. We set Figure 4 deadfall for game, baited it with wild turnip root. Some states prohibit traps, so check.

# LOST AT NIGHT

**"Robert took a step and found himself falling through space."**

**BY ED HEIM**

**B**y the time Robert stopped fishing, daylight was gone. The fact that it was getting dark had not worried him. His dad was close by. They had been enjoying the quiet lake, listening to the birds and catching bluegills. When they finally left the lake, the sky was filled with stars. This was when Robert made a mistake.

Both he and his dad knew the way back to his uncle's old farm house. All they had to do was follow the path. "But I know a shortcut," Robert said. "We can go straight out that way through the woods and come out right beside the house."

Half an hour later both Robert and his dad had to admit they were lost. Neither had the slightest idea where he was. They could find no trails. They could see no lights. They could hear no cars. No matter how loudly they yelled, nobody answered.

Then they made their second mistake. When they realized they were lost, they began hurrying through the forest faster than ever. Branches hit them in the face, and briars caught their clothes.

Robert took a step and found himself falling through space. He tumbled down a steep slope all the way to the bottom of a rocky hollow. He was lucky. He was scratched and bruised, but did not break any bones.

After two hours of tramping through the dark woods in big circles, they heard a dog bark in the distance. It might be his uncle's dog in the barn near the old farm house. They turned around and headed in that direction. The dog continued to bark and guided them home.

After this experience Robert did a lot of thinking about getting lost, especially at night. If he had done this thinking *before* getting lost, he and his dad might never have had any trouble.

To avoid getting lost at night, stay on the trails. Even when you are close to camp, you can become lost in the woods if you leave the trails. This can happen when you are playing games or hiding from friends. Taking "short cuts" through strange woods is a bad idea!

Trying to travel through the woods after dark is dangerous. You can't see the trail or know when you are going to stumble over rocks or logs. You can step in a hole, fall over a cliff or splash into a lake or stream. If you injure yourself, your troubles are multiplied.

If you are lost during the day, do not wait for darkness to settle down. Before dark, gather firewood so you can have a fire through the night.

Once people are lost, they have a tendency to keep moving. And if they begin moving they may start running and forget all the lessons they ever heard about trying not to panic.

When you get lost, day or night, *sit down*. Stay there a while, maybe 15 minutes or more. Think everything through. Try to remember landmarks you have seen, or the direction in which you followed a creek. In daylight you may be able to unravel your route and backtrack.

This is also a good time to go through your pockets and see what you are carrying that can help you. First of all you should have a knife and matches. The matches must be either in a waterproof container or waxed to protect them.

A map and compass would also be helpful, providing you have practiced enough to know how to use them. In addition, you will wish you had some dried fruit, hard candy, or nuts stored in a watertight bag in your coat pocket or pack. If you always carry these emergency items when you go into the outdoors, they may help you weather a rough night in the woods.

Try to pile up enough firewood before dark to keep your fire going all night. Somebody may be out looking for you, and the fire will help guide him. If the weather is bad, you may need to take shelter. Some pine boughs or even a thick-growing evergreen tree will help.

The best protection against getting lost is learning to feel at home outdoors. The night may seem spooky. You imagine all kinds of strange creatures out there. But the truth is that there isn't anything out there at night that wasn't there in the daylight. If you don't panic, you are probably safer in the woods than in the city.

When morning comes, stay with your fire. Make it as smoky as possible so people searching for you will see it. Then, when you hear them coming toward you, stay right where you are. They will find you quicker this way than if you go running through the woods to meet them.

Robert and his dad both agreed later on what they will do if they're ever lost again at night. They will settle down right where they are until morning or until they are rescued. ♣

The Scouts of Troop 67 of Jackson, Wyo., live within eyeshot of the Grand Teton, one of America's most beautiful mountains. They have often wondered what it would be like to climb it. Last August, seven of them found out.

The cone-shaped mountain sits proudly between Middle Teton to the south and Mount Owen to the north. "Ever since I was a kid I've looked up at it," said Scout Justin Bybee. Grand Teton rules over its own national park and attracts thousands of climbers.

The Scouts were headed for the summit, at 13,770 feet, and would

before leaving. Their first-day goal was base camp on the Lower Saddle. To get there, they would have to gain more than 5,000 feet of elevation from their starting point.

At lunch break, the Scouts "bouldered" on car-sized rocks, practicing the moves they would use later on bigger rocks. That afternoon, they reached their first big obstacle: "the upper headwall," a 150-foot rock face. Everyone was able to get up without trouble, thanks to a fixed rope left by rangers. Base camp was nearby. That evening Scouts

They were fed and on the trail *by 5 A.M.* To reach the summit and get back to camp, they would need all the daylight they could get.

At first, everyone seemed nervous. Some questioned Berkenfield and Burgette about "Wall Street." This pitch, or section of the climb, is a ledge that starts as wide as a school desk but narrows sharply as it slopes up. What's worse, only a step away is a 1,000-foot drop. The climbing term for being one step away from thin air is "exposure."

But the Scouts were prepared;

# A Grand Climb

*Troop 67, Jackson, Wyo., tackled the Grand Teton last summer. They followed the Exum Route going up and the Owen Spalding Route coming down. Above: Rappelling. Left: Helmets are a must for safety.*

need three days to get up and back. They would follow the popular Exum Route (see sidebar).

Lending advice were expert guides Scott Berkenfield and Dan Burgette. Both were climbing rangers at Grand Teton National Park and also fathers of Scouts in the troop. They were rewarding Troop 67 for a year's worth of service projects done within the park.

The group got the proper permits and signed in at the ranger station

*The Tetons, in northwestern Wyoming, are some of the most beautiful mountains in America. They draw thousands of climbers each summer.*

swapped stories and shared meals. A chill pushed everyone into their sleeping bags early.

Next morning, camp stoves could be heard hissing before dawn. (Open fires are prohibited in the backcountry.) The Grand's summit beckoned from 2,200 feet above. You could tell the Scouts were pumped.

climbing lessons had taught them rope handling, safety and basic climbing maneuvers. Now it was time to put it all together.

As morning's light edged the coal-black sky, the Scouts headed uphill. They slipped through Eye of the Needle, a hole through rock, and then gathered to hear Ranger Berkenfield's instructions.

"Well, this is the infamous Wall Street," Berkenfield began. Before tackling it, the climbers would need to rope up for protection, he said.

"This ledge is not as bad as everyone makes it out to be," he added thoughtfully.

Focus on the rock, he advised. "If the exposure starts to bother you," he continued, "don't look down. Concentrate on your handholds."

Then it was time to go. The group moved quickly and with precision, scrambling up the narrow catwalk and around the corner at the end. Their training paid off. The Scouts moved with confidence.

Next came the Golden Staircase, a big crack. It was here, as they reached and stepped for holds, that Scouts had their first true test of belaying (securing) one another by rope.

The climbers cruised the Staircase

## THE EXUM ROUTE

Glen Exum, now in his 70's, is one of the living legends of mountaineering in the Tetons. Many years ago, he pioneered the route that Troop 67 followed to the summit of Grand Teton.

When he got to the pitch now called "Wall Street," he was climbing alone and unroped, which most climbers consider extremely dangerous. He retreated from the narrow end of Wall Street seven times before summoning enough courage to take the dangerous steps around the blind corner at the end. Unable to retreat, he continued to the summit on his new route, now the most popular way up the Grand.    —Don Cushman

*Above: Scouts climbing on the Exum Route, above the pitch called Wall Street. Right: Jason Stauth rappels a 120-foot cliff.*

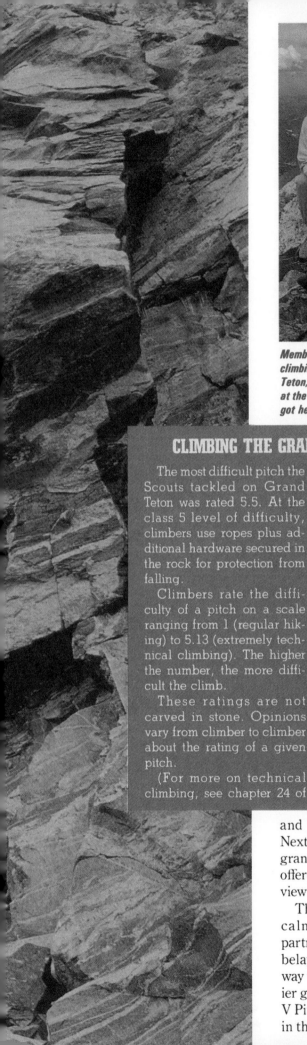

*Members of Troop 67, along with their adult climbing guides, enjoy the view atop Grand Teton, at 13,770 feet. "It is really fun being at the top, because I can't believe I actually got here," said Scout Scott McDowell.*

## CLIMBING THE GRAND IS NO CAKEWALK

The most difficult pitch the Scouts tackled on Grand Teton was rated 5.5. At the class 5 level of difficulty, climbers use ropes plus additional hardware secured in the rock for protection from falling.

Climbers rate the difficulty of a pitch on a scale ranging from 1 (regular hiking) to 5.13 (extremely technical climbing). The higher the number, the more difficult the climb.

These ratings are not carved in stone. Opinions vary from climber to climber about the rating of a given pitch.

(For more on technical climbing, see chapter 24 of the Boy Scout "Fieldbook.")

Before tackling the Grand, the Scouts of Troop 67 enrolled in a climbing school in Grand Teton National Park. Two good schools in the area are Exum Mountain Guides [telephone (307) 733-2297] and Jackson Hole Mountain Guides [(307) 733-4979]. Park rangers advise against climbing the Grand without prior climbing instruction.

All visitors to the park backcountry should register, get the proper permits, and obey park rules. For more information, write to Grand Teton National Park, P.O. Drawer 170, Moose, WY 83012. —*Chuck Harper*

and breezed past Windy Tunnel. Next came Friction Pitch, a large, granite plate that tilts backward. It offered few handholds and a nasty view of a chasm.

The Scouts took deep breaths to calm themselves. Their safety partners assured them they were "on belay." The climbers inched their way up. They climbed 100 feet to easier ground, only to be greeted by the V Pitch. This 120-foot pitch was split in the center by a large crack known as an "open book."

Scout Jason Stauth recalled later: "The exposure of the V Pitch was the wildest thing I encountered."

This stretch had what Burgette called "a slanting awkward crack with an overhang." Scout Stauth found it troublesome. "I got sorta wedged in the crack," he said. "It was freaky."

One obstacle remained: a large slanting crack with a difficulty of 5.5 (see sidebar), according to Burgette.

As the Scouts climbed, the rocks hid the climber from his own partner on the rope, so everyone had to be especially careful. Slowly, they groped their way up to a flat knife-edge of rock several hundred feet below the summit.

Here, the world opened up. The climbers scampered across a snowfield to the last bit of the Grand's rocky spine leading to the summit's knob. Then they were there: 13,770 feet above sea level. "Awesome," "Wow," the Scouts yelled into the rushing wind. Ravens soared below. Justin Bybee found the climb humbling. "It was scary," he said. "You have to put a lot of trust in your friends."

After 30 minutes of enjoying the view, the Scouts started their descent. Not far from the summit, the return route included a 120-foot overhang rappel. One at a time, each boy slid down a double length of rope. Safely off the rope, the Scouts hiked down a trail toward base camp.

It was all downhill from there.✣

*Each year thousands of Scouts in national high-adventure programs learn their lessons from the best teacher of all—the wilderness.*

*Sommers insignia (top) means canoe adventure. Wild blueberries simmer (below) for a cobbler. Troop 60 (top, right) finds a wet portage.*

# Here's High Adventure

**By William B. McMorris**

A late July heat wave baked the northern Minnesota country around the town of Ely. A faint breeze scarcely ruffled the waters of the region's many sparkling lakes, but eight Scouts from Troop 60 of Waucousta, Mich. were keeping cool. They had no choice. They were on the first portage of their 8½-day high-adventure trip out of Charles L. Sommers Wilderness Canoe Base and up to their necks in swift water.

"Keep the bow into the current," Sommers guide Eric Edwards warned Tom Schaefer, Jeff Main, and Kevin Wells as the three edged

PHOTOGRAPHS BY WILLIAM B. McMORRIS

*A rare bald eagle's nest (top) with a pair of young, on a portage near the Sommers base. Curious loon (below) eyes Scout canoeists. Eerie loon call echoes often in the northwoods.*

their heavily laden canoe out of a deep pool into a narrow chute where the water was so swift it almost yanked the craft from their chilly hands.

Upstream Chris Main, Tommy Morefield, and crew advisor Tom Morefield battled slippery rocks and knee-deep current. Just beyond them, assistant advisor Clint Wells clung to a rock in another shoulder-deep hole while he anchored the guide's canoe.

The Michigan Scouts had been fighting the little stream for almost an hour, slipping over boulders and plunging into holes, dragging the canoes behind them. Now the end was in sight.

Half swimming, half wading, they eased the canoes across the worn timbers of an old logging dam and paddled into the narrow arm of a quiet lake.

As the three canoes of the crew drew close together Chris Main asked nobody in particular, "Do we really need a guide to find those uphill rivers?" He grinned slyly in the direction of Eric Edwards.

Eric pretended not to hear, and just then his eye caught a movement near the top of a big jack pine. "You need a guide to point out eagles," he said.

Almost as he spoke, two huge adult bald eagles rose from their nest. One soared far out over the lake, but the other swooped to the top of a nearby snag. The white feathers of its head and tail shone in the sun but its body and folded wings were almost black. It fixed a fierce yellow eye on the canoeists as they stared up at the enormous bundle of sticks that were woven into the crown of the jack pine to form the eagle's nest.

The reason for the eagle's watch- ➤

60

PHOTOGRAPHS BY BRIAN PAYNE

PHOTOGRAPH BY WILLIAM B. McMORRIS

*Scouts at Philmont (right and below) study Indian writings, hike high mountains as part of a half dozen camping opportunity plans. In Manitoba (far right), crew at Northern Expeditions breaks a new portage trail.*

*Lean back and trust the rope. Member of a Philmont crew (above) tries the spine-tingling art of rappeling down a smooth cliff face.*

fulness became clear. Two young birds, nearly as big as their parents, but bearing the mottled dark-brown and black plumage of immature eagles, flapped their wings at the edge of the eyrie.

Eric was as surprised as any of the Scouts at finding the nest and young. Eagles occasionally are sighted soaring over the lakes in the wilderness canoeing waters around Sommers and north into Canada, but an active nest is a rare sight. This was one of an estimated 800 to 1,000 to be found in the 48 states south of Canada.

They were also intruding on the old eagle's territory, so the Scouts stayed only long enough to snap a few photographs before they quietly paddled into the main body of the lake. Ahead lay many other adven-

tures, but the sight of the eagle's nest would remain one of the high points of the trip.

•

In finding this kind of unexpected adventure the Scouts of Troop 60 were not so different from similar crews across the nation who were setting out on their own treks. Not all the crews found eagles, but in each high-adventure base in Maine, Wisconsin, Kentucky, Florida, Minnesota, Canada, and New Mexico they found a special outdoor experience they would always remember.

## Northern Expeditions

At a satellite base in Bissett, Manitoba, 175 miles north of Winnipeg, Scouts tried a different version of the Sommers program. They ven-

*Six high-adventure bases and gateways plus one satellite base offer the best in wilderness living and training at low cost.*

*A crew of guides from Land Between the Lakes Gateway test a powered pontoon boat on Lake Barkley, Ky.*

tured into a region of unmarked portages and unspoiled lakes where they would often use maps and compasses to find their way. Rarely would they see another human being during their trip. In addition to regular 8½-day expeditions, some crews made even longer trips—with the extra-cost option of a float-plane pickup at journey's end.

## Philmont Scout Ranch and Explorer Base

Far to the west near Cimarron, N. Mex., Scouts set out for the towering Sangre de Cristo Mountains of Philmont Scout Ranch and Explorer Base. They would experience high-altitude backpacking, horseback riding, gold-panning, trout fishing, and dozens of other activities chosen from six different camping opportunity plans. They would complete conservation projects, find fossils, see traces of ancient Indian cultures, practice mountaineering techniques, and sharpen all their outdoor skills.

In addition they would find the bonus of unexpected adventures that come with any trek into 137,000 acres of wilderness.

## Land Between the Lakes Gateway

In mid-America among the rolling green hills of Kentucky and Tennessee, Scout crews prepared for a different kind of high-adventure experience. They would explore the ridges and hollows of a wild peninsula created by two giant man-made lakes. Some would backpack through country rich in plant and animal life, but most would travel in canoes, sailboats, or powered pontoon boats along more than 3,000 miles of shoreline. From lakeside camps they would explore inland on day trips. Wherever they went they would nev-

er be far from prime fishing, swimming, and boating waters.

## Northern Wisconsin National Canoe Base

The cool lakes and evergreens near Boulder Junction, Wis. were the goal of Scouts intent on doing battle with the muskelunge, one of America's fiercest fresh-water fish. And while they sought the elusive musky—or perhaps bass or pike—they would become expert canoeists through a unique training plan.

At this base, one member of each crew is selected for intensive Voyageur training before the arrival of his unit. Most crews send a second

member for advanced training in environmental awareness. He assists the crew in gaining a greater appreciation of the ecology of the northern Wisconsin country. When the crew assembles, a base guide accompanies the group for the first day. Then the crew is on its own with its Voyageur leading the way.

## Florida Gateway High Adventure Base

In a totally different setting, still other crews were ready to sail the tropical waters of Florida and the Bahamas in ocean-going sailboats. They would also look in on the underwater world of reefs teeming with ➤

*Any good outdoors troop will be even better after it meets these challenges.*

*Sailing into a campsite at sundown (above) at Land Between the Lakes. Learning the best way to pack a canoe (right) in Northern Wisconsin. Exploring a tropical reef (far right) at the Florida High Adventure Gateway.*

bright-colored fish and strange vegetation. They would train with SCUBA gear, snorkels, masks, and flippers, learn the fine points of sailing and water safety. They might also venture inland along the mysterious bends of the Withlacoochee River by canoe, and study the delicate ecology of that tropical waterworld.

## Maine National High Adventure Area

In the northeast corner of the United States in the rugged Maine wilderness, crews of Scouts would leave from two separate bases in the Maine National High Adventure Area for adventures in five million acres of managed backcountry forest

PHOTOGRAPHS BY NORMAN LERNER

*High-adventure bases are
popular, so hurry to get
in on your summer of fun.*

PHOTOGRAPH BY FLIP SCHULKE

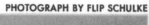

*Kayaking white water, canoeing, hiking, and mountain climbing in the famous
Travelers Range are just a few of the thrills to be found at Maine National High
Adventure Area.*

land. These Scouts could tailor trips to suit their special time requirements and interests. They could choose from canoeing, backpacking, or bushwhacking through trackless country. They could try kayaking swift rapids or learn to pole a canoe like a Maine guide. Lakes, streams, and the peaks of the famous Travelers Range were theirs to enjoy.

•

Wherever they went in high-adventure bases across the nation, Scouts like Waucousta's Troop 60 learned some things about themselves. If they were good campers, canoeists, sailors, or hikers before they left, they were better when they came back. There is no better teacher than the wilderness. ❖

If your troop has some Scouts who will be at least 14 by September 1976, they can obtain details about registration and costs for Charles L. Sommers Wilderness Canoe Base, Northern Expeditions Satellite Base, Northern Wisconsin National Canoe Base, and Land Between the Lakes High Adventure Gateway from their local council service center or 720 Franklin Square, Suite 200A, Michigan City, Ind. 46360.

For information about other high-adventure expeditions, write to:

Philmont Scout Ranch and Explorer Base
Cimarron, N. Mex. 87714

Maine National High Adventure Area
Box 150
Orrington, Maine 04474

Florida Gateway High Adventure Base
High Adventure Programs
Boy Scouts of America
North Brunswick, N. J. 08902

Also available to older Scouts are seven one-week-long hikes and climbs in the Washington Cascades and the Mt. Rainier area from the second week in July until the third week in August. If mountaineering is what you love, write for information to Chief Seattle Council, 3120 Rainier Avenue South, Seattle, Wash. 98144.

## Scout Program: Nature in Winter

# FUN IN THE SNOW

**BY JOHN TRACY**
PHOTOGRAPHS BY GENE DANIELS
Featuring Scouts of the River Bend District,
Central Wyoming Council.

If you spend all those snowy winter days in front of the television, you're missing a lot of outdoor fun. Scouts of the River Bend District of the Central Wyoming Council know this first hand. Every January, when winter is at its worst, these Scouts bundle up and go to the top of 8,000-foot Casper Mountain for their annual Winter Camporee and Klondike Derby.

What can Scouts do for winter fun? Try snowshoeing, skiing, sledding, skating, ice fishing and throwing snowballs —all things they can't do in summer. There are not enough winter hours to get to everything.

You can also read signs and find out what the wild creatures are doing. Tracks of the fox are there in the snow, as well as bobcat, wild turkey, grouse and squirrel. You may even see where an owl swooped down on a rabbit, left the outline of its wings in the snow and

took off with its prey.

Once you have become a winter camper, you may also learn some things about yourself. You find that you can be comfortable in cold weather. You learn how good you are at woodsmanship and whether you need more experience in such basic outdoor skills as cooking, staying warm and making a comfortable winter camp. As you sharpen these skills you gain confidence in your ability to survive in the cold if you should ever face a winter emergency or get lost in the wilderness during the cold months.

To enjoy the outdoors in winter you need the right *attitude*. If you think you can be comfortable and have fun out in the snow, you are probably right. Besides, in this season there are no bugs to fight.

Scouts of the River Bend District go to Casper Mountain for their January

campout. Much of their time is spent in competitions. Cooking and eating are important too, because the human body needs plenty of energy in winter.

If you get out into the cold weather for camping, or any winter sports, plan how to stay both comfortable and safe. This means, first of all, outfitting yourself with the right clothes.

Remember that the best insulation is dead air. For this reason, several layers of clothing will keep you warmer than a single heavy outfit because there is air between the layers. This is why some outdoorsmen wear several pairs of socks or two or three shirts.

The clothes you wear do not provide a bit of heat. They can only preserve the heat created by your body. If you let too much heat escape through your clothes, you are not getting the full benefit from them. You might even become a hypothermia victim.

**DON'T SPEND WINTER INDOORS!
SKIING, SLEDDING, SKATING,
SNOWSHOEING, ICE FISHING
AND TRACKING WILDLIFE ARE JUST
SOME OF THE EXCITING
WINTER ACTIVITIES YOUR
TROOP CAN DO ON
A COLD-WEATHER CAMPOUT.**

Knowing basic skills makes winter camping fun for these Wyoming Scouts. They dress properly (all wear hats to keep body heat from escaping). They build cooking fires with some slope to drain away melting snow (right), practice rescue techniques (below) and can keep warm inside a snow shelter.

**YOU CAN STAY DRY AND WARM WHEN CAMPING IN WINTER IF YOU KNOW HOW TO DRESS RIGHT, WHAT KIND OF EQUIPMENT TO BRING, AND SOME SNOWTIME SKILLS LIKE BUILDING A SHELTER FROM BLOCKS OF COMPACTED SNOW.**

You can short-stop these losses of body heat if you think ahead and wear the right clothing in your winter camp.

Heat is lost around the neck, wrists and ankles. You can block its escape at the neck by wearing a hat and a scarf or a parka with an attached hood. The hat or hood is especially good because much heat can be lost if your head is not covered. Experienced outdoor people wear a hat day and night when living in cold country. A knit stocking cap makes an excellent night cap to help you stay snug and warm in your sleeping bag.

Gloves that cover the wrists help prevent heat loss. So does fastening your pants legs around your boot tops.

Modern clothes make it easier to stay comfortable in cold weather. You'll get good protection from a jacket filled with synthetic fiber. (This is preferable to down, which can lose its insulating quality if it gets wet.) A windbreaker is important too. Wool clothing is a long-time favorite of experienced woodsmen, and a wool shirt is a sound choice.

If you are wearing Scout uniform trousers or blue jeans, wear long underwear with them. Thermal underwear with the waffle pattern is a good choice, and for sub-zero weather you may need down-insulated underwear.

The feet are especially important. Be sure to wear boots that are not too tight. Shoe pacs, the kind with rubber bottoms and leather tops, are excellent if they are equipped with felt liners and are big enough so you can wear one or two pairs of wool socks without their pinching your feet. A pair of cotton socks next to the feet give greater comfort.

If the weather is really cold, mittens are better protection than gloves for the hands. It's awkward using mittens, however, when cooking outdoors, or participating in competitions, so you may also need a pair of gloves.

Sleeping comfortably is vital to a successful winter camp. The Wyoming Scouts take a lesson from the Eskimos and make snow shelters.

One kind is a snow tunnel or cave. Another is the igloo made from blocks of compacted snow. The smaller the snow shelter, the warmer you can keep it with your body heat. The Wyoming Scouts make snow caves after packing down the snow.

Do not make the top of the shelter too thick. To insure correct thickness, push sticks 12- to 15-inches long into the cave top from the outside, so when you reach the sticks from the inside, you'll know you've hollowed out the roof the proper amount. To guard against roof cave-ins, be sure to make your inside ceiling dome-shaped (a convex arch). Avoid any squared wall-ceiling corners, which will make a weaker roof.

Make a raised platform out of snow for your sleeping bag inside the shelter, to provide extra insulation.

You will need fresh air in a snow shelter, so ventilation is important. Be especially careful if you use any kind of heater, even a candle, that might consume oxygen.

If you remember these tips, you will be comfortable and safe in the cold. And you will have fun in your winter camp. ♣

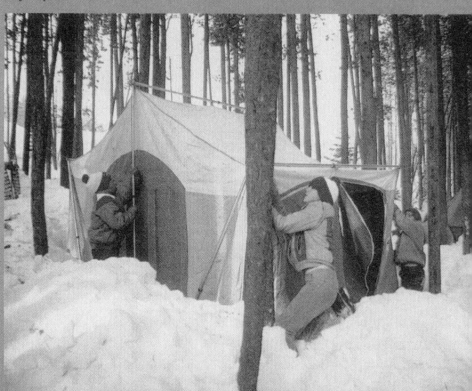

Snowshoes (opposite page) make walking in deep snow easier. Pioneering (left) doesn't stop in winter, but deep snow may force you to anchor your tents to trees. A stretcher race (bottom) is a fun way to practice first aid.

# Hiking Hells Canyon

A jet-boat ride on the thundering Snake River is a
thrill, but there's even more adventure
in hiking the trail through the canyon carved by the
river. Scouts of Pullman, Wash., had it all.

BY SAM CURTIS
Photographs by David Falconer

STARTING AS A SNOW-MELT
trickle on the Pacific slopes of the Conti-
nental Divide in Wyoming, the headwa-
ters of the Snake River are hardly worthy
of a jet boat ride. But by the time the
Snake has curled around the bottom of
Idaho to head north and form the bound-
ary between that state and Oregon, it has
become a boisterous river. In Hells Canyon,
the Snake pours through a gorge thousands of feet deep. People come to its
shores attracted by the scenery and usually mild climate.

The Indians came first, over 7,000 years
ago. By the middle of the 19th century,
prospectors and ranchers had entered
Hells Canyon. And in April of 1984, Troop
460 of Pullman, Wash., arrived to discover for itself what the canyon had to
offer. The thirty Scouts and eight adult
leaders found a fascinating array of history,
scenery, people and weather.

The first leg of their journey was easy.
After winding down into the canyon over
17 miles of dirt road, the troop—chartered
to Simpson United Methodist Church of
Pullman—reached Pittsburg Landing. In
two trips with his 32-foot jet boat, Norm
Riddle shuttled the troop and its gear 16

miles upstream to the mouth of Sheep
Creek. By jet boat, it was a journey of 45
minutes, but starting the next morning
the Scouts would take three days to hike
back to the cars.

The troop's campsite at Sheep Creek
was at the spot where Scotsman Bill
McLeod scratched out his homestead
exactly 100 years earlier. Later, the
McGaffee brothers purchased the land
and built the house and barn that now
stand abandoned here.

Despite the gray skies, the Scouts set-
tled in, pitching their tarp shelters and
poking about the old homestead. Not to
be without some of the comforts of home,
Brent Peters improvised a hammock. And
Trevor Meade discovered an aged and
bleached sheep vertebra that he adapted
as a neckerchief slide.

Meanwhile, Senior Patrol Leader Ken
Hillers caught a large carp in a backwater
of the river. Reid Alisch, Brian Hayton
and Joe Worthy assisted in its landing, as
Ken chuckled, "Carp don't bite, I don't
think."

From the steep hillside above Sheep
Creek a hiker can look across the river
into Oregon and see the fire lookout on

Above: On a chilly morn-
ing, Robert Riggs begins
the daily camp chores
for the Alligator Patrol.
Below, left: Members of
the Crazy Eagle Patrol
sit on a safe perch to
let a wrangler and his
pack train pass on the
trail. The rider, Jerry
Winegar, was headed
upriver to make trail
repairs for the U.S. For-
est Service.

Opposite: Alongside the
powerful Snake River,
Scouts from Pullman,
Wash., hike in Idaho with
a view of Oregon just
across the river. The weather had as many changes
as the Snake had bends in
this portion of the Hells
Canyon Recreation Area,
but the Scouts survived
them all in good shape.
They even got by Suicide
Point where "if you step
off the trail, you're not
going to step back on."

on the bar by the river. A camp there might be somewhat sheltered from the wind, and it seemed senseless to keep on hiking.

To everyone's relief, blue sky showed downstream by the time the tarps were being set up, and within an hour and a half, the sun was shining and clothes were drying.

It was right after all the tarps had been pitched that the sheepherder arrived. He strode into camp with a large six-shooter strapped to his hip, and his first words were, "I don't know how to tell you this, but your camp is right where my horses run. And I've got a white mule who'll walk into any tent he can stick his head into."

Fortunately, he assured us that he'd try to keep the horses away, and he figured a few barks from Maggie ought to scare the horses off.

The sheepherder had been living in a

Hat Point. The lookout, according to the topo map, is situated at 6,982 feet. The river at Sheep Creek is at 1,282 feet. It's that difference of 5,700 feet that accounted for the fact that the lookout was still surrounded by snow, while syringa bloomed along the banks of the Snake. The canyon rim and the canyon floor were in two different seasons.

Nevertheless, the evening sky was the color of slate. Tim Slabaugh, David Crain, Nate Ullrich, Shawn Gaymon and Jeff Loughney of the Crazy Eagle Patrol were taking no chances on having a soggy supper. By 5:00 P.M. they were the first of six patrols to be eating.

The rain didn't set in until 8:00, after everyone had eaten and washed up. It was a steady rain that lasted all night, stopping conveniently at 6:00 A.M. just in time for breakfast preparations. But morning light revealed a snowline that had crept down to the 4,000 foot level. The seasons were getting uncomfortably close together.

Maggie, Joe Stock's dog, must have felt the seasons shifting. She was with Joe in his sleeping bag when morning arrived.

It was after 10:00 when the Scouts got on the trail—a trail that camelbacks up over ridges and then down to the water's edge, over and over. At one point, Mike Gaskins, Matt Alisch and Eric Knapp discussed the merits of having skis along if the weather took a turn for the worse.

Other Scouts seemed to envy Leigh Juve and Jerry Winegar who passed in the opposite direction with their horses and a string of mules. They were on their way to Sheep Creek where they would live in the old McGaffee place while they improved sections of the trail.

Leigh and Jerry work for the U.S. Forest Service, which is the government agency responsible for managing Hells Canyon National Recreation Area through which the Snake River flows. The section of river along which the Scouts were hiking is part of the National Wild and Scenic Rivers System.

Above: A dog's best friend is her master's sleeping bag when the temperature takes a dive. (By the way, there are no fleas in this part of Idaho.) Top, right: Haakon Latvala and Jay Hutton decide they have found a horse's jaw bone. Below, right: Snow on the mountains stayed at the 4,000-foot level, but it gave a chilly edge to the wind on the canyon floor at 1,282 feet.

Despite thoughts of skis and horses, the Scouts continued on foot, reaching a high bench above Big Bar (a wide, grass covered gravel bar) at about 3:00 P.M. Their arrival here coincided with the arrival of a gray wall of clouds that had been moving steadily upstream as the Scouts moved downstream. The gray wall consisted of rain driven by a wild wind. It stopped the Scouts in their tracks. Behind the first blast of rain there appeared to be much more of the same.

Assistant Scoutmaster Charley Gaskins made the decision to get the troop down

wall tent in the canyon since December. The temperature had plunged to 30 below that month according to his figuring. He thought 160 to 180 sheep out of several thousand that he and another herder tended might have died because of the weather. (We had seen and smelled a number of dead sheep since our arrival in the canyon.) It was a winter to be reckoned with, the sheepherder told us.

He, along with the other people we met on the trip, are a part of the on going history of Hells Canyon—a history filled with stories just made to tell around a campfire at night. And so it seemed fitting that Ken Hillers related one of these tales at that evening's fire.

"Some of you may have noticed, back where we had lunch, there was a cabin that's sort of falling apart. Well, there was this old guy who lived in the cabin, and he had a lot of gardens. And one day these two gentlemen—one was named Brownlee—were trailing cattle along Big Bar, and they let the cattle have lunch in this guy's gardens.

"Well, when he came home and saw that cattle had been in his garden, he followed Brownlee to the rocks right up here where we came across. The place is now called Brownlee Saddle because, from there, the old guy shot Brownlee and tried to shoot the other man too. The old guy's name was Myers; he was later hung by vigilantes near the town of White Bird.

"That's just a bit of interesting history about this place." Ken paused and then added, "Hope you all sleep well tonight...."

The next morning dawned windy—so windy that it blew Andrew Crain's lounge (yes, lounge) chair into the fire. And it pulled Haakon Latvala into a clump of prickly pear cactus when it made a sail out of the tarp he was helping fold.

The wind continued as the Scouts climbed up the trail around Suicide Point. And, as Troop Committee Member Joe Hillers had said the night before, "You don't want to go foolin' around on the trail over there at Suicide Point, because I'll tell you, if you step off, you're not going to step back on."

Once around the point, the wind died down, and by early afternoon the Scouts had reached their day's destination—Kirkwood Historic Ranch. Homesteaded by Dr. Jay Kirkwood and his family in the 1880s, the ranch has had a number of owners, including Len Jordan who later became Governor of Idaho and then a U.S. Senator. Today, the small ranch is managed as a historic site by Lori and Dave Clark who work for the Forest Service and who greeted the Scouts on their arrival.

After setting up camp in a hayfield downstream from the ranchhouse, Scouts visited the museum that is housed in the log bunkhouse. There, Lori answered questions and commented on the ranch's past, and that evening Dave and jet boat operator Norm Riddle stood around the fire telling stories of Hells Canyon. They spoke of homesteading, mining and murders, and they told tales of ranching, river travel and Indians.

Finally, Dave Clark put some of the history into perspective.

"It's fascinating to me to think that until 400 years ago the Indians didn't have horses. They traveled through here on foot, and when they carried their winter supply of camas and cous bulbs from the high country down to here, they did it in their hands and in baskets.

"You guys have hiked through here, so you know how tough it is. Just think about

**Right: Leigh Juve stops her horse to chat with Jeff Loughney. Ms. Juve works on trail improvements, is a wrangler, and a recreational ranger for the Forest Service.**

**Above: The jet boat used just 45 minutes to take the Scouts on a three-day hike up Hells Canyon. Right: Robert Riggs set up a clothes line to dry his socks, but the weather had other ideas. He tries to squeeze out the rainwater but the socks (and most other clothing) stayed damp for the rest of the trip.**

carrying your whole winter supply of food with you, not just 3 or 4 days' worth. And they sure didn't have nylon bags and pack frames."

Later Scoutmaster Dick Crain would say, "the combination of history, scenery and weather made this a trip the Scouts will never forget."

Part of the reason the Scoutmaster included the weather was that next morning, with no food left to carry but lunch, the Scouts awoke to a steady rain and to thoughts of foot travel— soggy foot travel. As several Scouts hopped around a sput-

tering fire beating on tin cups with their spoons, someone suggested it might be a rain dance.

"I sure hope they're doing it backwards," said Matt Maring.

Unfortunately, the Scouts around the cooking fire didn't seem to know how to reverse a rain dance. The water continued to fall from the sky and the clouds dogged their tracks every step of the way back to the cars. But even though the trail was soggy, the Scouts were grateful they didn't have to haul an entire winter's food supply. ♣

Use duel contests at your patrol meetings. For STICK FIGHT you need a staff, about five feet long. Two fellows grab hold of it. The winner is the one who first touches an end of the staff to the floor.

# MAKE THEM EAT BEAR MEAT

"**E**VERY PATROL HIKE should have an objective" they tell me. So who's disagreeing? Not I! That's what I've been preaching all along—although I haven't used such a highbrow word.

"So what's a hike objective, daddy?" Usually something in the line of general Second and First Class work, first aid, signaling, cooking, nature.

But how about making HIKING your hike objective this month? In other words—have a hike for the sake of hiking!

It's about time for all of us to re-discover hiking. It is one of the best exercises known. It strengthens the lungs and heart, straightens the back, develops the muscles, makes the blood run tingling through your veins.

The old vikings used to eat bear meat for strength—it was tough to chew and full of red blood. Well, there's another kind of "bear meat" that'll make you strong—an imaginary kind, the kind you "eat" the last couple of miles of a twenty-mile hike, the kind you "chew" when you fight your way through brambles and underbrush on an orienteering race, when you climb to the summit of a mountain.

Cook up a lot of that kind of "bear meat" in the form of real hiking and serve it red-hot to your patrol as often as possible.

As a patrol leader it is your responsibility to help your boys become "physically strong." Making them eat "bear meat" is one of the best ways of doing it.

**After you're once in the swing** of real hiking, keep it up! Go whole-hog and set your sights for the Hiking merit badge for every boy in the patrol.

What's involved in getting this He-man badge?

Check the requirements in your HANDBOOK FOR BOYS and you'll see that they amount to this:
● Five hikes of ten miles each over a six-month period. One hike of twenty miles. A written report of each of the six hikes. And finally, a demonstration before an examiner of proper hiking techniques and a written plan for a ten-mile hike.
● See what I mean now? In the first requirement you have the challenge of a definite schedule of real hiking. A regular patrol hike each month—and by the time six months are up, there'll be a Hiking merit badge on the uniform sleeve or sash of each of your boys.

So get tough! Get them out! Onward to the Hiking merit badge!

**The outdoors is the best possible** place for your toughening-up process. But bring fitness and fun into your patrol meetings as well.

How'll you do it? By using duel contests—they're absolutely the most for this purpose.
● Which will it be? Just take a look at the pictures on this page and take your pick. Then, on your next patrol date, imitate! Run each of the duel contests on a championship basis: Pair the fellows against each other and let the winners fight it out until you've crowned a patrol champion.
● Or, even better, go in the opposite direction: Let the losers fight each other and find out who's the patrol "champ-nit." In this system, the weaker fellows get more practice and become better able to win the next time.
● Now don't stop with the four games on these pages. Use also other games from the Patrol Stunts chapter of your HANDBOOK FOR PATROL LEADERS as well as the physical fitness tricks we give you in the Duffel Bag section of every issue of BOYS' LIFE.

**Still wondering how to get** your fellows over the first aid hurdles for their Second and First Class badges? Nothing to it if you go about the job systematically.
● Get a large sheet of brown paper, a ruler, and a pencil. Draw as many horizontal columns as there are fellows in the patrol and put in their names. Next draw as many vertical columns as there are first aid items for Second and First Class and write in the items starting from the beginning: artificial respiration, shock, fainting, arterial bleeding of arm, arterial bleeding of leg, cuts, scratches, and so on and so forth. Now get the whole gang into the act.
● Demonstrate the first item yourself, then have the fellows perform. Watch to see that every boy does it right. When you're satisfied, check off that item on your chart for each fellow. Next item. You demonstrate, each fellow does it, you check him off. Next and next and next—until time's up or you've done as much as you'd planned to do at *that* patrol meeting. Then more next time.

With this system you'll get your fellows through the first aid requirements in no man's time—and you'll have your patrol ready for the big first aid event that I have a suspicion your troop will spring on you in December (but don't tell anybody that I told you).

HAND WRESTLING—Two fellows place the outside of their right feet together, clasp right hands, try to throw each other off balance without moving their feet.

TRACTOR PULL—Two boys get down on all fours, facing away from each other. Two riders grasp hands. "Tractors" pull away from each other until a rider is unseated.

COCK FIGHT—Two opponents hop around on one leg, holding on to the other leg. Each of them tries to knock the other fellow off balance using his shoulders only.

BY BUCK TILTON ✴ ILLUSTRATIONS BY JONATHAN CARLSON

 Heat Exhaustion

 Altitude Sickness

 Hypothermia

 Frostbite

THE SILENT KILLERS

Losing body heat happens in all seasons, and it can kill. Know the symptoms and how to treat them.

Twelve-year-old Erick Cole was sick at heart, and scared.

Erick and his little brother, Andy, 4, had been sledding together out in the Nebraska snow. When it came time to go home, Erick decided to make another run; Andy said he'd wait for his big brother at the bottom of the hill. But as Erick reached the end of his final slide, he discovered Andy

# HEAT LOSS

Your body gets rid of its excess heat in four ways:

**Conduction** occurs when you touch something colder than you. For instance, when you sit down on cold ground it draws heat from your body.

**Convection** occurs when air blows around you. That's why you feel colder on a windy day.

When liquid sweat on your skin turns to water vapor in the process of **evaporation**, you also lose a lot of heat.

When warm objects, including you, release heat, it is given off as **radiation** in the form of infrared rays.

---

had vanished! The temperature was dropping quickly, and soon Erick was desperate in his search for Andy. Where could he be?

The older boy walked near an abandoned construction pit, calling "Andy! Andy!" That's when Erick heard a weak cry. His brother had slipped into the pit and was too small to climb out.

Erick jumped down into the pit to rescue him. Andy was dazed, crying and unable to walk. Gently, Erick picked him up and carried Andy to the nearest house. It was a close call. Andy survived, but the cold had almost killed him.

## Heat Balance

Your body gets energy from the food and water you consume. As you process food and water, heat is released, keeping you warm inside. Usually you make more heat than you need. Your body sheds the excess heat through conduction, convection, evaporation, and radiation (see "Heat Loss") to stabilize your inner (core) temperature at 98.6 degrees Fahrenheit.

## Too Much Cold

When you lose heat faster than you make it—Andy's problem—your

internal temperature begins to fall. A drop in core temperature is called hypothermia. A hypothermic person develops increasingly serious problems as his body continues to cool down. They are:

1) Confusion and trouble solving problems, plus mild shivering.

2) Stumbling and stronger shivering, pale skin, having trouble speaking and an "I-don't-care" attitude.

3) Inability to walk and horrible shivers.

4) Slow heartbeat and breathing. Skin turns blue. Muscles grow rigid. Shivering stops for the same reason a motor dies—there's no more fuel. Then, death.

## Warming Up

Someone who can still shiver, walk and talk has mild hypothermia. You can warm that person back up to normal body temperature.

It's simple. Here's how:

Change any wet clothing for dry stuff. Add extra dry layers of clothing to provide more insulation. Also, use blankets or something similar to insulate the person from the cold ground. Offer him fluids, especially warm, sweet fluids like hot cider or sweetened tea, as well

as high-energy foods, such as candy. If you can, get the person to a source of heat, such as a fire.

Severe hypothermia starts when someone can't shiver anymore. Handle the person with care. No rough stuff. Take off his damp clothing. Bundle him in warm, dry layers and make sure there's insulation underneath him.

Wrap him in something waterproof and windproof, such as a tent fly, and be careful that his head is protected from the cold, too. Then go for help.

The best medicine is prevention. Here are some ways to prevent hypothermia:

1) Wear clothes designed to keep you warm in the cold.

2) Wear lots of thin layers of clothes instead of one heavy garment, such as a coat. If you get warm and sweaty, take off a layer to let the sweat dry. If you start feeling cold again, add layers of clothing.

3) Drink and eat a lot, so your body has plenty of "fuel" to generate heat.

4) In a group, watch out for hypothermia's symptoms in others. They may not realize they are becoming hypothermic.✢

## FURTHER READING

"Basic Essentials of Hypothermia," 2nd Edition, by William W. Forgey, M.D. (Globe Pequot Press).

"First Aid for Youths," by Buck Tilton, M.S., and Steve Griffin (Globe Pequot Press).

"Hypothermia, Frostbite and Other Cold Injuries," by James Wilkerson, M.D., Cameron Bangs, M.D., and John Hayward, Ph.D. (The Mountaineers).

*Ranger Dave Mahler briefs his crew.*

# PHILMONT RANGER

By Gene Daniels

*The two-man saw is a test of skill.*

*Easy as rolling a log, if you know how.*

*A good Philmont Ranger is a psychologist, cook, hiker, camper, first aid man, burro handler, and orienteer. And every Philmont Ranger is a good Ranger.*

*Tying a taut-line hitch to a tent stake. Going up a tree on climbing spikes.*

**B**oys and burros are a daily part of a Philmont Ranger's life, and he or she comes to understand both very well. The Ranger's job is to escort an expedition for the first three of its 12 days on the trails—but there is more to it than that.

During that time the Ranger hopes to steer each group into becoming competent enough in the fine art of mountain packing to go it alone the rest of the way. Last year almost 19,000 Scouts and Explorers hiked the high country at Philmont Scout Ranch and Explorer Base in northern New Mexico, and that meant work for a lot of Rangers.

Their job includes teaching the crews the proper use of all camp gear, food preparation, mapping, and the knack of being safe and comfortable in the wilderness with a minimum of equipment. Their own training is so thorough that they may even try to get a couple of blisters early in the season—so that they'll understand the blister problems that campers may have.

Typical of the Rangers is Dave Mahler, who takes such a personal interest in each of his crews that at the end of the first three days on the trail—when he has the option of leaving or staying with them—he knows them well enough to make the right decision. (It's very rare for a Ranger to find it necessary to break the normal pattern and continue to shepherd his crew after the first three days.)

As a species, the Rangers have two things in common. They like to hike and camp. And they are among the elite of the Philmont staff—only the horsemen get as much attention from the campers.

Otherwise they are individualists. Some read poetry, one carries her violin strapped to her back pack, several are guitarists, some are photographers, and back at home they may have been house painters, pre-med students, football players, or science majors. Many hike or climb a mountain on their "days off."

The crew Dave worked with in the pictures on these pages came from West Palm Beach, Fla. On the evening of their third day in the mountains, Dave gave them his final instructions, and cooked the traditional peach cobbler in a Dutch oven. The cobbler is a Ranger's way of saying, "Here's a reward for learning your wilderness lessons well. Now you're on your own." ❖

# Search for a Wilderness Lake

TEXT AND PHOTOGRAPHS
BY GENE DANIELS

THE ANGRY RATTLESNAKE was monstrous—much larger than those Troop 84 usually saw in the high desert that lies east of California's Sierra Nevada mountain range. For a moment, Star Scout Bobby Stockman wondered if the horse he was riding was going to rear up on its hind legs and dump him into the cactus. You know, like horses always do in the movies, when they hear the chilling rattle of a diamondback.

But the desert-wise steeds, carrying the Scouts upward toward Sawmill Pass, barely blinked. *Thank heaven,* thought Scoutmaster Bob Stockman, Bobby's dad. *I hope nothing else goes wrong.*

The fishing and camping trip into the mountains had been planned by Bobby and his Scout buddies—Frank Nikolaus and Chris Riesen—for more than a year. Just because they live in the desert town of Independence (where the troop is chartered to the Independence Civic Club), almost in the shadow of 14,495-foot Mount Whitney, doesn't mean they weren't looking forward to the trip.

But things had not gone well. One of the horses of the outfitter they'd hired had escaped into the desert, delaying their start. Next, the animal that I was riding—I'm a photographer-writer for *Boys' Life*—had collapsed. Getting the sick horse on its feet and headed back toward home, along with the outfitter, had taken another half hour.

That's when the snake started buzzing. But almost without missing stride, the horses plodded upward. Behind the Scouts, the desert became a vast panorama. As the climb became steeper, sand, sage, and rock

**If you don't count falling horses and angry rattlesnakes, this was Troop 84's smoothest Sierra trip.**

The sign reads:

ENTERING
KINGS CANYON NATIONAL PARK
SAWMILL PASS
ELEVATION 11,347
U.S. DEPARTMENT OF INTERIOR
NATIONAL PARK SERVICE

Horses got the Scouts started (below), but the high-altitude climb (above) was a matter of putting one foot in front of the other.

changed to grass, trees, and a little snow. By lunchtime, the party had climbed the 5000 feet to Sawmill Lake, with the pass still 1,350 feet above them.

The wrangler called them together. It was true, he conceded, that the troop had hired his boss to take them to Sawmill Pass. But because of the late start and the sick horse and all—well-l-l, it was already one o'clock. And if he didn't start back now with the horses, they'd be fighting their way through the sage in the dark.

The Scouts got the picture. They grabbed their packs and headed off on foot. Two grinding hours later, they sat down by the sign welcoming hikers to Kings Canyon National Park, where they waited 40 minutes for the adults to catch up. Two thousand feet below, and a mile-and-a-half west, lay their destination—Woods Lake—gleaming like a precious diamond surrounded by several smaller jewels.

Another group had beaten them to the big lake. So they walked on by. Troop 84 was looking for the best wilderness experience they could find.

Quickly, they set up tents, gathered wood, and ate. Then they pulled out their spinning rods. A few dark shapes followed their lures, but until the Scoutmaster began to fish, they had no luck. He finally caught a seven-inch brook trout.

What a crazy day! They had spent $200 for horses that pooped out, been threatened by a rattler, come close to losing the reporter under a falling horse, and climbed the toughest part of the trail with 40-pound packs. And now, after all that, their reward was a single, seven-inch trout!

Their laughter rang through the cold,

bright Sierra night. And off to bed they went.

The next morning, the Scouts and the sun rose together. No longer tired, they looked for new worlds to conquer. On a topographical map, Bobby and Frank spotted a tiny, blue dot not far away.

"That's the place to fish," promised Frank. "I'm sure that those tourists we saw didn't fish there."

In 10 minutes the Scouts had hiked to a clearing flanked by a massive, granite cliff. Lying peacefully in front of the cliff was a lake, ringed by a white collar of snow and ice.

Bobby shivered as he waded waist-deep into the icy water, determined to claim the farthest cast. Frank climbed a granite boulder, and Chris hid behind some pines. There was no need for them to have gone to all that trouble, for almost instantly, all three had hooked into fish.

Bobby reeled in the first one. "Goldens!" he shouted when he saw flashing orange color. But then he shook his head. He had not hooked one of the fabulously beautiful golden trout that inhabit some high Sierra lakes. His fish was a brook trout, as beautiful in its own way as a golden. And the fish was half as long as Bobby's arm. He leaned over and carefully unhooked the brookie, slid it gently back into the water, and watched as it swam away.

Then he looked over toward Frank and Chris, who also were releasing trout. Later in the day, they'd catch fish to save for dinner. Right now, all they wanted to do was have fun catching fish. They'd found their fish. And they'd discovered that the kind of wilderness they came looking for was still there. Why not enjoy it? ♣

"Good-bye, Old Paint" (above) was said a few hours up the trail. Troop 84 didn't stop until they reached a small, icy lake.

The water was clear and freezing cold, but those who braved the chill could bring in a brook trout on every cast.

# KEEP WARM

# In Winter Camp

### BY WILLIAM HILLCOURT

**National Director of Scoutcraft**

WINTER CAMPING is one of the grandest experiences you can have in Scouting—provided you are warm and comfortable. And keeping warm is simply a matter of knowing how—of having on the proper kind of clothing, of building the right type of fires, of making up your bed correctly.

As far as CLOTHING is concerned, spell it W-O-O-L. Wool absorbs moisture and is full of insulating air pockets. So it's wool underwear, wool shirt, wool pants—but with a closely-woven, water-repellent cotton jacket on top to keep the wind out and the body heat in. Use woolen ski socks to keep your feet warm in thick-soled, well-oiled, high-cut shoes or, better, ski boots. Use a Scout winter cap or a ski cap for head gear, and wool or fur-lined gloves for your hands.

You'll find four types of FIRES described on these pages. Pick those that suit your purpose. If you choose the tent stove, be POSITIVE that the chimney is thoroughly insulated where it goes out through the tent wall, and that the chimney opening is provided with wire netting for spark control. Let the fire go out at night when you turn in, and start it up again in the morning.

When it comes to your BED, the best stunt is to make a log frame, filling it with light brush, dead leaves, spruce or hemlock twigs, and covering it with a waterproof ground sheet. Then put in your sleeping bag or blankets—plenty of them. For night wear, get into a sweat suit or one of the popular flannel ski-pajamas, and a pair of heavy wool socks.

Here's to a glorious winter camping experience for you and your gang!

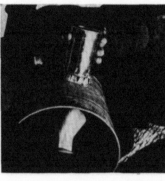

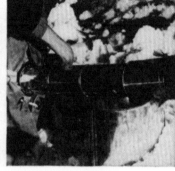

**TENT STOVE**—Cut square hole at edge of 10 qt. pail, with slits for sliding door. Opposite door, near pail bottom, cut hole with pointed tongues for chimney of No. 2 cans. Attach first can with four of the tongues through slits. Connect chimney parts with No. 2½ cans, slit lengthwise, pushed halfway into each.

Where chimney goes through tent corner, insulate it with collar of No. 3 can. Cut hole in bottom of this can to fit chimney; at other end cut tongues to form slips to hold can to canvas. Pack asbestos between collar and chimney. Cover chimney opening with wire netting for spark control. Brace the chimney firmly.

**NYING FIRE**—In Northern Scandinavia they use a special fire that will burn through the night; in Sweden and Norway they call it a *nying*, in Finland a *rakovalkea*. Split a dry log in two, using wedges. Rough up the split surfaces. Place one half on the ground, the other half on top of it, but raised above it

with two short, arm-thick cross pieces of wood. Put shavings and kindling between the log halves. When the fire has been going for a while, one or both of the cross pieces may be removed; they work as draft regulators. If properly prepared, the *nying* will go on burning without any attending whatever.

**COOKING FIRE**—Scoop snow aside and place floor of sticks on the ground on which to build the fire. Use two heavy logs to support your frying pans. For hanging your pots, make two tripods by lashing together short poles. Set up tripods four feet apart. Place lug pole on them. Hang pots in rustic pot hooks.

**REFLECTOR FIRE**—This is traditional fire for heating open-front tent: Prop up two stakes about six feet in front of the tent, then stack green logs against them to form reflector. Scoop snow away, and place floor of green logs on the ground. Build the fire on the log floor. Have generous supply of dry wood.

**ACTIVITIES**—Numerous activities, such as skiing, snowshoeing, tobogganing, will help to keep you warm in winter camp. Peel off some of your heavy clothing so that you have just enough on to be comfortable. In this way you avoid perspiration that may chill you afterwards. Put it all back on when you rest.

# QUEST BEYOND EAGLE

**BY ROBERT GRAY**
PHOTOGRAPHS BY BRIAN PAYNE

Six Eagle Scouts picked their way among the boulders along the slope of Mt. Conness, high in California's Sierra Nevada range. Ahead, the peak towered almost 13,000 feet above sea level, its flanks covered with snow and ice, parts of the summit swept bare by wind.

Eagle Scout Larry Landauer looked at the peak ahead. "It's gonna be a hot, long climb," he said. "Let's take a break. Be sure to put on sun-screen and goggles. The glare will be awful out on the snow."

The Scouts had been climbing since five o'clock that morning. This was the day they had been working toward for almost two weeks, ever since they had come north from Los Angeles with 18 other Eagle Scouts. They were involved in this high adventure as part of a program called, "Quest Beyond Eagle."

Its setting was Log Cabin Boy Scout Camp in the northern Sierra, 10,000 feet above sea level. But the camp served primarily as a jumping off point, for the quest took these Eagles far afield.

When they first arrived in camp, they were assigned to the crews of six persons with whom they would live and work. Each crew took the name of a famous Californian of earlier years. The Huntingtons were named for one of the builders of the first transcontinental railroad; the Bidwells, for a discoverer of gold in the state; the Drakes, for the navigator who was the first Englishman to set foot in California; the Fremonts, for the colorful Army officer who became the state's first military governor. Four crews had six Eagle Scouts each.

At Log Cabin camp they learned about mountain geology, plant and animal life, and ecology along with their training in rock climbing, search and rescue techniques, orienteering, and camp housekeeping. Evenings were given over to rap sessions when the four crews discussed what they had done during the day.

It wasn't all work, though. There were activities meant for nothing more than old-fashioned fun. The log jam, for instance, put the crews into competition in pole climbing, caber tossing (throwing a young tree trunk, a Scottish sport), log carrying and sawing. There was a black powder rifle shoot during which the Scouts learned how to load and fire a musket. They went on a tour of a gold mine. And, perhaps most appreciated of all at the end of hot, tiring days, there was a dunking in the gold mine's water tank.

By the beginning of the second week, the Scouts were down to fighting trim, lean and well-trained for a two-day cross-country backpack and an ascent of Mt. Conness. The distance from Log Cabin to base ▶

A rock-climbing Eagle (top) rides the
mountaineer's elevator, a rappel
rope. At the bottom of the cliff he
will climb back up for practice.
Near the summit of Mt. Conness, one
team (above) was forced back by dangerous
snow conditions. Team log rolling
(right) was a base camp sport.
Lumberjack's peaveys are the tools,
and muscle makes the log roll.

camp at Greenstone Lake was only about eight miles as the crow flies, but since backpacking Scouts aren't crows, they had to hike quite a bit farther. An adult advisor tagged along with each crew to make sure nobody got into serious trouble. Otherwise the Scouts were completely on their own.

The Huntingtons were the final crew to leave Log Cabin. Earlier these Eagles had elected Larry Landauer as their leader for the hike. So on the appointed morning he assembled them at trail head. "OK, let's saddle up," he drawled, and the six Scouts shouldered their packs and hiked up the hill.

A reporter from *Boys' Life* struggled along behind them.

En route to their campsite for the night, they scrambled up 12,000-foot Mt. Warren, and later bedded down in a deep, green valley beside one of the Sierra's ice-cold streams. Everything around them seemed larger than real life—the mountains, rocks, stars, moon—and mosquitoes. "Man, do they ever bite!" Gregory Kearney from Hollywood yowled. This was his first experience with mountain mosquitoes.

Shortly after chow that first day, the Scouts hit the sack. It had been a long, tiring hike. The *Boys' Life* reporter had gone to bed immediately after reaching the campsite.

At first light the next morning, the crew was up and getting ready for another day's hike. They reached base camp in late afternoon. A staff of volunteers was waiting to help complete their basic mountaineering training.

The first thing to learn was use of an ice axe. "This tool is used throughout the world by mountaineers," trainer Gary Gustin explained. "It can save your life, and it can also cause a lot of damage if used incorrectly. *I never* want to see anybody fooling around with it. O.K.? Now I'm going to demonstrate a few basics of self-arrest using an axe. Then you're going to practice them. Remember, they could keep you from falling down a slope and into a crevasse."

He fell face downward into the snow. "I want you to dig in. Shoulder into the axe. Toes in. Lift on the handle. Now try it."

Six eager Eagle Scouts fell face forward and tried it.

"Dig in! Lift that handle!" Gary barked, sounding like a Marine Corps Drill Instructor.

He walked up the hill and sat down on the snow. "Here's a basic arrest," he said, and slid downhill. He flipped onto his stomach and made an arrest. "Try it."

The Scouts tried it.

Next Gary dived head first down the hill and arrested. Finally, he fell over backward and slid upside down, head first.

"Wow!" Gregory gasped.

After practicing self-arrest techniques for an hour or so, the Scouts roped up to learn team arrests. After that, Marvin Lowe taught them crampon techniques.

"You have to walk flat-footed with your feet parallel to the snow or ice surface," he advised. "And be careful to walk with your feet apart. More than one person has stabbed himself in the ankle with these 12 points."

Lights-out came early that evening, for the next day was the big ascent. The crew was up at four o'clock and ready to go by five. So by the time the sun was rising, they were well up the glacier on their way to the top.

The three other crews of the Quest had already made their ascents. The first crew had attempted to climb along the traditional route—straight up. But the hot weather (it was 95 degrees at the 10,000 foot high base camp) had softened the snow badly. The snow bridges across the bergschrund—the deep, broad crevasses at the head of the glacier—were unsafe. So the first crew had to abandon the climb. Crew two explored a new route, longer, still very steep, but safe. They achieved the summit. So did the third crew, kicking even deeper footsteps into the route pioneered the previous day. So crew number four, the Huntingtons, made its ascent along an established route, although it was still a tough one. At the foot of the steep snow chute they took a breather.

"It's rugged," admitted Marvin Lowe, the climb leader. "But you won't have any trouble if you stay in the middle where there's still shade and the snow is firm. And by the way, it's perfectly acceptable in mountaineering situations such as this to be scared. Jim Whittaker, the famous American climber, once said that he didn't want somebody on the end of his rope who wasn't scared—that is, who didn't respect the mountain. O.K., let's go."

Once up the chute, the rest of the climb was a "cakewalk," as Larry called it—a tough but technically easy climb to the top.

"I can see forever!" one of the Scouts cried from the summit.

And he seemed to be right. The views were breathtaking. To the east and far below, the Conness glacier, up which they had climbed, glistened in the late morning sunlight. Base camp lay beyond, out of sight behind a ridge. Southward some of the grandest peaks in the northern Sierra—Mts. Dana, Ritter and Banner—cut jagged edges into the horizon. The western face of Mt. Conness fell vertically away directly in front of them—1,200 feet straight down to a tiny alpine meadow. Beyond lay one of the grandest and most spectacular sights in the world—the valley of Yosemite. It looked small and toy-like from this distance and elevation, but all of the familiar landmarks were visible —Liberty Cap, Half Dome, Cathedral Spires, El Capitan.

The Scouts stayed on top long enough to appreciate the view and take pictures. Then it was time to leave. "We've got to get off the mountain before the snow turns to slush," climb leader Lowe advised.

The descent seemed simple compared with the earlier, strenuous climb. At the base of the snow chute, the Scouts plunked down and took off on a wild, long, steep glissade down the glacier.

"Glissade" is a French word meaning to slide. In mountaineering, it refers to sliding on snow or ice without using skis or a sled. It's done in one of two ways—sitting or standing. The Scouts of Huntington crew chose to sit.

What a trip! A good glissade usually involves an elevation loss of a few hundred feet at most. That slide down Conness glacier dropped the Scouts 1,200 feet! More than one of them got wiped out and saved himself only by applying ice axe arrest techniques learned the previous day.

"It took us two hours to climb that slope and only five minutes to come down," one of the Scouts observed.

Back in base camp, they were still excited. "We did it! We did it!"

"That's right, you did," Marvin Lowe agreed. "And you have reason to be proud. It was a tough climb. But remember, you couldn't have made it if the other crews hadn't pioneered the way. 'You stood on the shoulders of giants.' That's an old mountaineering way of saying that a climb takes team effort. Everything you've done this week has been possible because you worked together."

That was one of the most valuable things those Scouts from Los Angeles learned during their two week experience in the Sierra. By working together, each had grown to become a bigger person. They thought about that on the last night, alone, away from camp, on their own Solo quests. They came back a bit larger. What had they gained from the mountains? Here is what a few of them had to say.

"It was different, challenging."

"I haven't had anything like it in Scouting."

"It made me more aware of nature and my relation to it."

"It helped me become more mature."

Finally there was the last campfire. Each Scout was awarded his own ice axe to keep forever. If there had to be a symbol of those two weeks, the ice axe was perfect. It was the tool which allowed the achievement of the ultimate goal—the summit. Whenever those Scouts used it, they'd be apt to remember that special summer when they made their Quest Beyond Eagle. ♣

# Winter Survival Tips

**Know them
before you go
on a hike.
They could
save your life.**

You are hiking in the mountains with your troop. Suddenly, the skies darken and a blizzard dumps two feet of snow on your trail. You'll have to spend the night in the woods.

Could you survive?

If you've come prepared and know how to handle yourself, you should have no problem. Here are some tips that will help:

• Be prepared for all types of weather. Take enough warm clothing to get you through wet and icy storms.

• Check weather forecasts before leaving on a hike. Don't be fooled by sunshine. Mountain weather can change in minutes.

• Remember the C.O.L.D. rule: Keep your body and clothes Clean; avoid Overheating; dress in loose Layers of clothing that will trap body heat; and keep clothes Dry.

• Always take along a wool stocking cap. Eighty percent of the body's heat is lost through the head and neck area.

• You've heard of frostbite, but how about immersion foot? This occurs when your feet get wet and the skin wrinkles and peels. The pain can keep you from walking.

Keep your feet dry by wearing a thin pair of polypropylene socks underneath heavy wool socks. The wool socks will wick moisture away from your feet. The thin socks will help prevent blisters.

Make sure you have room to wiggle your toes inside your boots. Boots that are too tight will cut off circulation and hasten frostbite. And always bring extra pairs of socks, even on day hikes.

• Carry an ample supply of waterproof matches and a candle. A candle is a great fire starter; it will burn for 10 minutes or longer.

• If you become lost and cannot retrace your steps, stay put. Carry a whistle for signaling rescuers. Remember, the universal distress signal: three quick yells or blasts from a whistle.

• Drink a lot of water, 8 to 12 glasses a day. But do not eat snow to satisfy your thirst. Eating snow can lower your body's core temperature, triggering deadly hypothermia. Melt ice for drinking water. If you don't have a fire, gather snow or ice in a waterproof container; hold it between layers of clothing until the ice melts.

• Remember the cat. Cattail plants can help you by providing two things—food and warmth. The roots are good to eat. Look for the horn-shaped sprouts growing from the tangle of roots. Peel off the outer covering and eat the white inner part raw or boiled. The rootstocks themselves can be ground and made into flour. The fuzz on the top of the stalk makes a good downy insulation to stuff between two pieces of clothing.

• Finally, never panic. Help yourself by using what you know. Think "shelter" first because staying warm and dry is the key to survival.♣

*(These tips came from the Air Force Survival School of the 3636 Combat Crew Training Wing at Fairchild Air Force Base, Wash.*

*Before going on a winter hike, review the sections in "The Boy Scout Handbook" and "Fieldbook" on how to treat frostbite and hypothermia, and how to make snow shelters.)*

ILLUSTRATED BY JOE SNYDER

**Glacier National Park offers a little bit of everything. If you can bear it.**

File photo.

# 'COME AND GET IT'

**"Hey, bear!"** a kid calls. It echoes across the rugged Rocky Mountains as Scouts continue their backpacking outing in Montana's Glacier National Park.

**"Fresh meat!"** another boy yells. "Come and get it!"

Naturally, the Scouts, from Troop 2, Madison, Wis., hope no grizzly takes them up on their offer. It's just that bears are more turned off by human voices than by the tinkling of bells tied to bootlaces. Glacier National Park is trying to minimize bear-human contact. Some bears have been trapped, moved and even destroyed.

And now a sign along the trail warns of mountain lion activity and advises hikers to stay in groups.

Scary? Sure. But it's all part of the backpacking experience in this sanctuary known for its glacier-carved valleys, rich forests and mountain scenery. Even bears.

### Back—and Up—to Nature

Troop 2 arrived at Glacier last August. While younger Scouts remained at base camp for day hikes or an overnight trip, four backpacking crews lit out into the wild for five-day, four-night excursions.

First, they had to get used to the thin mountain air. Although altitude sickness is usually not a problem at Glacier, spending a day or two in base camp to get used to low oxygen is wise. Glacier's trails can reach 8,100 feet above sea level. The average elevation back in Madison is 845.6 feet. ▶

*Left: Glacier's mountains began 170 million years ago along the Lewis Overthrust Fault. Right: Bear alert! Luckily, Carl Davis identifies a faraway visitor as a mountain sheep—maybe.*

TEXT BY JOHNNY D. BOGGS
PHOTOS BY GARTH DOWLING

## BE BEAR AWARE

**Y**ou've just rounded the corner on a backcountry trail, and standing before you is a grizzly bear. What do you do?

"Certainly you should never approach the bear," Chief Park Ranger Stephen J. Frye says. "You should detour, back around, somehow remove yourself from the situation if you have the opportunity."

Like humans, bears have different personalities. "You need to decide for yourself what action you're going to take," Ranger Frye says.

**HERE ARE SOME TIPS:**

• Hike in groups—never alone. Avoid hiking early in the morning, late in the day or after dark.

• Avoid surprising the bear. Talk while hiking. Tie bells to your pack. Be noisy.

• Be aware of your surroundings, especially on wildlife trails or near streams. Watch for signs of bear activity such as tracks, diggings and dung.

• Never take pets into the backcountry.

• Never leave food, beverages or backpacks unattended.

• Carry refuse and garbage out.

**IF YOU RUN INTO A BEAR ON THE TRAIL:**

• Turn around and make a wide detour around the bear. Retreat slowly.

• Try to keep upwind of the bear so the animal knows you are there and is not surprised.

• Remain calm, and talk in a firm voice.

• If a bear charges, as a last resort lie facedown and cover your neck with your arms and hands. Don't move.

• Never run. A bear can run faster than 35 miles per hour.

• Always give the bear plenty of space.

"If you follow our rules and recommendations, your trip should be as safe as any backcountry trip, recognizing the fact that safety cannot be guaranteed in a wilderness setting," Ranger Frye says.

*A glacier forms when more snow falls each winter than melts in the summer. In the park, all the glaciers are shrinking—making possible ice-cold swims for weary backpackers.*

### Up and Down

Life Scout Tim Gruenisen, 15, leads the group that will hike from Ptarmigan Tunnel to Elizabeth Lake on this sunny first day out. That's less than 10 miles, but it's 2,480 feet up and 2,518 feet down—and backpacks are heaviest on Day One.

Even though the packs will be a day's supply lighter, the second day won't be a picnic either. That's obvious when the Scouts reach a river about 20 feet wide, with only a cable stretching across the swift water. They'll have to hold on to the cable and walk across the rocks.

One problem: The six-person crew has only one pair of sandals to wear crossing the river. Glacial water is cold. The rocks are slippery. One wrong step and...*brrrrr.*

Once one Scout gets across, he ties the sandals to a rope and flings them across the river for the next person to wear. Everyone stays dry.

### Where's the Hot Water?

Life Scout Justin Stangel, 13, knows the water at Iceberg Lake must be cold too. One clue: Chunks of ice float on the surface. But after a long hike on a hot day, he can't resist.

Though the water is cold enough to knock the breath out of you, Justin calls his swim "quite refreshing."

It can be dangerous. As a lifeguard, Eagle Scout Alex Nepple, 16, knows hypothermia can set in quickly. He makes sure these swims don't last more than a minute.

### The Bear Necessities

Later on the Highline Trail, Life Scout Zack Cuellar, 15, looks through his binoculars and spots a grizzly about a half-mile away.

"That's close enough for me," he says.

Back at base camp, Tenderfoot Scout Jacob Chadderdon, 12, gets a closer look when a cub runs across the campground.

"I was a little scared," he admits, "because normally the mom would be pretty close." Thankfully, no adult bear is seen.

Bear safety is important, especially in the backcountry. Bears have a keen sense of smell, so food and anything else that might draw a bear is stored at night in bear-resistant containers or "bear bags" suspended at least 12 feet up and well away from the campsite.

After a day's hike, the Scouts have

*Using bear bags is wise even in bear-free areas. They keep smellables from ground squirrels, mice and raccoons.*

only a couple of hours to set up camp. It's hectic. Tents must be pitched, food cooked and the dirty dishes thoroughly cleaned and properly stored.

If another bear were to wander by despite their precautions, the Scouts know to keep their distance. Rangers told them to stay at least 500 feet from a bear and at least 1,000 feet from a bear with cubs.

That's no problem for the Scouts of Troop 2, who want no part of the animals. Even if their shouts say otherwise.✤

### LEAVE NO TRACE

Do your part in protecting America's natural resources by following the principles of Leave No Trace:

1. Plan ahead and prepare.
2. Travel and camp on durable surfaces.
3. Dispose of waste properly.
4. Leave what you find.
5. Minimize campfire impact.
6. Respect wildlife.
7. Be considerate of other visitors.

From "Leave No Trace" (Bin No. 21-105, available from your local council service center).

### MOUNTAIN MISTAKE

Even Scouts make mistakes. After reaching Dawson Pass, some Scouts from Troop 2 noticed a cairn with names scratched into rocks. "Excited" to be at the pass and "not thinking" (their words), they decided to scratch their own names and "Troop 2" into a small stone.

That, however, is a violation of both the Wilderness Act and the BSA's Leave No Trace policy (left), which prohibit the disturbance of natural objects.

A Glacier National Park ranger caught the boys and issued them a warning. They missed the troop's raft trip because they had to meet with a ranger.

The Scouts wrote letters of apology and made donations to the park's Search and Rescue fund.

It was, one Scout said, "a very tough lesson."

### KNOW BEFORE YOU GO

The million-acre Glacier National Park in northwestern Montana offers hiking, camping, fishing, bird-watching, cycling and, in the winter, cross-country skiing. Whitewater rafting is available outside, but adjacent to, the park.

Glacier National Park, one of the last grizzly strongholds, contains 30 to 40 glaciers, 200 lakes or streams and more than 730 miles of trails.

Backcountry hikers planning to camp overnight must obtain permits at a visitor center or ranger station. Backcountry permits are issued first-come, first-served no more than 24 hours before the trip, or may be reserved in advance in person or by mail.

For more information: Glacier National Park, P.O. Box 128, West Glacier, MT 59936. Telephone: (406) 888-7800. On the Internet: www.nps.gov/glac.

*A trail that had become hazardous forced Troop 2 to take a longer return route than planned. The extra miles took their toll.*

# Lost in the Bridger Wilderness   By ERNEST DOCLAR

**W**e were inching our way up the steep trail when we stumbled into an ambush. They struck like lightning from the sky—buzzing and swarming, peppering our hands and the backs of our sun-scorched necks. Wyoming mosquitoes!

Swatting with one hand and spraying repellent with the other, I danced the Rocky Mountain two-step in the middle of the pebbly path. Scout Doug Smith, a slim red-head from Nebraska, gave me a deadpan look: "Why are you hopping around like that? Why, back home in Lincoln these mosquitoes wouldn't even be keeping size!"

"That's a fact," piped up blond Ricky Ganz. "And besides that, you oughta be ashamed to murder these defenseless little things!"

Here I was on the annual Troop 2 wilderness trip, high in the Jim Bridger Wilderness, being attacked by hordes of bloodthirsty pests. Did I get any pity? No, nothing but wisecracks—hardly effective first aid for insect bites. But after being on the trail for three days with these guys, I was getting used to their kidding. I pushed on and resolved to try to forget the mosquitoes.

We came to Clark Creek, a torrent shallow enough to be forded by carefree Scouts, but which I approached with dry boots and hopes of keeping them that way. The Nebraskans simply plodded through the stream and onto the opposite shore, water oozing from their boots, pant legs sopping.

Hugging my boots against my chest, I baby-stepped into the creek. I hadn't even reached the middle when CRASH! The racing water, the sharp stones, and the 40-pound pack on a 40-year-old back upended me. I landed bottom first in the icy cur-

*Here the Green River begins its 730-mile journey.*                    *Granite Peak dwarfs hikers.*

## Add a swift Wyoming mountain stream, a thunderstorm, an unfamiliar fork in the trail to a hike and you've got trouble—plus 11 strayed Nebraskans

rent. Brrrrrr! What a way to find out the temperature of a mountain creek!

Ricky Ganz and Dan Warlick whinnied like a pair of stallions that had just feasted on locoweed. "Thatsaway to keep your shoes dry!" Dan yelled.

Shortly after, we came to a fork in the trail. The troop was stretched out like knots on a long rope. There were clusters of hikers a half mile in front and behind us. Near-

by hikers and I checked our map, chose the path to the left, and began the steep climb.

Two hours later, we finally topped Green River Pass, 10,-370 feet above sea level. Before our eyes to the north were brown waves of towering mountains; to the south lay a green ocean of treetops. For a few moments we were fascinated by the vista, almost unchanged since Jim Bridger led fur-trapping ex-

peditions and railroad survey teams through these forests more than a hundred years ago.

But we were drawn back to reality by the rumble of thunder. Dark clouds rolled in from the west and screened out the sun. Beneath the blackness a thick curtain of rain fell.

The troop assembled at the trail sign marking the pass and the junction of several trails. Scoutmaster Loren Wil-

son took out his little notebook and counted off the hikers, ". . . 28, 29, 30, 31 . . ." But we had started with 42! Trail blazers Warren and "Rusty" Brauer were sure that nobody had passed them. There was only one conclusion. Eleven Scouts must have taken the wrong turn at the Clark Creek fork.

I might have panicked, but Scoutmaster Wilson assured me that there was no cause for worry. ➡

*Doug Smith eases out lure.*     *Log aids stream crossing.*     *Spinning tackle snares trout.*     *Bright ponchos dot forest.*

"For one thing," he explained, "most of the 11 are experienced campers. Several made the trip here in '68. They have tents, food, compasses, and maps. Besides, Dr. Brauer, the troop physician, is with them." I thought of all the first aid gear Doc Brauer carries tucked away in his pack, and decided that the wanderers probably were in better shape than our group.

Troop leaders decided that half the gang would wait at the pass and corral the strayed Scouts if they tried to catch up with the main body. The other half and I would proceed toward our overnight stop, Borum Lake. I was comforted by thoughts of a soft bed, dry socks, and a full stomach.

Borum was peaceful—a clear, quiet pool about a quarter of a mile long. Just what Doc Brauer would have prescribed for tired Scouts. Rusty and Warren Brauer wrote their own prescription. They raced ahead for some fishing. As we descended from the crest of the trail overlooking the lake, we saw Rusty waving a string of four fat trout. He yelled, "Hey! Look at these!" Mike and Doug Smith took off, dropping their packs and assembling fishing rods as they ran toward the lake.

In the next two hours the gang netted about 20 trout, mostly cutthroats. By nightfall the rest of the guys lumbered into camp—the 11 stragglers hadn't shown up at Green River Pass. However, the hikers who reached Borum perked up at the sight and smell of fried fish and bubbling stew.

Next day was clear, but the 11 still hadn't appeared. After a breakfast of freshly caught cutthroats, we decided to keep hiking south to Trapper Lake, our base for the next few days.

By early afternoon we arrived at Trapper Lake, breathtaking, mirror-slick, rippled here and there by surfacing fish.

When the troop finished setting up camp, they turned to sampling the Trapper Lake fishing. There were long tales of good catches and short stories of failing to hook anything but underwater snags. Owen Kelly sat dejected and

*Being prepared with optimism, know-how, and rugged hike equipment helped Troop 2 bring its adventure to a happy ending.*

Photos by GENE DANIELS—Black Star

*Meadows oozed water from melted snow.*

empty-handed. "Whatsa matter, Owen, can't get any trout?" someone teased. That did it! Owen jumped right in, fully clothed, and scooped up six cutthroats with his hands. Nobody questioned his fishing after that.

Late next morning a forest ranger rode up on horseback. "You the group with the missing hikers? I ran into them along the trail. They're going to wait for you back at the Scout camp at New Forks."

That night we celebrated the good news with a pizza and fish fry. Stuffing ourselves like bears about to hibernate, we had to roll into our sleeping bags to sack out.

Two days later we reached Camp New Forks and had a happy reunion with the lost 11. Each group bragged about what the other had missed: The strays telling about their pine-tree conservation work at camp, the hikers describing the fishing and the trail cleanup they did for the 50-Miler Award.

Someone asked Tony Vidlak how it felt to be lost. The chunky, sandy-haired senior patrol leader faced the group and spoke like an old soldier back from the war; "Well, it was like this: We found trail markers that told us where we were. But when we realized that it was the wrong trail, it was too late to backtrack and catch up. Our maps showed us the way out. We had plenty of food, so we knew we'd get out all right."

Were they afraid? "Only thing we were afraid of," Tony said, "was what Mr. Wilson would say about our missing the trail." The Scouts laughed.

I'd have laughed too, if I hadn't been so limp with relief at seeing the lost 11. All I had strength for was to lean against a pine, mop out my damp hat, and say to myself: *That's the last time I grow any gray hairs over a troop of Scouts! Mosquitoes, fast-running streams, wrong trails— they handle all of them better than I do.*

Struck by a disturbing thought, I glanced around at the grinning faces. Had they been worried about getting me out of the Bridger Wilderness safely? ●

Wind River Range is backdrop for Troop 2 hikers.

Backpack covers add color to the trail.

**BOYS' LIFE**

# KNOW HOW

One of the great reasons to join Scouting is to learn how to be comfortable and competent in the outdoors (or in any setting). Scouting teaches Scoutcraft (leadership, citizenship, fitness, first aid, and aquatics), woodcraft (nature and the ethos of Leave No Trace), and campcraft (hiking, camping, cooking, navigation, and tools). Beginning its second century, *Boys' Life* offers its readers tips and how-to's on all of these.

These Scouting skills promote service to the community and nation, good decision-making, and an appreciation of nature. They present challenges that build confidence, give a boy the opportunity to explore the world around him, and become the building blocks for the boy to become a responsible young man. Mastering the tools for outdoor adventures prepares a boy for life.

If you want to know how to camp in the rain or snow, the magazine offers the best methods on how to do it in relative comfort. You want to shoot a shotgun or rifle? Safety rules, games, and instructions for a backyard range are offered (a range for air rifles, that is). Feeling like William Tell? The magazine gives you tips on mastering a bow and arrow. You spot a set of animal tracks—the magazine has drawings to help you identify them and tips on how to track the animal that made them. Even flag signaling is explained (but texting is easier).

When Scouts go into the backcountry, they need to take everything they will need to have a successful adventure. That means food, shelter, clothing—and a first aid kit. The magazine explains different ways to build fires, how to catch fish (even under the ice) and then fillet them, how to pitch a tent (or camp without one), what you need in your personal first aid kit, and how to treat snakebites. Columns in the magazine show how to camp on the beach or in the snow (and have fun in the powder) and how to take shelter from a snowstorm. Going into bear country requires certain precautions—and the magazine spells them out.

Rigorous activity calls for stamina, and *Boys' Life* explains how to keep physically fit and healthy. As part of the Scout Oath, a Scout promises to keep himself "physically strong." Hiking, climbing, canoeing—all of the activities that Scouts enjoy—require strength and endurance. Exercise, healthy eating, and plenty of rest are necessary to participate fully in the programs Scouting offers.

Modern camping clothing and gear allow Scouts to explore further into the backcountry. For example, backpacking stoves allow Scouts to camp where traditional fires might have scarred the land. Scouts know more about protecting the environment as campcraft skills have evolved. But the skills presented in this chapter link Scouts through the decades—how to use, and when not to use, a pocketknife, saw, and axe; how to build lashing towers and bridges; lighting a fire without a match on a cold, rainy day; primitive cooking; tracking animals. "Be Prepared" has been the Scouting motto since its inception, and the outdoors is the classroom that Scouting uses to teach boys how to take care of themselves—and how to take care of the outdoors.

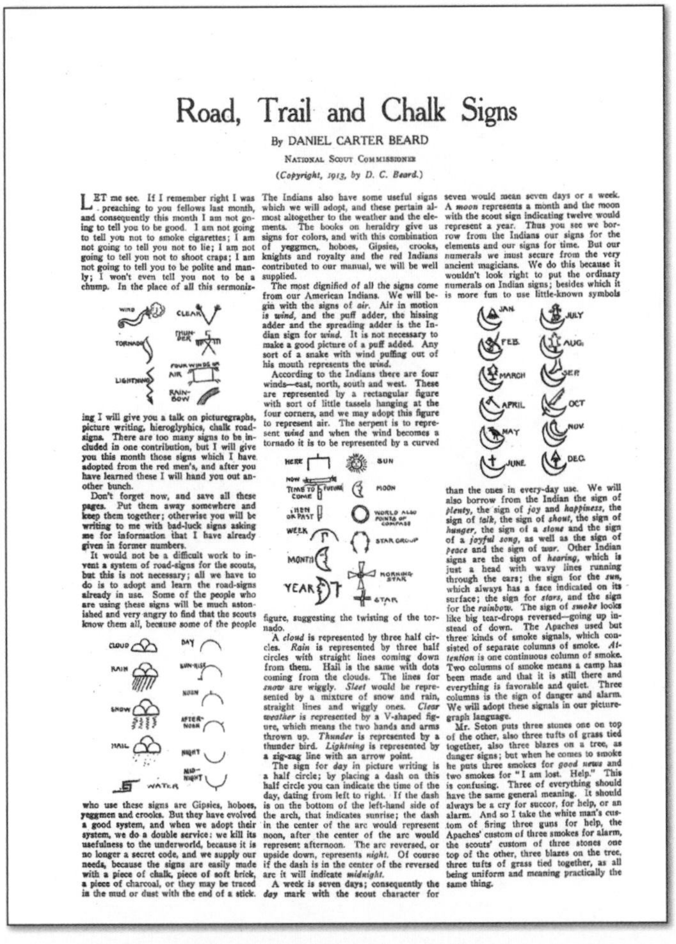

# Ice-Fishing Tip-Ups

## With these ice-fishing tip-ups, you'll always know when you have a bite.

### Text and illustrations by David J. Brooks

**What You'll Need:**

- Tape measure
- Saw
- Drill
- Screwdriver
- Sandpaper
- Glue
- Pocketknife
- 2 L screws
- 2 Finish nails
- Spring doorstop
- Metal coat hanger
- Bright-colored felt or cloth
- Braided fishing line and snelled hooks
- 1¾-inch x 22-inch dowel or straight branch
- 10-inch dowel or straight branch that fits into the end of the doorstop spring

**What You'll Do:**

1. Cut the dowels to length and sand smooth.
2. Drill pilot holes, then hammer in the finish nails about two inches from the base of the spring doorstop and four to five inches apart.
3. Screw both the L screws in place as shown.
4. Drill a snug hole for the coat hanger, push it through and bend to shape.
5. Screw the spring doorstop to the end of the large dowel.
6. Screw the small dowel into the end of the spring doorstop.
7. Glue on the flag.
8. Tie the braided fishing line off around one nail, and wrap about 25 yards of line around both nails. Add a snelled hook.

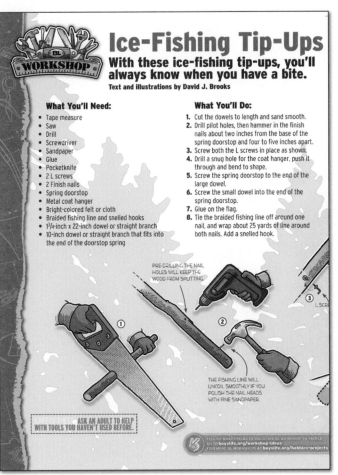

PRE-DRILLING THE NAIL HOLES WILL KEEP THE WOOD FROM SPLITTING.

THE FISHING LINE WILL UNCOIL SMOOTHLY IF YOU POLISH THE NAIL HEADS WITH FINE SANDPAPER.

ASK AN ADULT TO HELP WITH TOOLS YOU HAVEN'T USED BEFORE.

TELL US WHAT PROJECTS YOU'D LIKE BL WORKSHOP TO TACKLE.
GO TO boyslife.org/workshop-ideas
FIND MORE BL WORKSHOPS AT boyslife.org/hobbies-projects

---

# SCOUTCRAFT
## YOUR FIRST CAMPOUT

### CHOOSING THE SITE

LOOK FOR A FAIRLY OPEN SPOT WHERE THE GROUND SLOPES GENTLY SO THAT RAINWATER DRAINS OFF QUICKLY. GRASS-COVERED, SANDY OR GRAVELLY GROUND IS BEST. THE SITE SHOULD BE NEAR WOODS, BUT NOT DIRECTLY UNDER TREES. SAFE DRINKING AND COOKING WATER SHOULD BE NEARBY.

A LAKE OR A STREAM WILL PROVIDE WATER FOR WASHING MESS GEAR, BUT DON'T WASH POTS OR MESS GEAR IN THE LAKE OR STREAM. PURIFY THIS WATER BEFORE DRINKING.

DON'T DIG A TRENCH AROUND YOUR TENT. IT'S UNNECESSARY IF YOU'VE CHOSEN A SUITABLE, WELL-DRAINED SPOT.

DIG A STRADDLE LATRINE IN THE BUSHES DOWNWIND FROM CAMP AND AT LEAST 75 FEET FROM ANY WATER. SAVE ALL DIRT FOR LIGHT COVER AFTER EACH USE, AND FOR REFILLING LATRINE BEFORE YOU LEAVE CAMP FOR GOOD. REPLACE SOIL.
FOR MORE INFORMATION, CHECK YOUR BOY SCOUT HANDBOOK, THE FIELDBOOK AND THE CAMPING MERIT BADGE PAMPHLET.

### A COMFORTABLE GROUND BED

SMOOTH OUT BUMPS AND REMOVE STONES FROM YOUR SLEEPING AREA. INSTEAD OF DIGGING HIP AND SHOULDER HOLLOWS, COVER YOUR BED AREA WITH LEAVES, STRAW, GRASS, OR PINE NEEDLES. PACK EXTRA PADDING WHERE YOUR BACK, HEAD AND MIDDLE THIGHS WILL LIE. SPREAD YOUR GROUND CLOTH OVER IT ALL. LAY YOUR SLEEPING BAG ON THIS—OR MAKE THIS BED SACK WITH TWO BLANKETS AND LARGE BLANKET PINS.

#### BLANKET BED SACK

① SPREAD FIRST BLANKET ON GROUND CLOTH. THEN PUT SECOND BLANKET HALFWAY OVER THE FIRST.

② FOLD BOTTOM BLANKET HALFWAY OVER TOP ONE.

③ FOLD TOP BLANKET OVER.

④ FOLD BACK FOOT PART OF BOTH BLANKETS.

⑤ PIN TOGETHER TO MAKE SACK.

A SHEET OF POLYETHYLENE (A PLASTIC) 4-6 MIL THICK MAKES A GOOD GROUND CLOTH. OR YOU CAN USE AN AIR MATTRESS INFLATED JUST ENOUGH TO KEEP YOUR BODY OFF THE GROUND. OR USE A PIECE OF POLYFOAM 5" THICK BY 24" WIDE AND THE LENGTH FROM YOUR HEAD TO SEAT. A GROUND CLOTH HELPS INSULATE YOU FROM DAMPNESS AND COLD.

MAKE THIS HANDY POCKET LIST OF PERSONAL EQUIPMENT TO TAKE WITH YOU. CUT IT OUT, FOLD BACK TO BACK, THEN LAMINATE IT IN PLASTIC. CHECK OFF THE ITEMS WITH A GREASE PENCIL AS YOU PACK, WIPE OFF FOR NEXT USE.

### CAMPOUT CHECKLIST

| WEAR | | |
|---|---|---|
| ☐ COMPLETE UNIFORM | ☐ INDIVIDUAL TOILET PAPER | ☐ MOCCASINS or SNEAKERS |
| ☐ HIKING SHOES | ☐ COMPASS | ☐ CLOTHESBAG WITH: |
| ☐ SWEATER or JACKET | ☐ 2 or 3 BAND-AIDS | ☐ EXTRA SHIRT |
| ☐ RAINCOAT or PONCHO | **FASTEN TO OR INSIDE YOUR PACK** | ☐ EXTRA PANTS |
| **CARRY IN POCKETS** | ☐ REPAIR KIT (NEEDLES, THREAD, ETC.) | ☐ PAJAMAS or SWEAT SUIT |
| ☐ SCOUT KNIFE | ☐ EATING UTENSILS | ☐ EXTRA HANDKERCHIEFS |
| ☐ MATCHES (IN WATER-PROOF CASE) | ☐ FLASHLIGHT (CHECK BATTERIES) | ☐ EXTRA SOCKS |
| ☐ HANDKERCHIEF | ☐ SLEEPING BAG (OR 2-3 BLANKETS) | ☐ CHANGE OF UNDERWEAR |
| ☐ WALLET (INCLUDE DIMES FOR PHONE) | ☐ WATERPROOF GROUND CLOTH | ☐ TOILET KIT CONTAINING: |

(continued) ☐ BATH TOWEL ☐ TOOTHBRUSH & TOOTHPASTE (PLASTIC OR COVERED) ☐ WASH RAGS ☐ **OPTIONAL ITEMS** ☐ WATCH ☐ SWIM TRUNKS ☐ CAMERA, FILM ☐ CANTEEN ☐ NOTEBOOK, PENCIL ☐ MAP ☐ FIRST AID KIT ☐ SCOUT HANDBOOK or FIELDBOOK ☐ MOSQUITO DOPE & NETTING ☐ LENGTH OF LINE or ROPE ☐ WASH CLOTH ☐ COMB ☐ SOAP ☐ HAND TOWEL

---

# Road, Trail and Chalk Signs

### By DANIEL CARTER BEARD
#### NATIONAL SCOUT COMMISSIONER
(Copyright, 1913, by D. C. Beard)

LET me see. If I remember right I was preaching to you fellows last month, and consequently this month I am not going to tell you to be good. I am not going to tell you not to smoke cigarettes; I am not going to tell you not to lie; I am not going to tell you not to shoot craps; I am not going to tell you to be polite and manly; I won't even tell you not to be a chump. In the place of all this sermonizing I will give you a talk on picturegraphs, picture writing, hieroglyphics, chalk road-signs. There are too many signs to be included in one contribution, but I will give you this month those signs which I have adopted from the red men's, and after you have learned these I will hand you out another bunch.

Don't forget now, and save all these pages. Put them away somewhere and keep them together; otherwise you will be writing to me with bad-luck signs asking me for information that I have already given in former numbers.

It would not be a difficult work to invent a system of road-signs for the scouts, but this is not necessary; all we have to do is to adopt and learn the road-signs already in use. Some of the people who are using these signs will be much astonished and very angry to find that the scouts know them all, because some of the people who use these signs are Gipsies, hoboes, yeggmen and crooks. But they have evolved a good system, and when we adopt their system, we do a double service; we kill its usefulness to the underworld, because it is no longer a secret code, and we supply our needs, because the signs are easily made with a piece of chalk, piece of soft brick, a piece of charcoal, or they may be traced in the mud or dust with the end of a stick.

The Indians also have some useful signs which we will adopt, and these pertain almost altogether to the weather and the elements. The books on heraldry give us signs for colors, and with this combination of yeggmen, hoboes, Gipsies, crooks, knights and royalty and the red Indians contributed to our manual, we will be well supplied.

The most dignified of all the signs come from our American Indians. We will begin with the signs of air. Air in motion is wind, and the puff adder, the hissing adder and the spreading adder is the Indian sign for wind. It is not necessary to make a good picture of a puff added. Any sort of a snake with wind puffing out of his mouth represents the wind.

According to the Indians there are four winds—east, north, south and west. These are represented by a rectangular figure with sort of little tassels hanging at the four corners, and we may adopt this figure to represent air. The serpent is to represent wind and when the wind becomes a tornado it is to be represented by a curved

figure, suggesting the twisting of the tornado.

A cloud is represented by three half circles. Rain is represented by three half circles with straight lines coming down from them. Hail is the same with dots coming from the clouds. The lines for snow are wiggly. Sleet would be represented by a mixture of snow and rain, straight lines and wiggly ones. Clear weather is represented by a V-shaped figure, which means the two hands and arms thrown up. Thunder is represented by a thunder bird. Lightning is represented by a zig-zag line with an arrow point.

The sign for day in picture writing is a half circle; by placing a dash on this half circle you can indicate the time of the day, dating from left to right. If the dash is on the bottom of the left-hand side of the arch, that indicates sunrise; the dash in the center of the arc would represent noon, after the center of the arc would represent afternoon. The arc reversed, or upside down, represents night. Of course if the dash is in the center of the reversed arc it will indicate midnight.

A week is seven days; consequently day mark with the scout character for

seven would mean seven days or a week. A moon represents a month and the moon with the scout sign indicating twelve would represent a year. Thus you see we borrow from the Indians our signs for the elements and our signs for time. But our numerals are not secure from the very ancient magicians. We do this because it wouldn't look right to put the ordinary numerals on Indian signs; besides which it is more fun to use little-known symbols

than the ones in every-day use. We will also borrow from the Indian the sign of plenty, the sign of joy and happiness, the sign of talk, the sign of about, the sign of hunger, the sign of a stone and the sign of a joyful song, as well as the sign of peace and the sign of war. Other Indian signs are the sign of hearing, which is just a head with wavy lines running through the ears; the sign for the sun, which always has a face indicated on its surface; the sign for stars, and the sign for the rainbow. The sign of smoke looks like big tear-drops reversed—going up instead of down. The Apaches used but three kinds of smoke signals, which consisted of separate columns of smoke. Attention is one continuous column of smoke. Two columns of smoke means a camp has been made and that it is still there and everything is favorable and quiet. Three columns is the sign of danger and alarm. We will adopt these signals in our picturegraph language.

Mr. Seton puts three stones one on top of the other, also three tufts of grass tied together, also three blazes on a tree, as danger signs; but when he comes to smoke he puts three smokes for good news and two smokes for "I am lost. Help." This is confusing. Three of everything should have the same general meaning. It should always be a cry for succor, for help, or an alarm. And so I take the white man's custom of firing three guns for help, the Apaches' custom of three smokes for alarm, the scouts' custom of three stones one on top of the other, three blazes on the tree, three tufts of grass tied together, as all being uniform and meaning practically the same thing.

---

# RESCUE RULES

TOO MANY SWIMMING ACCIDENTS OCCUR WITHIN A SHORT DISTANCE OF SAFETY. PRACTICALLY EVERY ONE CAN BE AVOIDED IF THE SWIMMER DOES NOT BECOME PANICKY AND IF THE RESCUER KEEPS CALM AND USES HIS HEAD. "KNOW-HOW" CAN PREVENT AN ACCIDENT FROM BECOMING A TRAGEDY.

KNOW THESE SIMPLE RULES SO THAT IN AN EMERGENCY YOU'LL FOLLOW THEM AUTOMATICALLY!

**REACH** IF THE PERSON IN DISTRESS IS WITHIN REACH, EXTEND ANY OBJECT TOWARD HIM THAT HE CAN GRAB.

**THROW** TOSS A LINE, A RING BUOY, AN INNER TUBE OR ANY OBJECT THAT WILL FLOAT AND THAT YOU CAN GET HOLD OF IN A HURRY. THROW IT OVER AND BEYOND HIM!

**ROW** IF THERE'S A BOAT HANDY, ROW OR PADDLE OUT TO GIVE HELP.

**GO** IF YOU MUST SWIM OUT TO REACH THE PERSON IN DISTRESS, JUMP IN—DON'T DIVE. CARRY YOUR SHIRT OR TOWEL IN YOUR MOUTH. FLIP ONE END OF TOWEL OR SHIRT TO PERSON AND TOW HIM IN. KEEP YOUR EYES ON PERSON AT ALL TIMES.

**HANG ON** SHOULD YOUR BOAT OVERTURN, HANG ON! A SWAMPED OR CAPSIZED CANOE OR ROWBOAT WILL SUPPORT MANY PEOPLE IF THEY JUST HOLD ON TO IT. IT'S BETTER TO WAIT FOR SOMEONE TO PICK YOU UP OR TO PADDLE THE CRAFT SLOWLY TO SHORE THAN TO LEAVE IT AND BECOME EXHAUSTED.

# Ice-Fishing Tip-Ups

## With these ice-fishing tip-ups, you'll always know when you have a bite.

Text and illustrations by David J. Brooks

## What You'll Need:

- Tape measure
- Saw
- Drill
- Screwdriver
- Sandpaper
- Glue
- Pocketknife
- 2 L screws
- 2 Finish nails
- Spring doorstop
- Metal coat hanger
- Bright-colored felt or cloth
- Braided fishing line and snelled hooks
- 1³/₄-inch x 22-inch dowel or straight branch
- 10-inch dowel or straight branch that fits into the end of the doorstop spring

## What You'll Do:

1. Cut the dowels to length and sand smooth.
2. Drill pilot holes, then hammer in the finish nails about two inches from the base of the spring doorstop and four to five inches apart.
3. Screw both the L screws in place as shown.
4. Drill a snug hole for the coat hanger, push it through and bend to shape.
5. Screw the spring doorstop to the end of the large dowel.
6. Screw the small dowel into the end of the spring doorstop.
7. Glue on the flag.
8. Tie the braided fishing line off around one nail, and wrap about 25 yards of line around both nails. Add a snelled hook.

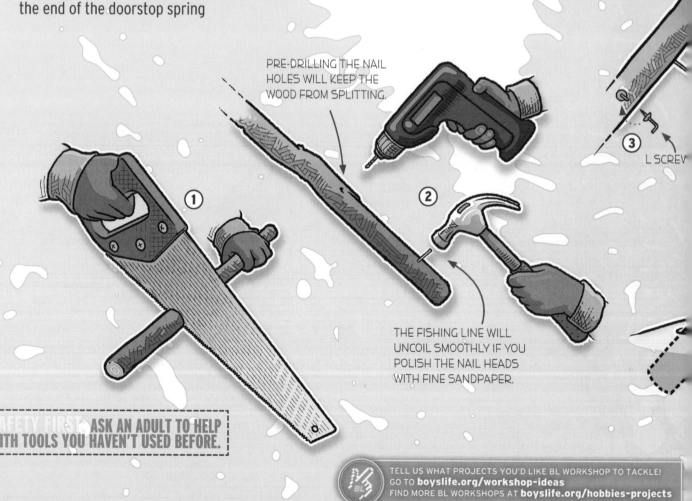

PRE-DRILLING THE NAIL HOLES WILL KEEP THE WOOD FROM SPLITTING.

L SCREW

THE FISHING LINE WILL UNCOIL SMOOTHLY IF YOU POLISH THE NAIL HEADS WITH FINE SANDPAPER.

**SAFETY FIRST** ASK AN ADULT TO HELP WITH TOOLS YOU HAVEN'T USED BEFORE.

TELL US WHAT PROJECTS YOU'D LIKE BL WORKSHOP TO TACKLE!
GO TO **boyslife.org/workshop-ideas**
FIND MORE BL WORKSHOPS AT **boyslife.org/hobbies-projects**

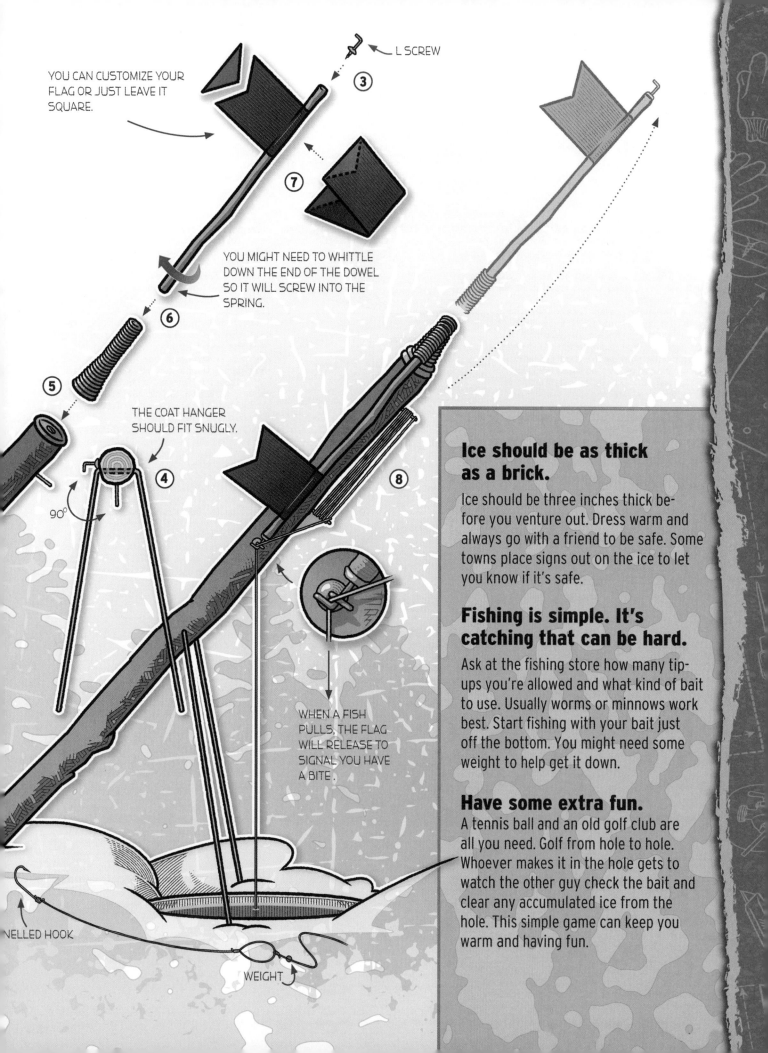

YOU CAN CUSTOMIZE YOUR FLAG OR JUST LEAVE IT SQUARE.

L SCREW

③

⑦

YOU MIGHT NEED TO WHITTLE DOWN THE END OF THE DOWEL SO IT WILL SCREW INTO THE SPRING.

⑥

⑤

THE COAT HANGER SHOULD FIT SNUGLY.

④

90°

⑧

WHEN A FISH PULLS, THE FLAG WILL RELEASE TO SIGNAL YOU HAVE A BITE.

NELLED HOOK

WEIGHT

## Ice should be as thick as a brick.

Ice should be three inches thick before you venture out. Dress warm and always go with a friend to be safe. Some towns place signs out on the ice to let you know if it's safe.

## Fishing is simple. It's catching that can be hard.

Ask at the fishing store how many tip-ups you're allowed and what kind of bait to use. Usually worms or minnows work best. Start fishing with your bait just off the bottom. You might need some weight to help get it down.

## Have some extra fun.

A tennis ball and an old golf club are all you need. Golf from hole to hole. Whoever makes it in the hole gets to watch the other guy check the bait and clear any accumulated ice from the hole. This simple game can keep you warm and having fun.

# The Indian Sign Language for Boy Scouts

## Part II.—Beginning the Dictionary

### By ERNEST THOMPSON SETON

#### CHIEF SCOUT, BOY SCOUTS OF AMERICA

#### (Copyright, 1913, by E. T. Seton)

TO conclude our introduction, started last month, we have but one more sign, and then we take up the dictionary. This sign, or combination of signs, really might come first of all, as it will be the first you will use in opening a conversation in the sign language.

*Sign Language.* Slap back of left hand with flat fingers of right, then back of right with flat fingers of left and add the sign *talk*, that is, hold right "G"* finger near mouth, pointing forward and advance it, working it up and down. (Sheeaka.)

*Illustration.* Do you talk sign language? Give *question, you* and *sign language.*

### THE DICTIONARY

*Abandon, Abandoned,* or *Drop it, Let it alone, Give it up.* (Thrown away, chucked.) Bring both closed hands, backs up, in front of and a little to left of body, hands near each other, lower the hands

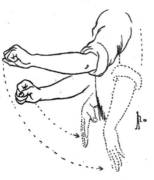

"GIVE IT UP"

quickly, at same time carry them to left and rear, and simultaneously open the hands with a snap of the fingers in extending them, drawing the hands back after the movement, as though throwing away something unpleasant. (C.) Often but one hand is used; two gives greater emphasis.

*Aboard.* (Sitting down on.) Left hand out,

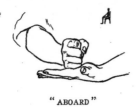

"ABOARD"

flat palm up, right "S" hand on it, thumb up. (C.)

*Above* or *Over.* (One thing above another.) Bring the flat left hand, back up, in front of and a little to the left of body; left forearm horizontal, fingers pointing to right and front; bring the flat right hand, back up, over the left in a semicircle upward, large or small according to

whether it is desired to represent a great or small distance. (C.)

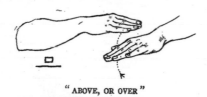

"ABOVE, OR OVER"

*Under, Below* or *Beneath* is the reverse of *Above,* i.e., swing right under instead of over the left. (C.)

*Absent, Gone,* or *Out of.* Place the right "5" hand back up in the left "C" hand

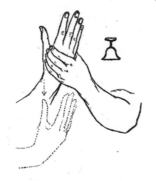

"ABSENT, OR GONE"

which is back down; drop the right hand down out of the left, closing left to "O." (T.F.)

*Afraid.* (Sinking heart.) Make the sign of *heart* by holding the compressed right hand with fingers straight down on left breast; then shake it up and down two or three times, to indicate the throbbing action of the heart under the influence of fear; others hold the hand as in *heart,* and then raise to make it stronger, finish by raising the hand until its back strikes the chin, to mean the heart rises in the throat. (C.)

*After* or *Behind.* Hands closed, except index fingers which are straight up, in front of body; place the left hand in front of body, then bring the right from the front to rear of left and drop it, at the same time clench the first. (T.F.)

*Ahead* or *Before.* Hold the fingers as in *after,* but bring the one from behind to in front of left, then clench and drop the hand. (T.F.).

*Alive* or *Lift.* (Walking about upright.) Hold index of right "G" hand upright, move it about shoulder high, forward in zigzags. (Roe.) Or hold the flat hands slightly curved near the ribs and move in and out as in breathing. (LaF.)

*All.* With right hand flat and back up, describe a large horizontal circle, shoulder high. (C.)

*Always* or *Forever.* (Going on in cycles.) With elbow at side, hold the right "G"

hand pointing forward back to right; move hand forward describing circles with the index, the result a spiral, ending with index raised. (T.F.)

*Angry.* (*Torn up inside.*) With fingers of one hand bent like talons make a tearing motion upward against the same side. (D.)

The Indians hold the fist near the forehead with tip of thumb touching it, then twist the first a little. (C.)

*Appear, Seem, Look like.* Hold up flat right hand thumb toward you, shoulder high; throw it forward a little and turn palm toward you, fixing the eyes on it; then add the sign for *look.* (T.F.).

*Approval, Applause* or *Praise.* Make the motion of clapping the hands. (Pop.)

*Arrive Here* or *Get Here.* Hold the flat left hand, back outward, in front of the breast and close to it, fingers pointing to right; carry right "G" hand well out in front of body, index finger pointing upward; back of hand to right, bring the right hand briskly against back of left, so the index projects but little above it. (C.)

*Arrive There, Get There* or *Reach.* Hold flat left hand, back to front, well out in front of body, about height of neck, pointing to right; bring right "G" hand, palm

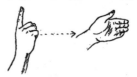

"ARRIVE THERE"

outward, in front of and close to neck, index finger pointing upward, carry the right hand out sharply and strike palm of the hand with the side of right index. (C.) This just reverses the preceding.

*Astonishment* or *Wonder.* (Stop, I am speechless.) Lay the flat palm of left hand over the mouth, and then draw the body backwards, holding right hand up, flat. (Sheeaka.)

*Autumn.* (Leaf-falling time.) Make the sign for *tree* with left hand, that is hold forearm upright with fingers spread, the other hand flat under the elbow, palm up, then the sign for *leaf-falling* with right, that is, the flat right hand back up slowly settles down in a succession of zigzags. (C.)

*Axe, Hatchet* or *Tomahawk.* Hold the right hand, with first three fingers straight

"AXE"

and touching, others closed, use it as a hatchet. (T.F.)

*Baby* or *Infant*. Swing the right arm in the hollow of the left as though it were a baby. (C.B.)

*Back, Backward* or *Past*. (In time.) Throw flat hand back over the shoulder, palm back. (T.F.)

*Bad*. Hold clenched fist back up near breast, throw it forward, down and aside, opening the hand which finishes palm down. (C.)

*Band* or *Patrol*. (Banded together.) Hold up the left hand, all fingers and thumb together and straight, encircle them with the right forefinger and thumb. (C.B.) (See *Tribe* or *Troop*.)

*Bar up*, or *Fines*, called also *King's X, King's Cross, Pax, Truce*, etc. Hold up right hand with first and second fingers crossed. (As in letter "R.") This means I claim privilege—what I now do is outside the game. (Universal in our schools and very ancient.) (Pop.)

*Battle-cry* or *War-cry*. Open the mouth as in saying "O" and pat it with the palm of the flat right hand. (C.B.)

*Beautiful, Handsome* or *Pretty*. Look on the flat right hand as in a mirror then make the sign *good*. (C.)

*Because*. Hold flat right hand palm down, near left breast, swing it to right side, palm

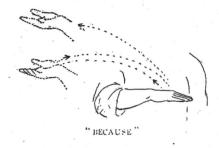

"BECAUSE"

up, then to left, palm down, then to right, palm up and a foot higher. (Roe.)

*Before, that is future*. Make the sign for *time*, that is with right index draw a circle on left palm, held up facing forward; then point and move forward with right "G" index, which describes a curve, forward and downward. (D.)

Or sign *after sleeps, many*. (Sheeaka.)

*Begin*. (You work now.) *You*, then with "B" right strike to left, then to right, always with little finger edge down. (Sheeaka.)

*Beyond*. Hold the flat left hand, back up in front of body about ten inches, fingers point to right; bring flat right hand, back up, between left and body same height, fingers pointing to left; swing the right hand upwards, forwards, and then downwards on curve, beyond left hand, turning right hand, back down, in the movement. (C.)

*Big*. Bring the flat hands out even, with palms toward each other, well out in front of body, a little lower than shoulders, a few inches apart, and pointing to front; separate hands carrying right to right, left to left, keeping them opposite each other. (C.)

*Bird*. With the flat hands near the shoulders, pointing forward, palms down, binding at wrists only, imitate the motion of wings. (Sheeaka.)

*Blanket* or *robe*. (Wrapping about shoulder.) Bring the closed hand, palms towards each other, opposite and near each

shoulder, move the right hand to left, and the left to right, terminating movement when wrists are crossed, right hand nearest body. (C.)

*Boat*. Bring the flat hands together, hollowed, fingers straight, little fingers touching, the thumbs farther apart, to represent the body of a boat. (M.)

*Book*. Open and close the flat hands like the covers of a book, then indicate writing. (Sheeaka.)

*Born, To be, Offspring*. (To come out of the hidden, into view.) Place the left hand a foot in front of the waist, the palm downward and slightly arched; pass the flat right hand fingers first from behind the left downward, forward and upward, forming a short curve underneath the left. (M.) Or omit the left hand. (C.)

*Brave*. (Strong heart.) For *calm fortitude* clinch the right fist and place it to the left breast. For *aggressive bravery*, raise and clench the hands until the fists are against breast near the shoulders and then push them far outward and lean forward. (D.)

Tap middle of breast with and then raise "G" finger in a curve, at first out, then straight up high, point up, that is, my heart is up high. (Sheeaka.)

Tap breast with and raise fists one behind other for brave in war. (Sheeaka.)

*Bring* or *Fetch*. Push the right "G" hand briskly forward back to right, then draw it back, at same time hooking index finger. (C.)

*Broad*. Same as *big*, but keep the flat hands palms down. (Sheeaka.)

*Brother*. (Suck together.) Lay the finger tips of nearly horizontal "N" of right hand on lips pointing straight at the mouth, then add *male*, that is, hold up right "G" hand palm forward. (C.)

*Buffalo*. (Curved horns.) Bring both "G" hand, palms toward and touching the sides of head, index fingers curved, and above the head. (C.)

To distinguish domestic cattle add *spotted*, by tapping the left forearm with tips of right fingers and thumb held touching each other in a point.

*But, except*, or *save*. (Of all, one picked out.) Hold up both "5" hands, palms forward and downward, then turn the left palm to you and tap the little finger with right "G" finger. (Sheeaka.)

*Called* or *Named*. Lay the right "G" finger on the lips, swing it over and forward toward the person, then strike down a little to left and right with it. (Sheeaka.)

*Camp*. (Form circle.) Make the sign for *tepee* or *lodge* (by crossing both "G" fingers at tips); then bring both curved "C" hands in front of center of body, palms toward each other, so the fingers and thumbs are about an inch apart, each forming an incomplete horizontal circle; lower the hands simultaneously and briskly some inches, as though forcing down a large vessel. (C.)

To indicate the size of the camp, give the number of lodges, or make sign for *tepees*, sign for *small*, if there are few lodges, and *many* if a large camp. If an unusually large village, add sign for *trees*, the idea being that the tips of the tepee-poles look like a forest. (C.)

To *Make camp*, omit the sign for *tepee*.

*Camp-fire*. (The wood laid ready.) Hold left hand flat, palm down, fingers a little spread, then lay right hand fingers similarly held, across the left fingers at right angles and add sign for *fire*. (Sheeaka.)

*Can* or *Able*. Hold the "S" hands in front, backs out, elbows at sides, drop the hands for six inches with a jerk. (Sheeaka.)

*Canoe*. Make sign for *boat*, and then sign for *paddling* same. (C.)

*Carry*. Both closed hands held opposite the temples as if holding the tump line, the shoulders slightly forward as though bearing a burden. (Scott.)

*Chicken*. *Bird*, then *red* (that is, rub the cheek lightly with the finger tips of one hand) and with "5" hand erect on crown show the comb. (C.)

*Chief*. (People, with one man rising above them.) Hold up left "5" hand, palm to right, pass index of right "G" hand several inches above left in a curve from the right up over the left. (Scott.)

*Child* or *Offspring*. When very small. Give the sign *baby* then indicate the size. To denote the sex add the signs *man* ("G" hand pointing up, palm forward) or *woman* (draw curved "5" hand past side of head like a comb). (C.)

*Choose, Make choice* or *Select*. Swing the "G" hand in a horizontal semi-circle, following it with eyes and at same time pointing forward with index finger; then end by throwing it forward in a curve. (Sheeaka.)

*Close*. (Draw near.) Bring the right hand back to right, fingers curved and touching, thumb resting on index finger, well out in front of body, hand about height of shoulder; draw the hand in toward the body and slightly downward. (C.)

*Coffee*. (Grinding coffee in mill.) Hold the extended left hand, back down, in front of body; bring the closed right hand a few inches over left palm, little finger nearest and parallel to it; move the right hand in small horizontal circles, representing the turning of crank, which causes the grinding of the coffee. (C.)

*Cold* (Shivering.) Bring the fists in front of and close to the body, height of shoulder, elbows at sides, shoulders drawn in, and shake the fists. (C.)

*Color*. With the fingers of right hand (thumb closed) rub circularly on the palm of the left hand as though rubbing color. (Sheeaka.)

*Black*. *Color* and touch the hair or eyebrow. (Sheeaka.)

*Blue*. (Sky when sun is there.) *Sun*, i.e., make a ring of left index and thumb, hold it up high, then with the "G" finger indicate the space around it, to mean "sky." (Sheeaka.)

*Gray*. Sign *Color, black, white* and *mix* by grinding on the left palm, with the heel of the right. For other colors touch or indicate some object of the tint meant. (Sheeaka.)

*Green*. *Color* and *grass* (i.e. hold "5" hand very low, palm up, fingers pointing upward and raise it with a little jerk). (Sheeaka.)

*Red*. (Cheek color.) *Color* and lightly brush right finger tips over the cheek. (Scott.)

# SCOUTCRAFT
## YOUR FIRST CAMPOUT

## CHOOSING THE SITE

LOOK FOR A FAIRLY OPEN SPOT WHERE THE GROUND SLOPES GENTLY SO THAT RAINWATER DRAINS OFF QUICKLY. GRASS-COVERED, SANDY OR GRAVELLY GROUND IS BEST. THE SITE SHOULD BE NEAR WOODS, BUT NOT DIRECTLY UNDER TREES. SAFE DRINKING AND COOKING WATER SHOULD BE NEARBY.

A LAKE OR A STREAM WILL PROVIDE WATER FOR WASHING MESS GEAR. BUT DON'T WASH POTS OR MESS GEAR IN THE LAKE OR STREAM. PURIFY THIS WATER BEFORE DRINKING.

DON'T DIG A TRENCH AROUND YOUR TENT. IT'S UNNECESSARY IF YOU'VE CHOSEN A SUITABLE, WELL-DRAINED SPOT.

DIG A STRADDLE LATRINE IN THE BUSHES DOWNWIND FROM CAMP AND AT LEAST 75 FEET FROM ANY WATER. SAVE ALL DIRT FOR LIGHT COVER AFTER EACH USE, AND FOR REFILLING LATRINE BEFORE YOU LEAVE CAMP FOR GOOD. REPLACE SOD.

FOR MORE INFORMATION, CHECK YOUR **BOY SCOUT HANDBOOK**, THE **FIELDBOOK** AND THE **CAMPING** MERIT BADGE PAMPHLET.

## A COMFORTABLE GROUND BED

SMOOTH OUT BUMPS AND REMOVE STONES FROM YOUR SLEEPING AREA. INSTEAD OF DIGGING HIP AND SHOULDER HOLLOWS, COVER YOUR BED AREA WITH LEAVES, STRAW, GRASS, OR PINE NEEDLES. PACK EXTRA PADDING WHERE YOUR BACK, HEAD AND MIDDLE THIGHS WILL LIE. SPREAD YOUR GROUND CLOTH OVER IT ALL. LAY YOUR SLEEPING BAG ON THIS—OR MAKE THIS BED SACK WITH TWO BLANKETS AND LARGE BLANKET PINS.

### BLANKET BED SACK

① SPREAD FIRST BLANKET ON GROUND CLOTH. THEN PUT SECOND BLANKET HALFWAY OVER THE FIRST.

② FOLD BOTTOM BLANKET HALFWAY OVER TOP ONE.

③ FOLD TOP BLANKET OVER.

④ FOLD BACK FOOT PART OF BOTH BLANKETS.

⑤ PIN TOGETHER TO MAKE SACK.

BLANKET PINS — GROUND CLOTH

A SHEET OF POLYETHYLENE (A PLASTIC) 4-6 MIL THICK MAKES A GOOD GROUND CLOTH. OR YOU CAN USE AN AIR MATTRESS INFLATED JUST ENOUGH TO KEEP YOUR BODY OFF THE GROUND. OR USE A PIECE OF POLYFOAM 3" THICK BY 24" WIDE AND THE LENGTH FROM YOUR HEAD TO SEAT. A GROUND CLOTH HELPS INSULATE YOU FROM DAMPNESS AND COLD.

**MAKE THIS** HANDY POCKET LIST OF PERSONAL EQUIPMENT TO TAKE WITH YOU. CUT IT OUT, FOLD BACK TO BACK, THEN LAMINATE IT IN PLASTIC. CHECK OFF THE ITEMS WITH A GREASE PENCIL AS YOU PACK. WIPE OFF FOR NEXT USE.

## CAMPOUT CHECKLIST

**WEAR**
- [ ] COMPLETE UNIFORM
- [ ] HIKING SHOES
- [ ] SWEATER or JACKET
- [ ] RAINCOAT or PONCHO

**CARRY IN POCKETS**
- [ ] SCOUT KNIFE
- [ ] MATCHES (IN WATER-PROOF CASE)
- [ ] HANDKERCHIEF
- [ ] WALLET (INCLUDE DIMES FOR PHONE)

- [ ] INDIVIDUAL TOILET PAPER
- [ ] COMPASS
- [ ] 2 or 3 BAND-AIDS

**FASTEN TO OR INSIDE YOUR PACK**
- [ ] REPAIR KIT (NEEDLES, THREAD, ETC.)
- [ ] EATING UTENSILS
- [ ] FLASHLIGHT (CHECK BATTERIES)
- [ ] SLEEPING BAG (OR 2-3 BLANKETS)
- [ ] WATERPROOF GROUND CLOTH

- [ ] MOCCASINS or SNEAKERS
- [ ] CLOTHESBAG WITH:
- [ ] EXTRA SHIRT
- [ ] EXTRA PANTS
- [ ] PAJAMAS or SWEAT SUIT
- [ ] EXTRA HANDKERCHIEFS
- [ ] EXTRA SOCKS
- [ ] CHANGE OF UNDERWEAR
- [ ] TOILET KIT CONTAINING:
- [ ] WASH CLOTH [ ] COMB
- [ ] SOAP [ ] HAND TOWEL

- [ ] BATH TOWEL
- [ ] TOOTHBRUSH & TOOTHPASTE
- [ ] WASH BASIN (PLASTIC OR CANVAS)

**OPTIONAL ITEMS**
- [ ] WATCH [ ] SWIM TRUNKS
- [ ] CAMERA, FILM [ ] CANTEEN
- [ ] NOTEBOOK, PENCIL [ ] MAP
- [ ] FIRST AID KIT
- [ ] SCOUT HANDBOOK or FIELDBOOK
- [ ] MOSQUITO DOPE & NETTING
- [ ] LENGTH of LINE or ROPE

68280

# CANOEING IN THE SURF

## GOING OUT

**K**EEP THE BOW AT RIGHT ANGLE TO THE WAVES.

IF YOU ALLOW THE WAVES TO HIT AT AN ANGLE THEY WILL TURN THE CANOE SIDEWAYS AND IT WILL BROACH...AND OVER YOU'LL GO!

**T**HE BOW MAN KNEELS BEHIND THE THWART...THE LARGER THE WAVES, THE FURTHER AFT HE SHOULD MOVE.

**M**AN IN STERN KNEELS AT AFTERSEAT.

RIDING A WAVE IS GREAT SPORT!

## COMING IN

**K**EEP STERN AT RIGHT ANGLE TO THE WAVES, FOR THE SAME REASON AS WHEN YOU'RE GOING OUT.

**S**TERN MAN, IN HIGH KNEELING POSITION, STRADDLES AFT THWART SO HE CAN QUICKLY MOVE FORWARD OR BACK TO TRIM THE CANOE.

**B**OW MAN KNEELS BEHIND FORWARD THWART. IN LARGER WAVES HE MAY HAVE TO MOVE FURTHER AFT IN ORDER TO KEEP WEIGHT CENTERED AND ALLOW BOW OR STERN TO LIFT EASILY.

**K**EEP A SHARP EYE OUT FOR SWIMMERS OR OBSTACLES IN YOUR PATH.

**T**HE BOW MUST BE KEPT LIGHT ENOUGH TO RIDE EASILY UP AND OVER INCOMING WAVES.

**I**F YOUR CANOE CAPSIZES, OR YOU GET TOSSED OUT IN DEEP WATER, HANG ON TO IT TO KEEP IT FROM HITTING YOU. IF YOU CAN'T HOLD ON TO IT, DIVE AS DEEP AS YOU CAN AND STAY DOWN AS LONG AS YOU CAN. COME UP WITH HANDS PROTECTING YOUR HEAD.

**I**N SHALLOW WATER, STAY AT ENDS OF CANOE SO THAT THE WAVES OR THE BACK WASH WON'T SMASH THE CANOE AGAINST YOUR LEGS OR ROLL IT OVER YOU.

**P**ADDLING IN ON THE BACK OF A WAVE IS THE SAFE, EASY METHOD TO COME IN. HOLD, OR BACK WATER, KEEPING WEIGHT AFT AS WAVE APPROACHES AND PASSES.

AS SOON AS WAVE HAS PASSED THE BOW, MOVE WEIGHT FORWARD AND PADDLE FOR SHORE. WATCH BEHIND FOR FOLLOWING WAVE.

**T**O RIDE THE WAVE IN...GET CANOE MOVING TO MATCH SPEED OF WAVE... AS WAVE APPROACHES...KEEP WEIGHT CENTERED.

WHEN STERN PICKS UP AND CANOE STARTS TO SLIDE DOWN AND FORWARD, MOVE WEIGHT AFT QUICKLY. *KEEP A STRAIGHT COURSE!*...WHICH REQUIRES STRONG RUDDER ACTION BY STERN MAN.

# A Fly Rod Carrier

Put a set of these easy-to-make fly rod carriers on top of your car and you'll save the unnecessary inconvenience of having to take apart your rod when you travel to a new fishing spot. A set of these carriers holds two rods.—G.W.

The wire caps are bent from coat hanger wire. The insides are lined with strips of ¼" sponge rubber to cushion. Screws hold the carriers on car gutter.

First saw the two slots inside 5/16" guide lines and just beyond 1" mark. With wood block and hammer bend center section at right angle at the 1" mark.

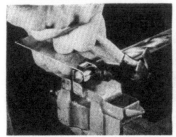

Now bend the two hooks around a ½" rod with a piece of metal 3/32" thick between the rod and the bent portion. Tap lightly with hammer. File corners.

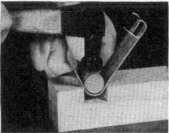

You can make clean bends if you use a jig like this. Use a ¾" wood dowel and a hardwood block underneath with a ⅞" wide slot cut across the block.

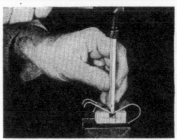

Use a ¼" x 1¼" x 4" strip of maple to make third bend. The block underneath is ⅝" x 1½" x 1⅝" with a ⅜" slot cut across it 11/16" from the left end.

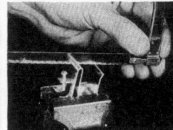

Drill and tap for an 8-32 machine screw; saw two slots following the guide lines, then file the notch for the wire cap 3/16" deep. File all the edges.

# Splittin' Wood'n Logs

A true woodsman takes pride in his ability to handle an axe. Like all sports, it takes lots of practice and a "know how" to be good at it. So if you're called upon next time to split wood for the fire or split logs for a construction job study these photos for "how to" kinks. Then go and try it for yourself. Practice will make you perfect!

Cut small branches at an angle. Slip one end under a second log to prevent its flying up in the air as it is cut. Feet behind block.

To split small pieces, start axe in the stick, then raise both together. This "contact method" saves energy, and wild swings.

Splitting hardwood requires good axemanship. Keep legs apart on side of block opposite wood. Now, eyes on target—fire!

Sometimes two axes can be used effectively to split a large chunk. One axe acts as a starter wedge; other finishes job.

Here's another way to split that heavy chunk. Use a hardwood wedge; hit it with the head of the axe. Use only light blows.

Now let's tackle a log. Start a notch in the end of the log with your axe, insert the wooden wedge; then drive it home hard!

To split a real heavy log, you'll need two iron wedges, one heavier than the other, and a maul to drive 'em. Axe is no maul.

Make axe notch, then drive your light wedge all the way into the log. Follow up with the heavy wedge, and, well, that's it!

# Quickie Fires

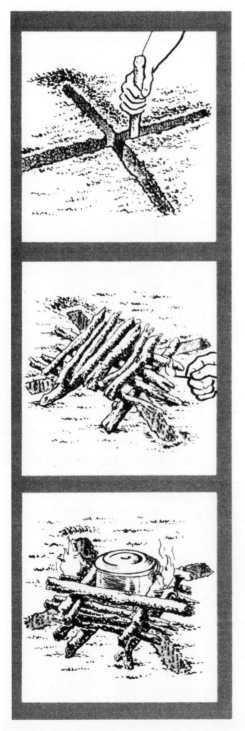

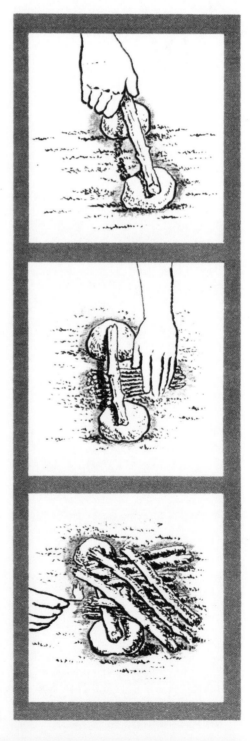

**T**HERE comes a time in every camper's life when he needs a fire in a hurry. You may need a roaring fire to dry by after a dunking in an icy stream. Or you may have to rustle up a meal to leave camp on time.

To build such a quick fire you must know where to find dry firewood that will ignite quickly. You also need to know how to lay a fire so that the heavier fuel doesn't fall and smother the flames when the tinder burns out.

Use either one of these two lays for a quick fire: the cross-ditch fire lay shown to the left or the fire-stick fire lay, to the right.

For the *cross-ditch fire*, first scrape a three-inch-deep cross in the ground. This shallow ditch lets air sweep in under the fire and provides a good draft. Place a large wad of tinder in the middle of the cross ditch. Now lay several foundation sticks diagonally over the cross. Build up on those, in crisscross fashion, enough wood for a speedy bed of coals for broiling (left center).

For rapid boiling, place a layer of foundation sticks diagonally over the cross ditch and place your pot on them. Then, in log-cabin style, build up fuel around the pot. When completely laid, light the tinder (left bottom).

For the *fire-stick fire*, place two small rocks on the ground, about ten inches apart (right top). If you can't find rocks, use two thick sticks. Now lay a "fire stick" across the two rocks. Push a large handful of tinder in under the fire stick (right center). Then lean thin kindling against the downwind side of the "fire stick." Build up the fire lay with thicker and thicker pieces of fuel wood, as much as is needed for your cooking. Now light your tinder close to the ground. ■

# Wild-Food Cookout

### BY JON C. HALTER
**Photographs by Gene Daniels**
Featuring the Scouts of North Essex Council, Lawrence, Mass.

**W**HAT'S for lunch?

How about watercress salad, boiled milkweed pods, and roasted cattail roots, with black walnuts, rose hips, and cranberries for dessert and sumac tea to drink?

The cost: zero. Nutrition: the highest. And taste? These wild foods can be just as good as apples, potatoes, carrots, and good ol' "bug juice."

"The Official Boy Scout Handbook" is a good place to start learning about wild foods. A library or bookstore will have other, more detailed guidebooks.

Knowing basic wild foods will add extra pleasure to any hike or camp-out. You'll be more aware of plant life and have a better understanding of nature.

Wild foods can certainly liven up any camp meal. And they can also help your family's food budget at home.

They're good for you too. Most wild foods are richer in vitamins and minerals than supermarket fruits and vegetables.

Finally, being able to live off the land prepares you for any survival situation.

## Find an Expert

All beginners should learn how to forage for wild foods with the help of an experienced outdoorsman who knows what to look for. (Never taste a plant unless you're sure that it is safe to eat.)

Ken Cole is just such a wild-food expert, and he gladly assisted the Massachusetts Scouts shown here. A former professional Scouter, Mr. Cole showed the Scouts how to prepare several foods from wild plants growing in a typical Northeastern meadowland.

At first glance many tasty plants do not seem appetizing. Who could imagine gobbling a milkweed pod, or munching on a giant puffball? But you already eat apples and berries and carrots and potatoes. Wild foods are closely related to, and in many cases taste much like, foods you already enjoy.

## What to Look For

These five rules help your selection. A food must be

**1.** eatable—easily chewed, either raw or cooked.

**2.** wholesome—not poisonous or contaminated, such as by motor oil and leaded gasoline along a highway.

**3.** digestible—tolerated by the human digestive system.

**4.** nutritive—rich in vitamins and minerals.

**5.** palatable—tastes good, or at least O.K.

Five general wild-food categories are greens for salads; breadstuffs; roots and tubers; beverages, and desserts. Many foods can be eaten raw. Others are best prepared by boiling, frying or roasting.

Acorns are best for making bread in the wild, but their bitter tannin must be removed first. You can also mix cattail pollen and regular flour to make bread.

Green, unripe milkweed seedpods also must have their natural bitterness removed. Boil them in water and drain several times. Then you can cook them in salted, boiling water until tender.

Mr. Cole showed the Scouts three root foods that make a hearty dish when cooked and seasoned. In cooking pots, they boiled wild carrot (from the plant commonly known as Queen Anne's Lace), the peeled stalks of cattail plants, and the fiddlehead sprouts of ferns.

Berries and nuts make great desserts, in camp or back home. Mr. Cole found cranberries, good for snacking and making jam, jelly, or a beverage.

The Scouts also sampled red, tangy rose hips, the fruit of the wild rose (which in winter can be a vital survival food). They opened the green husk of black walnuts to try the sweet nuts inside.

For a beverage, the Scouts made tea from staghorn sumac. They heated the reddish fruit in water and then strained out the solids. Adding sugar to the remaining liquid produced a tasty drink.

Every season of the year offers an endless assortment of wild foods to campers. You only need the key of knowledge to unlock nature's wild pantry.♣

You can't always tell a wild food's use by its appearance. The herb yarrow (far left, top), when rolled and crushed, can relieve toothache pain when you bite on it. A wild carrot root (far left, middle) doesn't look much like the garden variety, but can be just as edible. Patridge-berries (far left, bottom) can be eaten raw, or dried for future use, while ground juniper (at left) is used mainly as a spice.

"Let's pick dinner," say these hungry Massachusetts Scouts as they forage for staghorn sumac (above), young milkweed pods (at right), and wild carrot (Queen Anne's Lace). When boiled (at left) these wild plants will yield nutritious camp foods. Strained, the sumac makes a tasty "pink lemonade." The boiled milkweed pods and wild carrot roots make a serving of truly unusual mixed vegetables.

Above: **Rose hips can be found in winter.** Below: **These patrol cooks prepare dinner completely with wild foods.**

The best part of a fern (above) is not its leaves, but is found in the "fiddlehead," or young shoot, which can be eaten raw or cooked like asparagus.

**You can open the door to nature's bountiful pantry of good eating if you learn which plants to look for.**

# Personal FIRST AID

ACCIDENTS HAPPEN, MANY OF THEM WHEN YOU'RE ALONE. THINKING AHEAD AND PRACTICING FOR EMERGENCIES COULD SAVE YOUR LIFE. HERE ARE SOME HINTS FOR WHEN THE CHIPS ARE DOWN AND YOU'RE ALL BY YOURSELF.

IF YOU **CUT AN ARTERY** IN YOUR ARM—*LIE DOWN* QUICKLY TO *KEEP SHOCK TO A MINIMUM.* RAISE YOUR ARM. TRY TO STOP BLEEDING BY HOLDING A COMPRESS **DIRECTLY OVER** THE WOUND.

IF THAT DOESN'T WORK, **TWIST A NECKERCHIEF** OR BELT **AROUND YOUR ARM.**

SHOULD YOU CUT YOUR LEG, **PRESS** A COMPRESS DIRECTLY **ON** THE WOUND TO STOP BLEEDING. IF BLEEDING DOESN'T STOP, PLACE ARM **UNDER KNEE, BENDING LEG SHARPLY** TO CUT BLOOD SUPPLY TO LEG.

FOR A **NOSEBLEED,** SIT DOWN AND BEND YOUR HEAD **BACK.** PINCH YOUR NOSTRILS TOGETHER, OR PRESS YOUR UPPER LIP **HARD** AGAINST YOUR TEETH WITH A FINGER.

IF YOUR CLOTHES SHOULD CATCH FIRE, **DON'T RUN!..** YOU'LL FAN THE FLAMES. PUT ONE HAND OVER YOUR MOUTH TO PREVENT INHALATION OF FLAMES. GET TO THE FLOOR OR GROUND QUICKLY. **ROLL** OVER AND OVER. THIS WILL EXTINGUISH THE FLAMES.

IF A BLANKET OR A COAT IS **HANDY,** GRAB IT AND WRAP IT AROUND YOUR-SELF TO SMOTHER THE FLAMES *AS YOU ROLL!*

WHEN YOU FEEL **FAINT, SIT DOWN** ON A LOG OR STUMP AND **LOWER** YOUR HEAD SO THAT IT'S **BELOW** YOUR HEART.

ANOTHER METHOD IS TO **LIE FLAT** ON YOUR BACK, WITH YOUR LEGS UP AGAINST A TREE. THE EXTRA BLOOD SUPPLY TO YOUR HEAD SHOULD REVIVE YOU.

A TRUE STORY of SCOUTS IN ACTION
by ALSTEN

ON THE EVENING OF APRIL 15, 1960 SOME BOYS WERE SAILING A MODEL HYDROPLANE ON LAKE PEMBROOK NEAR FERGUSON, MISSOURI...

IT'S GETTING DARK. I CAN'T SEE THE BOAT.

THERE IT IS—ABOUT SEVENTY-FIVE YARDS OFF SHORE. I'LL ASK MY MOTHER IF I CAN SWIM OUT AND GET IT.

IT'LL NEVER DRIFT ASHORE, MOM. THERE'S NO WIND.

THAT WATER'S PRETTY COLD—BUT GO AHEAD—AND HURRY—IT'S TIME WE DROVE HOME.

SO HE WALKED INTO THE SMALL, BUT DEEP LAKE...

BR-R-R IT IS COLD!

ABOUT 20-YARDS FROM SHORE...

HELP! HELP!

I'LL GET HIM!

KICKING OFF HIS SHOES, CLARENCE GOOD, 14-YEAR-OLD EXPLORER RUSHED INTO THE WATER...

...SWAM TO HIS EXHAUSTED BUDDY AND PUSHED HIM TO SHORE!

I'M COLD. LET'S HURRY HOME AND WARM UP.

BOY! YOU DIDN'T HESITATE A SECOND TO GO AFTER HIM.

FOR HIS PROMPT AND EFFICIENT ACTION IN THIS EMERGENCY, EXPLORER CLARENCE GOOD WAS AWARDED THE CERTIFICATE OF MERIT BY THE NATIONAL COURT OF HONOR, BOY SCOUTS OF AMERICA.

CLARENCE IS A MEMBER OF SHIP 244, FLORISSANT, MISSOURI, SPONSORED BY AMERICAN LEGION POST 444.

# HOW TO CATCH A FISH
by TED PETTIT

TEN PER CENT OF ALL FISHERMEN CATCH 90% OF THE FISH! PRETTY DISCOURAGING?... BUT HERE ARE SOME FISHING SECRETS THAT WILL HELP YOU BECOME ONE OF THOSE TEN-PER CENTERS!

YELLOW PERCH & WHITE PERCH

YELLOW BASS

BULLHEAD

BLUEGILL

DON'T JUST GO FISHING...GO AFTER SPECIFIC FISH LIKE THOSE PICTURED ABOVE. FISH DIFFER IN THEIR HABITS—SO THE FIRST SECRET IS **KNOW YOUR FISH!**

IF I KNEW I'D FISH THERE MYSELF!

YOU MIGHT TRY AND ASK LOCAL FISHERMEN WHERE FISH USUALLY ARE AT DIFFERENT SEASONS OF THE YEAR AND TIMES OF DAY. TYPICAL PLACES—EDGES OF WEED BEDS, AROUND UNDERWATER LOGS, STUMPS, ROCKY AREAS. TEST VARIOUS SPOTS.

FISH AT DIFFERENT DEPTHS. SOME FISH PREFER THE DEEPER, COLDER WATER. SOME FEED ON BOTTOM, SOME NEAR SURFACE, OTHERS IN-BETWEEN. A FLOAT WILL HELP YOU CONTROL THE DEPTH OF YOUR BAIT.

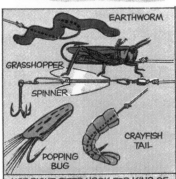

EARTHWORM

GRASSHOPPER

SPINNER

POPPING BUG

CRAYFISH TAIL

USE RIGHT-SIZED HOOK FOR KIND OF FISH YOU'RE AFTER. KEEP HOOKS CLEAN AND SHARP. A SMALL SHARPENING STONE OR FILE WILL DO THE TRICK.

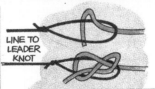

LINE TO LEADER KNOT

TURTLE KNOT LEADER TO HOOK

PRACTICE TYING THE CORRECT KNOTS FOR SECURING HOOKS AND LEADERS—ESPECIALLY WITH THE NEW SYNTHETIC LEADER MATERIALS.

PRACTICE CASTING. ACCURACY FIRST—THEN GO FOR DISTANCE.

WE'LL TOSS THIS IN THE GARBAGE PAIL AT HOME.

DON'T BE A LITTER-FISHER! PUT TRASH IN BAG TO DISPOSE IN A PROPER PLACE LATER. MANY WATERS HAVE BEEN CLOSED TO FISHERMEN BECAUSE OF LITTERING.

# WINTER Camping

## There's fun in that thar white stuff...
### By WILLIAM HILLCOURT

Before you put up your tent, scoop away as much snow as possible, and trample down the rest.

Pitch tent with the closed back to the wind. Arrange a place in front of tent for your fire.

For your bed, make a frame of dead logs and fill it with dry leaves. Newspapers make an excellent insulation under your sleeping bag.

EVER HEAR OF "Radiator Scouts?" Those are the guys who are enthusiastic about camping in the middle of summer —but retire to their steam-heated rooms to spend the winter. You couldn't get them out-of-doors on a bet when the temperature hovers around freezing and below.

Then there's the other kind—the "All-Year Scouts." Always on the go, always excited about experiencing new thrills. To these fellows winter camping is a challenge and a cinch. They go cold-weather camping the right way and have a marvelous time.

There are five important points to successful winter camping: Proper clothing, shelter, bedding, food, and activities.

CLOTHING—Dry and warm clothing is the secret of comfortable winter camping. You are better off with several layers of light clothing instead of one or two heavy layers. Start with loose-fitting "long-johns," then tightly-woven, water-repellent trousers, a heavy flannel shirt, and a windproof jacket. Use two pairs of light, woolen socks to keep your feet warm and dry in high-cut, watertight shoes or ski boots. Wear a ski cap with ear flaps and woolen gloves with waterproof cover mittens.

SHELTER—Pick a camp site that is sheltered by trees or by the side of a hill. Use baker or Explorer tents with open fronts—you can build a reflector fire in front of them and keep the fire going all night.

BEDDING—To sleep warm, you must have at least as much under you as over you. Make a bed frame and fill it with light brush, dead leaves or evergreen twigs. Cover with several layers of newspapers and with your waterproof groundsheet. Then spread out your sleeping bag, or turn four heavy blankets into a sleeping bag with the help of blanket pins.

FOOD—Meals for winter camping must be high in calories to keep your engine stoked. Plenty of fats and sugars, hot cereal, bacon, hot soups. Stew is tops for the main meal.

ACTIVITIES—To keep yourself warm in winter camp, you need to be on the move. Wood cutting will give you some of your warm-up exercise—and then there's skiing, tobogganing, snowball fighting, and a snappy hike through the countryside.

Winter camp is the perfect place for exploring nature. Take a hike through the surrounding landscape and see what you can find. Look for bird nests, and for plants under the snow.

Animal tracks are at their best in snow. Can you identify the animals that made the tracks? How far can you follow the tracks?

PHOTOS BY ILMAR PLEER

Plan a number of vigorous activities for your days in winter camp. Skiing and tobogganing will be high on your list. So will snowball fighting.

Or try a snow tug-o-war: Build a snow wall and run your rope through it, half of the gang on each side—and no one is permitted to let go of the rope.

For cooking, clear the ground of snow and place down a floor of sticks. Over them, make a hunter's fire from two logs. Erect a tripod over fire. Hang pots from top of tripod or from cross-stick lashed to it.

For warmth, build a reflector fire place about six feet in front of the tent. Prop up two stakes and stack green logs against them to form a reflector. Collect enough fire wood to last the night.

## OVERHAND KNOT>

Start with the simplest of all knots. The overhand is an example of a stopper knot. Stoppers are tied to prevent the end of a rope from unraveling, slipping through another knot or passing back through a hole.

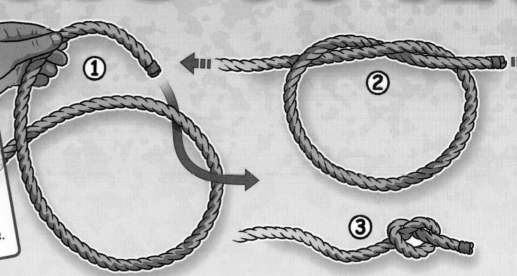

## <SQUARE KNOT

This is a binding knot that can keep loose objects together. It is a first-aid basic, used for tying bandages.

# OW

**Here are four simple knots every guy should know how to tie.**

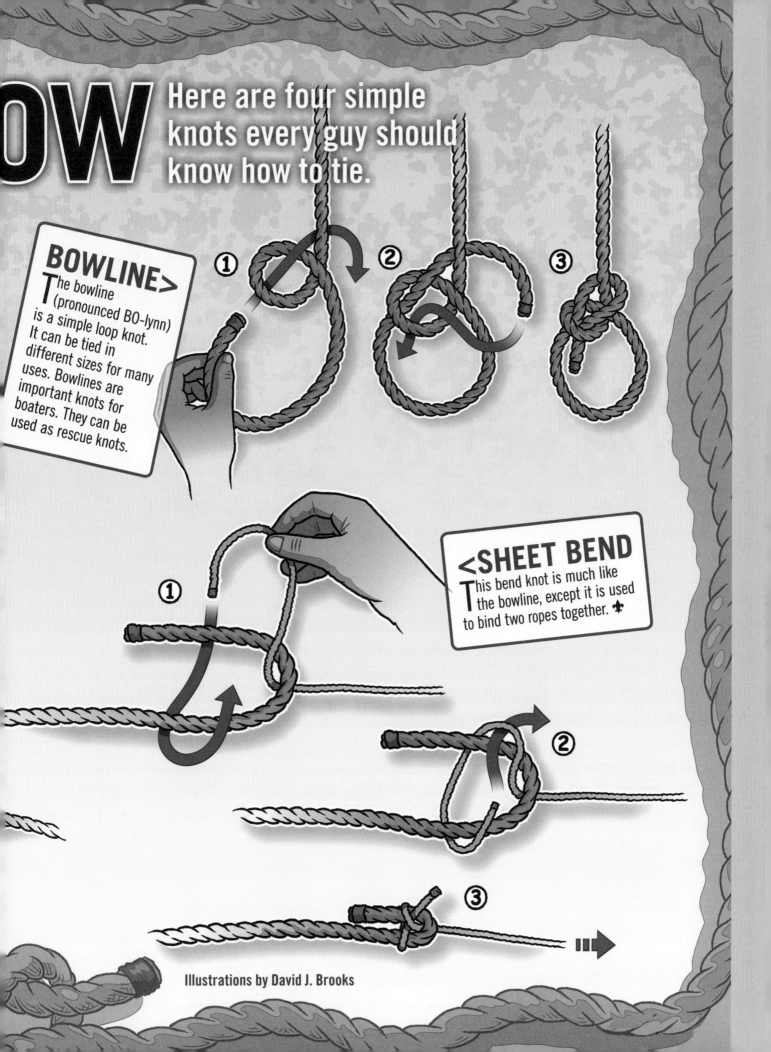

## BOWLINE>

The bowline (pronounced BO~lynn) is a simple loop knot. It can be tied in different sizes for many uses. Bowlines are important knots for boaters. They can be used as rescue knots.

① ② ③

## <SHEET BEND

This bend knot is much like the bowline, except it is used to bind two ropes together. ✤

① ② ③

**Illustrations by David J. Brooks**

# CAMPING WITHOUT TENTS

## A Clever Article for All Scouts

SCOUTS who are not well off rarely have very good camps because they can't afford to buy carts to lug their tents and stuff about in.

For if you have to carry your baggage along on your shoulder, you don't get very far out into the country. Instead of going out to those delightful camping-pitches a few miles away, you're only too glad to put your tents upon the nearest field you can find—right

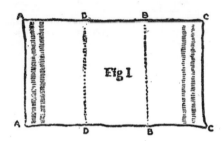

Fig 1

up close to the town, which is a bad thing to do, in my opinion, because you're inclined to spend your time in the town instead of round the camp-fire. It ins't the real thing at all.

### Showing Points of Folding the Blanket.

So this issue I'm going to tell you how to pack up a kit with which, in the fine weather, you can camp out in the open, without tents, or anything.

You want to be comfortable, of course, but if you're going to camp, why, do it in a proper scouting way, and "go light." I've no patience with fellows who can't go for a week-end camp unless they're lumbered up with folding-tables, and eiderdown quilts, and tin buckets, and camp kettles, and goodness knows what!

### What You Really Need.

Well, now, here's a list of the absolutely necessary things to take with you: Water-

proof ground-sheet, blanket, sweater and flannel trousers for sleeping in or sleeping-bag, two spare pairs of socks, soap and towel, hairbrush, tothbrush, and two handkerchiefs.

With these as a pack, and with your mess-tin or billy, scoutknife, one or two axes between you, knife, fork, and spoon in your

haversack, string, matches, and plenty of grub, you ought to be able to camp quite comfortably, if you are a healthy chap—and a scout.

Now to make up your pack.

Lay your blanket flat as in figure 1. Fold A, A to B, B, and C, C to D, D, so as to fold the blanket evenly in three.

Now turn up one end, about three inches, as at A, Fig. 2. On top of this turn-up put your sleep-suit, socks, soap, towel, and whatever other oddments you are packing, folded up and stowed away as small as you can get 'm. Keep them well in the midde. Don't let them stray away towards the sides.

At the other end turn up about six inches, as at B, so that the top of the turn-up forms a kind of deep pocket (C). This pocket is the important thing of the whole affair.

### How to Pack Your Kit.

Now start rolling up from A, with your odd articles in the middle of the roll. Make

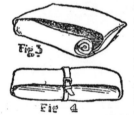

Fig 3

Fig 4

this roll as tight and neat as you can. For prefererence, get another fellow to roll up at one side while you do the other. Roll on till you get to the pocket (C). Then tuck in as in Fig. 3.

Roll it right in, so as to have a firm, close-up roll as in Fig. 4. Wrap the ground-sheet tightly round it. Now put a strap or a piece of cord round the middle, and you have the thing complete. All your odd articles are safely and securely stowed away in a bundle that you can strap on to your belt where your coat usually goes, or sling on your back, and carry for miles.

But don't pack it across your shoulders above your haversack. That's the way to tire yourself out. A burden carried in that position is twice as fagging as one which hangs well down on the small of the back.

When you pitch camp, you either lay down your ground-sheets and blankets to make big beds to hold three of four of you, or you can roll up in your own blanket, and all of you sleep in a circle, with your fee to the camp fire.

Mind you, this is no scheme for wct weather. If you try to do it on rainy days you'll be wretchedly uncomfortable, and probably get a chill. It isn't good enough. And I wouldn't let little chaps do it, unless they're very sturdy. They're far better stowed away in a warm tent. But for good healthy chaps over thirteen on so, in good summer weather, it's a model way to camp.

# AXEMANSHIP

THE AXE AND THE FLINTLOCK RIFLE WERE TWO OF THE MOST IMPORTANT TOOLS OF OUR PIONEER FOREFATHERS. WE NO LONGER NEED THE FLINTLOCK, BUT THE AXE IS AS NECESSARY TO EVERY OUTDOORSMAN TODAY AS IT EVER WAS. AND THE TEST OF A GOOD WOODSMAN IS HOW WELL HE USES AND CARES FOR HIS AXE.

## A SHARP AXE IS SAFEST!
TO KEEP YOUR AXE IN SHAPE, USE A NICE FILE. KEEP THE ACTUAL CUTTING EDGE OF YOUR AXE KEEN WITH A SHARPENING STONE.

IF YOU'RE THE RIGHT KIND OF AXEMAN YOU'LL BE ABLE TO MAKE A PERFECTLY SQUARE-POINTED TENT PEG WITH JUST FOUR CUTS! TRY IT...

SHARPENING STONE

MILL FILE

PLACE HEAD OF YOUR AXE AGAINST A LOG, EDGE UP. HOLD IT FIRMLY IN POSITION WITH WOODEN PEGS. PUSH FILE DOWN OVER THE EDGE. WHEN ONE SIDE IS FILED, TURN THE AXE OVER AND FILE OTHER SIDE.

FILE STRAIGHT AWAY— NOT OBLIQUELY. FILE CUTS ON DOWNWARD STROKE, LIFT FILE ON RETURN STROKE.

KEEP THE AXE HANDLE TIGHT!

HONE YOUR AXE AFTER FILING WITH A CIRCULAR MOTION ALONG THE EDGE WITH THE SHARPENING STONE.

PASS AN AXE OR HATCHET BY OFFERING THE HANDLE. DON'T LET GO UNTIL THE OTHER FELLOW HAS A FIRM GRASP ON IT.

## KEEP YOUR AXE MASKED WHEN NOT IN USE

## WHEN READY TO USE...

CARRY THE HAND AXE BY ITS HEAD—EDGE POINTED AWAY FROM YOU—DON'T SWING YOUR ARM TOO WIDE.

MASKED IN A LEATHER SHEATH

MASKED IN A LOG.

IN AN EMERGENCY, MASK YOUR AXE WITH A FLATTENED TIN CAN WITH HOLES PUNCHED THROUGH. TIE WITH STRING OR THONG AROUND THE AXE AS SHOWN.

## USING YOUR HAND AXE

CUTTING
USE THE CONTACT METHOD

SPLITTING
TAP AXE AND STICK TOGETHER TO START

PLACE THE EDGE OF AXE ON STICK... LIFT STICK AND AXE TOGETHER, BRING THEM DOWN TOGETHER HARD ON BLOCK.

...LIFT AXE AND STICK TOGETHER, BRING DOWN HARD TOGETHER. AS YOU HIT BLOCK, TWIST AXE HAND SLIGHTLY TO SEPARATE THE PIECES.

WHEN HIKING CARRY YOUR SHEATHED HAND AXE INSIDE, OR ATTACHED TO YOUR KNAPSACK.

## TWO AXE GAMES THAT YOU CAN PLAY...

←MATCH

STRING

STICK A MATCH IN A STUMP CRACK OR CHOPPING BLOCK. MEMBERS OF RIVAL PATROLS TAKE TURNS TRYING TO IGNITE THE MATCH WITH STROKE OF AXE. SEE WHICH PATROL LIGHTS MORE MATCHES.

MASK AXE IN LOG BETWEEN EACH STROKE.

PLACE TWO INCH STRING ALONG CHOPPING BLOCK. COMPETING PATROL MEMBERS ATTEMPT TO HALVE THE EVER-SHORTENING STRING. SEE WHICH PATROL WINDS UP WITH MOST PIECES OF STRING.

Just one more soft, warm branch, and First Class Scout Jeremy Moon will be ready to move in.

BY LAURA READ ~ PHOTOGRAPHS BY LARRY PROSOR

# HOME, SNOW HOME

YOU'RE LOST AND COLD IN THE BACKCOUNTRY. START DIGGING.

NOT A GRAVE—A SNOW CAVE. IT CAN SAVE YOUR LIFE.

High in the mountains of the Sierra Nevada, Jeremy Moon is racing to finish his emergency shelter. The 14-year-old First Class Scout quickly sticks his head inside the snow cave, finds it too small, then picks up his snowboard and shovels out more snow.

All along the snowy Truckee, Calif., slope—an area that gets serious snow each year—other Scouts from Jeremy's Troop 267 are doing the same. Nearby, Northstar-at-Tahoe Ski Resort patrollers who earlier this January day taught the Scouts the shelter-building skills now remind the boys to make sure they build safe structures.

### Snow Caves Save Lives

Jeremy remembers the life-or-death questions a builder of an emergency shelter must ask himself:

Would the cave hold up if a storm piled snow on top of it? Would the person inside get soaked or cramped? Would searchers be able to spot the cave's location?

"We live in snow country," Jeremy says. "At least three or four people get lost or get caught in avalanches every year. The ones who build snow caves survive more often than not."

Rescue team members can spend all night searching for a lost person. Sometimes the search stretches into two or three days. That's when a snow cave makes a difference.

### All the Comforts Of Home (Sorta)

The patrollers taught the boys well: Not just any cave will save a life.

"It should be one and one-half body lengths long," Life Scout Galen Vandergriff, 15, says. "It should be wide enough

## STAY BUSY, ALERT—AND ALIVE

You're inside a snow cave awaiting rescue. With the wind howling, the night ahead appears long and foreboding. You wonder when help will arrive. Worse, you wonder if it's going to arrive at all.

Things are getting depressing.

What do you do?

Keep your chin up. Traveling with a buddy will give you someone to talk and laugh with. Someone to share warmth to help survive deadly cold.

To fight boredom, Life Scout Ryan Ochoa, 16, says he would go outside every once in a while and stomp paths that would direct searchers to his spot.

First Class Scout Jeremy Moon says he would keep his mind busy.

"I would do math problems or five-minute puzzles," he says. "Your psychological condition affects your body. Panicking skyrockets your heart rate and drains the energy you need to survive."

so you don't have to lie on your side, but not too wide or you'll have more snow surface area to cool the air."

Body heat warms the air inside the cave. When two people get in together, Galen says, they have a better chance of keeping warm.

The shape of the cave is important too, Jeremy adds. "Try to make the entrance lower than where you will be sitting because heat rises."

Jeremy finishes digging his cave. He throws some pine boughs on the floor for a carpet that will help keep him dry, jumps inside and closes the entrance with more pine boughs.

"It's comfy," he calls to the Scouts who are working on their own caves.

"Where's the bathroom?" inquires Star Scout Andy Lynch, 14.

▲ 1. Dig a tunnel into a snowdrift, angling it several feet upward.

▼ 2. Excavate a dome-shaped room at the top of the tunnel, judging the thickness of the roof by uncovering the ends of 18-inch-long sticks poked in from the outside.

*Above: A message in the snow helps lead to a rescue. Left: A Scout is thrifty—Joey Rzeplinski uses a snowboard, not special digging tools.*

Everyone chuckles. The survival caves aren't *that* comfortable.

## Sweat Means Wet Means Trouble

The guys know it is important to build a snow cave quickly. And they know that in an emergency, it is important to save energy and stay dry.

"If possible, don't use your hands and feet to dig," Jeremy says, holding his snowboard "shovel."

## WISE WINTER WAYS

There's a good reason Be Prepared is the Scout motto—it's a lifesaver. Careful preparation before any outing can mean the difference between a one-way or roundtrip trek. Here's how to have safe winter outings:

• **DRINK WATER.** The body needs plenty of water to work well. Drink a lot of it—before you get thirsty. A good rule of thumb: If your urine is yellow, you're not drinking enough. (And if you're not urinating, you're dangerously not drinking enough.)

• **REMEMBER THE FOUR W'S.** Tell a responsible person **what** you will be doing, **when** you will return, **where** you are going, **who** you are traveling with.

• **TRAVEL WITH A BUDDY.** Buddies can help each other and—should a problem occur—can sustain spirits until searchers arrive.

• **WEAR THE RIGHT CLOTHING.** Remember, "cotton kills." Cotton material (jeans, shirts, socks, underwear) gets wet and stays wet, holding dangerous moisture (sweat, melted snow, etc.) next to your skin. Polypropylene shirts worn next to the skin move sweat away from your body to the outer clothing layers, keeping you drier and warmer. Wear gloves. And a hat; at least 40 percent of body heat escapes from your head.

• **EAT THE RIGHT FOOD.** An energy bar or high-protein snack can be tucked easily into your pack. The extra energy can make the difference between finishing your cave and shivering outside all night in the cold, too tired and hungry to move.

**WILDERNESS SURVIVAL MERIT BADGE**

Work quickly, he adds, but not so fast that you overheat and sweat.

Wet clothes and skin speed hypothermia, a condition in which the body loses more heat than it can generate. Victims of hypothermia become disoriented and have shivering attacks that can lead to a coma—and death.

## Location, Location, Location

With their caves finished, the Scouts check out one another's digs.

A long, narrow snow cave wins the design award; it offers a comfortable place to spend the night, and its small

▼ **4. Poke a couple of ventilation holes in the ceiling at a 45-degree angle to the floor. Move in and stay warm.**

size will help preserve body heat.

All the caves were dug into a hillside where snow had gathered a little deeper than on wind-exposed slopes. "You wouldn't want to build a cave just anywhere," Galen says.

"A hillside is a good spot as long as it is stable and won't avalanche," he says. "Under a tree is also good because you have a little protected spot you can dig into."

Tree limbs also act as a roof to protect the cave from weather. Sometimes the tree limbs come all the way to the snowpack, forming an extra wall.

"If you get lost, plop down where you are and build a snow cave," Jeremy says. "If you move around, the searchers will keep missing you."

Then Jeremy gives perhaps the best advice of all: "First of all, try not to get lost."✦

▲ **3. Smooth the curved roof and carve niches in the walls for candles.**

Dave Albers

*Ski patrollers praise the cave of Kevin Emley and his team. "It's narrow and easy to heat with your body," John Holoday says.*

# HOW TO PITCH A TENT

"Too many cooks spoil the broth," they say. Well, there's another similar saying that goes: "Too many tent pitchers spoil the tent pitching." It may be fun, when you get a new tent for the whole gang, to play around pitching it. But for efficiency you need two tent pitchers only and, when you're good at it, one fellow can do the job. Provided, of course, he goes about it in the right manner.

You start your camp making by picking a spot for your tent that's almost level and, preferably, slightly elevated above its surroundings so that you won't have to ditch the tent for rainy weather. Then get down on your hands and knees and go over every inch of the ground to clear away sticks and stones and hard bumps of grass.

Now unroll your tent and lay out tent poles and pegs. The poles should be exactly the correct height, otherwise the tent won't stand right. Unless you have permission to cut poles on the campsite, you'll have brought the poles from home— sectional aluminum poles for a lightweight tent, wooden poles for a heavyweight. Your tent pegs may be lightweight, of metal, or heavyweight, of hardwood, or cut on the spot from sticks about 1 inch thick, 9 to 12 inches long. For guy lines you may be using nylon line or light rope.

There's one main secret to quick tent pitching: Close the tent door before you do anything else—that is, tie up the door flaps. When that's done you're all set for the four steps shown in the four photographs on these pages.

When you're finished, step back and look at your handiwork. If you're a good camper, the ridge should have little sway, the sides and walls should be smooth, with few wrinkles.

*There's one easy way and nine hard ways to pitch a tent. Why not do it the easy way?*

*The Voyageur tent uses two 6-foot poles and 15 tent pegs. It is 7'6" wide, 8' deep, 6' high.*

## By WILLIAM HILLCOURT

*Peg down the two front corners so that the tent is facing the way you want it. Then peg down the two rear corners, making all floor corners right angles.*

*Have a buddy raise a pole at one tent peak and hold it in upright position while you put in a peg at a proper distance and fasten the guy line to it.*

*If you use wooden pegs, attach line with two half hitches, run line through ring or loop on tent and finish with taut-line hitch. It's even simpler if you use light metal pegs and have lines provided with metal rings and metal or wooden slides.*

*Now go around the tent. Peg the tent sides to the ground and put in pegs for the side lines (if your tent has them). Finally, tighten all lines.*

*Then have your buddy raise the other pole while you peg down the other guy line and stretch the tent ridge taut between the two poles.*

# MOUTH-TO-MOUTH
# ARTIFICIAL RESPIRATION

THE MOST EFFECTIVE METHOD OF ARTIFICIAL RESPIRATION IS **MOUTH-TO-MOUTH BREATHING!** YOU BREATHE AIR INTO THE VICTIM'S LUNGS WITH YOUR OWN MOUTH. THIS METHOD HAS BEEN ADOPTED BY THE U.S. ARMY, THE AMERICAN RED CROSS, AND THE BOY SCOUTS OF AMERICA.

IN TRAINING FOR THIS METHOD, _DO NOT DEMONSTRATE NOR PRACTICE THE BLOWING PART._ IT ISN'T NECESSARY. IF YOU LEARN THE CORRECT PLACEMENT OF YOUR HANDS AND THE VICTIM'S HEAD, YOU SHOULD HAVE NO DIFFICULTY PUTTING YOUR MOUTH IN THE RIGHT POSITION WHEN YOU COME UP AGAINST A REAL ACCIDENT.

WHEN A PERSON HAS STOPPED BREATHING, ARTIFICIAL RESPIRATION SHOULD BE STARTED IMMEDIATELY. SPEED IS IMPORTANT. FIRST—PLACE THE VICTIM FACE UP. IF THERE IS FOREIGN MATTER IN THE MOUTH, WIPE IT OUT QUICKLY WITH YOUR FINGERS OR A CLOTH WRAPPED AROUND YOUR FINGERS. BEGIN ARTIFICIAL RESPIRATION AS FOLLOWS:

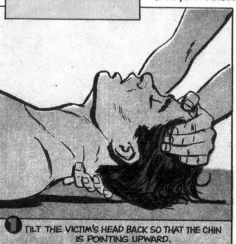

**1** TILT THE VICTIM'S HEAD BACK SO THAT THE CHIN IS POINTING UPWARD.

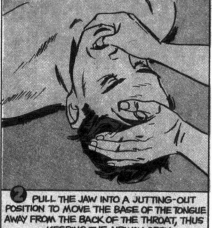

**2** PULL THE JAW INTO A JUTTING-OUT POSITION TO MOVE THE BASE OF THE TONGUE AWAY FROM THE BACK OF THE THROAT, THUS KEEPING THE AIRWAY OPEN.

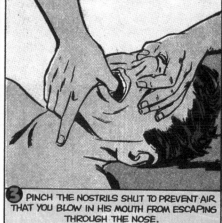

**3** PINCH THE NOSTRILS SHUT TO PREVENT AIR THAT YOU BLOW IN HIS MOUTH FROM ESCAPING THROUGH THE NOSE.

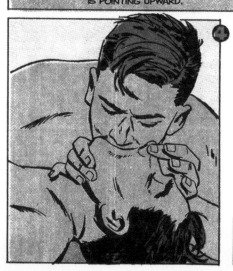

**4** BREATHE INTO MOUTH. OPEN YOUR MOUTH AND PLACE IT TIGHTLY OVER THE VICTIM'S MOUTH. _IN CASE OF A YOUNG CHILD, PLACE YOUR MOUTH OVER BOTH THE MOUTH AND NOSE OF THE VICTIM._

BLOW INTO THE MOUTH UNTIL YOU SEE CHEST RISE. REMOVE YOUR MOUTH, TURN YOUR HEAD TO THE SIDE, AND LISTEN TO THE OUTRUSH OF AIR THAT INDICATES AIR EXCHANGE. REPEAT BLOWING. ON AN ADULT, BLOW VIGOROUSLY AT A RATE OF 12 BREATHS PER MINUTE. FOR A YOUNG CHILD, TAKE RELATIVELY SHALLOW BREATHS APPROPRIATE FOR THE CHILD'S SIZE AT THE RATE OF ABOUT 20 PER MINUTE.

IF YOU ARE NOT GETTING AIR EXCHANGE, RECHECK HEAD AND JAW POSITION, TURN VICTIM ON HIS SIDE, AND GIVE SEVERAL SHARP BLOWS BETWEEN THE SHOULDER BLADES TO JAR FOREIGN MATTER FREE. SWEEP FINGERS THROUGH VICTIM'S MOUTH TO REMOVE FOREIGN MATTER.

**_DO NOT QUIT!_** LET THE DOCTOR DECIDE WHEN TO STOP. WHEN THE VICTIM'S BREATHING STARTS, TIME YOUR EFFORTS TO COINCIDE WITH HIS EFFORTS TO BREATHE FOR HIMSELF. KEEP HIM LYING DOWN AND WARM HIM WITH BLANKETS OR OTHER COVERINGS. GET HIM UNDER A DOCTOR'S CARE DURING THE RECOVERY PERIOD.

RESCUERS WHO CANNOT OR WILL NOT USE MOUTH-TO-MOUTH TECHNIQUES SHOULD USE A MANUAL METHOD—THE BACK-PRESSURE ARM-LIFT (NIELSEN) METHOD AS DESCRIBED IN THE BOY SCOUT HANDBOOK. THE CHEST-PRESSURE, ARM-LIFT (SILVESTER METHOD) IS ALSO RECOMMENDED.

# Road, Trail and Chalk Signs

## By DANIEL CARTER BEARD

### NATIONAL SCOUT COMMISSIONER

*(Copyright, 1913, by D. C. Beard.)*

LET me see. If I remember right I was preaching to you fellows last month, and consequently this month I am not going to tell you to be good. I am not going to tell you not to smoke cigarettes; I am not going to tell you not to lie; I am not going to tell you not to shoot craps; I am not going to tell you to be polite and manly; I won't even tell you not to be a chump. In the place of all this sermoniz-

ing I will give you a talk on picturegraphs, picture writing, hieroglyphics, chalk road-signs. There are too many signs to be included in one contribution, but I will give you this month those signs which I have adopted from the red men's, and after you have learned these I will hand you out another bunch.

Don't forget now, and save all these pages. Put them away somewhere and keep them together; otherwise you will be writing to me with bad-luck signs asking me for information that I have already given in former numbers.

It would not be a difficult work to invent a system of road-signs for the scouts, but this is not necessary; all we have to do is to adopt and learn the road-signs already in use. Some of the people who are using these signs will be much astonished and very angry to find that the scouts know them all, because some of the people

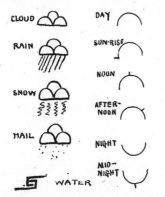

who use these signs are Gipsies, hoboes, yeggmen and crooks. But they have evolved a good system, and when we adopt their system, we do a double service: we kill its usefulness to the underworld, because it is no longer a secret code, and we supply our needs, because the signs are easily made with a piece of chalk, piece of soft brick, a piece of charcoal, or they may be traced in the mud or dust with the end of a stick.

The Indians also have some useful signs which we will adopt, and these pertain almost altogether to the weather and the elements. The books on heraldry give us signs for colors, and with this combination of yeggmen, hoboes, Gipsies, crooks, knights and royalty and the red Indians contributed to our manual, we will be well supplied.

The most dignified of all the signs come from our American Indians. We will begin with the signs of *air*. Air in motion is *wind*, and the puff adder, the hissing adder and the spreading adder is the Indian sign for *wind*. It is not necessary to make a good picture of a puff adder. Any sort of a snake with wind puffing out of his mouth represents the *wind*.

According to the Indians there are four winds—east, north, south and west. These are represented by a rectangular figure with sort of little tassels hanging at the four corners, and we may adopt this figure to represent air. The serpent is to represent *wind* and when the wind becomes a tornado it is to be represented by a curved

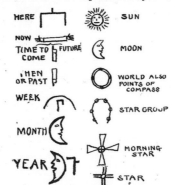

figure, suggesting the twisting of the tornado.

A *cloud* is represented by three half circles. *Rain* is represented by three half circles with straight lines coming down from them. Hail is the same with dots coming from the clouds. The lines for *snow* are wiggly. *Sleet* would be represented by a mixture of snow and rain, straight lines and wiggly ones. *Clear weather* is represented by a V-shaped figure, which means the two hands and arms thrown up. *Thunder* is represented by a thunder bird. *Lightning* is represented by a zig-zag line with an arrow point.

The sign for *day* in picture writing is a half circle; by placing a dash on this half circle you can indicate the time of the day, dating from left to right. If the dash is on the bottom of the left-hand side of the arch, that indicates sunrise; the dash in the center of the arc would represent noon, after the center of the arc would represent afternoon. The arc reversed, or upside down, represents *night*. Of course if the dash is in the center of the reversed arc it will indicate *midnight*.

A *week* is seven days; consequently the *day* mark with the scout character for

seven would mean seven days or a week. A *moon* represents a month and the moon with the scout sign indicating twelve would represent a year. Thus you see we borrow from the Indians our signs for the elements and our signs for time. But our numerals we must secure from the very ancient magicians. We do this because it wouldn't look right to put the ordinary numerals on Indian signs; besides which it is more fun to use little-known symbols

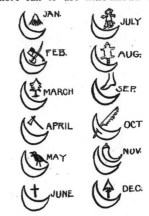

than the ones in every-day use. We will also borrow from the Indian the sign of *plenty*, the sign of *joy* and *happiness*, the sign of *talk*, the sign of *shout*, the sign of *hunger*, the sign of a *stone* and the sign of a *joyful song*, as well as the sign of *peace* and the sign of *war*. Other Indian signs are the sign of *hearing*, which is just a head with wavy lines running through the ears; the sign for the *sun*, which always has a face indicated on its surface; the sign for *stars*, and the sign for the *rainbow*. The sign of *smoke* looks like big tear-drops reversed—going up instead of down. The Apaches used but three kinds of smoke signals, which consisted of separate columns of smoke. *Attention* is one continuous column of smoke. Two columns of smoke means a camp has been made and that it is still there and everything is favorable and quiet. Three columns is the sign of danger and alarm. We will adopt these signals in our picture-graph language.

Mr. Seton puts three stones one on top of the other, also three tufts of grass tied together, also three blazes on a tree, as danger signs; but when he comes to smoke he puts three smokes for *good news* and two smokes for "I am lost. Help." This is confusing. Three of everything should have the same general meaning. It should always be a cry for succor, for help, or an alarm. And so I take the white man's custom of firing three guns for help, the Apaches' custom of three smokes for alarm, the scouts' custom of three stones one top of the other, three blazes on the tree, three tufts of grass tied together, as all being uniform and meaning practically the same thing.

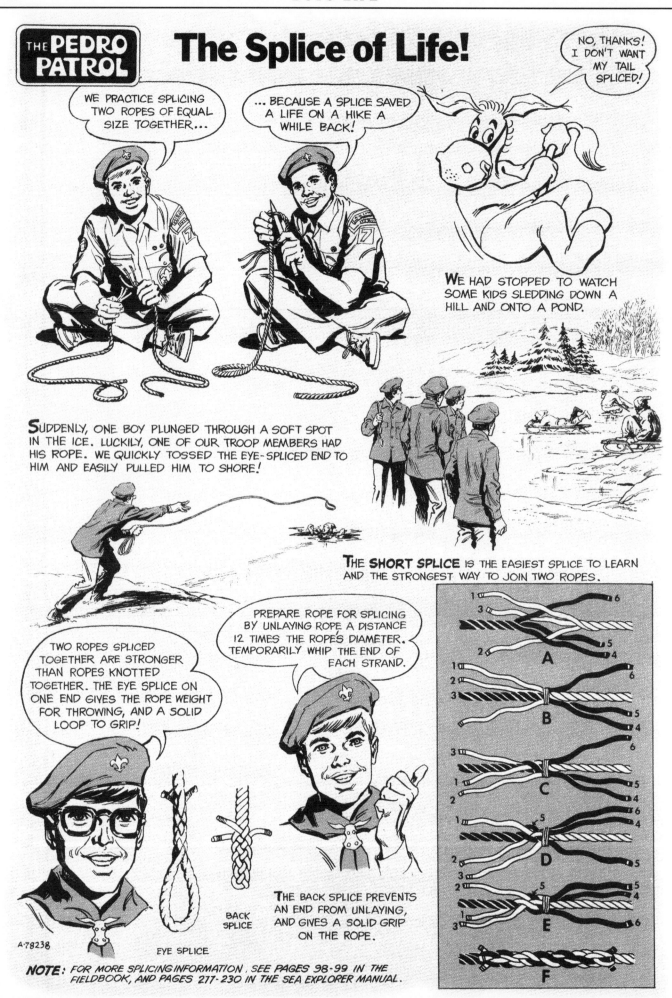

# About Man-Eating Lions

## By THEODORE ROOSEVELT

MAN - EATING lions have always been fairly common in East Africa. The most noted, but far from exceptional, case was that of the two man-eaters which for a time stopped the building of the Uganda railroad by their ravages among the workmen, until they were finally shot by the engineer in charge, Mr. (afterward Colonel) Patterson. Another lion, after killing several men around a station on the railroad, carried off and ate the superintendent of the division; the latter had come down in his private car, which was run on a siding, and he sat up at a window that night to watch for the lion; but he fell asleep and the lion climbed on the platform, entered the car by the door, and carried off his would-be slayer through the window.

Near Machakos-boma a white traveler was taken out of his tent by a man-eater one night, a good many years ago; a gruesome feature of the incident was that on its first attempt the lion was driven off, after having seized and wounded its victim; the wounds of the latter were dressed, and he was again put to bed, but soon after he had been left alone the lion again forced his way into the tent and this time carried the man off and ate him.

Every year in East Africa natives are carried off from their villages or from hunting-camps by man-eating lions.

The attack of a man eater is always delivered at night, and is practically always by surprise; but, if the first attack fails, a bold lion will sometimes persevere and do his best to seize another victim.

Even a man-eater thoroughly realizes that men are dangerous; he is no more apt to make a hard fight when himself hunted than is any other lion of like vigor, and when he is the hunter he always retires with his victim, as soon as he has caught it, out of reach of vengeance, although he may only go for a distance of a few hundred yards, being confident in the shelter yielded by a dark night. This is entirely unlike the lion's conduct with other prey; if a zebra or hartebeest is killed, the lion stays on the spot with his victim, and may eat it where it has fallen or drag it a few yards to a more convenient spot.

During the last twenty years scores of white hunters have been killed by lions, elephants, buffaloes and rhinos in East and Middle Africa; and the lions have killed much more than half of the total number. Except Mr. Rainey, who worked with dogs, Lord Delamere has killed more lions than any other man I know—fifty-three; he was badly mauled on one occasion, and has now given up hunting them, stating that no man can count on killing more than fifty lions without himself being killed or fatally injured.

Kermit and I killed only seventeen lions between us, two being cubs and two not

LION AND LIONESS FROM NAIROBI, BRITISH EAST AFRICA.
Presented to the Washington Zoological Park, by W. N. McMillan.
From a Photograph by Herman F. Carl

THE stories told by Colonel Roosevelt on this page of BOYS' LIFE are, as he has explained, based mainly on first-hand information gathered in his explorations in the African wilds, but are also in part based on the cumulative observations of many other men. They are from "The Life History of the African Lion," published in a recent number of Scribner's magazine, to the editors of which we are indebted for permission to reproduce both stories and illustration for American boys.

much more than half-grown; and thirteen full-grown lions are too few to permit of free generalization as to their fighting capacity. Three of these thirteen lions—two big-maned males and a lioness—charged with the utmost resolution from a distance of nearly two hundred yards when wounded and brought to bay by the pursuing horsemen; three others (all male lions) were at bay and were about to charge—one had begun to trot forward—when killed; five were killed or disabled under circumstances that gave them no opportunity to charge; two (both lionesses) were killed close up, after being wounded, under circumstances which seemed to invite a charge, yet they made no effort to charge. Only one other lion was shot by any other member of our party, a lioness killed by Alden Loring; she charged with the utmost resolution when mortally wounded, and died while still charging.

A beginner might readily kill three or four lions without danger; and he might be charged and killed by the first one he attacked. If the sport is persevered in, the man who achieves success must possess coolness, wariness, resolution and reasonable skill with the rifle; and now and then he will need to show all these qualities.

Except when resting, and in the breeding-season, the whole career of a lion may be summed up in the single word, rapine. For all the creatures of the wilderness, save the full-grown elephant, rhinoceros, and hippopotamus, he is the terror that stalks by night.

His prowess is extraordinary. His tactics are stealth, surprise, and sudden overwhelming fury of attack. Occasionally he hunts by day, but in the great majority of cases by night; and the darker the night the bolder he is and the more to be feared.

If an animal passes close to his resting place in the daytime he will often attack it; and in wild regions he may, if hungry, begin to hunt early in the afternoon or continue to hunt late in the morning; but that this is not common seems to me to be shown by the fact that if lions are abroad in the daytime the game does not seem especially disturbed by their proximity; hartebeests, zebra, and gazelle will keep a watch on a lion thus moving by, and will not go very near it, but show no special alarm or excitement. Where game swarms, and beasts of prey are abundant, and therefore, often seen, the animals that are preyed on are so constantly exposed to assault that although always on the watch and often very nervous if they suspect the presence of a lion or leopard without being able to place it exactly. they yet grow to reckon their chances with coolness if the creature they dread can be seen, and show a curious indifference to the presence of the marauders if they believe themselves safe; their moments of mad and panic terror are only when the foe actually charges, especially if he has been hitherto unseen.

Unquestionably a party of lions will sometimes drive game; they spread out and those on one side, by grunting, or merely by their smell, stampede the game so that those on the other side may catch it. Ordinarily, however, the lion crouches motionless as his prey grazes toward him, or himself crawls toward it, with almost inconceivable noiselessness and stealth. The darker the night the bolder the lion; under the bright moonlight a lion is apt to be somewhat cautious, whereas there is almost no limit to its daring in black, stormy weather.

No matter how pitch dark the night, the lion seems to have no difficulty in seizing its prey in such manner as to insure it well-nigh instant death.

Except full-grown elephant, rhinoceros, and hippopotamus. there is no animal in Africa which the lion does not attack.

**PACKSACK:** Build a criss-cross fire lay, placing half a dozen small stones in with the fuel; then light the fire. When stones are red-hot, pick them up with two sticks and drop them into cavity of cleaned chicken. Working fast, tie string around bird, wrap in brown paper. Place package in packsack filled with dry leaves; pack leaves firmly around it. Close pack, and leave chicken to cook for three to four hours.

For a patrol feast, get the gang to try

# STUNT COOKING

## By WILLIAM HILLCOURT

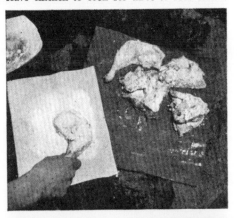

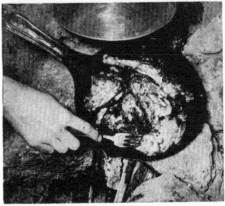

**FRYING:** Cut chicken in suitable serving pieces. Flour pieces by shaking them in paper bag with small amount of flour. Fry in fat until brown. Then add half a cup of water, cover the pan, steam for approximately half an hour.

HOT DOGS and hamburgers are for the tenderest kind of Tenderfoot Scouts. By the time you've done your share of hiking and camping, you'll want to be different—very different. That's when stunt cookery enters the picture—the preparation of ordinary food in dozens of exciting ways.

Chicken adapts itself admirably to stunt cooking, as long as you realize that chicken cookery is slow cookery if you want the meat to be tender and juicy—and who doesn't?

Frying and roasting are the two most popular ways of preparing chicken.

In frying—whether you use a pan or Dutch oven—you brown the chicken first, then steam it until tender, with the cover on the pot or pan. The aluminum foil or clay method works along the same line. But here you don't need to add liquid; foil or clay keeps in all the natural juices of the bird.

For roasting, you can place the chicken before the fire on a spit or hang it in a string. Or you can go Hawaiian and prepare a chicken *imu,* as described in your *Scout Field Book.* For this, you heat a number of stones in a hole to almost white heat, then throw in a layer of moistened leaves. On top of the leaves go chicken, sweet potatoes, corn, green bananas. Then more leaves, a wet burlap bag to cover, and a layer of dirt to prevent the steam from escaping. You leave the *imu* to cook, and come back two hours later for your patrol feast.

Some other time, you may want to cook your chicken in a packsack—which is simply an *imu* in reverse, with the hot stones *inside* the chicken. This cookery stunt is particularly good for a canoe expedition: You can prepare your hot stones and your chicken in the morning, and can serve hot roast chicken for dinner at journey's end.

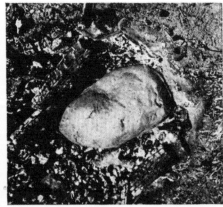

**IN CLAY:** Fill inside of cleaned but unplucked chicken with stones. Rub a thin clay mixture into the feathers, then cover bird completely with a one-inch layer of clay. Dig shallow hole in the ground; burn a fire in it down to a good bed of coals. Place clay-covered chicken in embers, keep fire going over it for about two hours. Crack open clay shell. Chicken will come out clean, all feathers sticking in the clay.

**HOLE:** Dig a hole 15″ wide, 24″ long, 15″ deep. Line one end with stones, and build brisk fire against them. Opposite the fire, push stick into ground. Tie looped string to it. Push two pointed sticks through chicken, one at wings, the other at legs. Slip loop over ends of one stick. Roast chicken before fire, twirling string repeatedly. When half-done, reverse bird, slip loop over ends of other stick; continue roasting, twirling.

**DUTCH OVEN:** Heat the Dutch oven and its cover on the coals. Flour the chicken pieces as for ordinary frying, by shaking in a paper bag with flour. Fry the pieces in hot fat, add half a cup of water, cover, and continue cooking for half an hour or until chicken is tender. **ALUMINUM FOIL:** Wrap each piece of chicken in greased foil, folding ends tight. Place on coals, turn occasionally. Cook 20 to 30 minutes.

# Fly Tying

### By WALTER REID and GLENN A. WAGNER

EVERY REAL fisherman likes to brag a little about the flies he's tied himself. And why not? There's nothing like landing a a big one on a fly you've made yourself.

To tie your own flies, all the tools you need are a fly tying vise, hackle pliers, and a pair of manicure scissors. For raw materials you'll want fly tying silk, wax, and a small bottle of lacquer. These supplies, and the special materials listed for each fly, you can get in any sportsman supply shop.

Probably you already know there are two kinds of flies—wet and dry. You fish a dry fly *on* the surface. Its hackles and tail keep it afloat. But you fish a wet fly *under* the surface. A wet fly resembles a drowned insect, an immature stage, or an aquatic form.

Most flies are made to look like some insect, although a few flies don't even *begin* to look like insects and are highly successful. Only the fish know why.

Each fisherman has his own favorites, and you'll probably have trouble finding two who agree. But here are a couple of flies that have a pretty good reputation as palate teasers for trout.

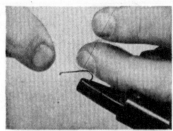
Anchor hook in fly vise. Wax 15" thread. Wrap one end on hook shank, and secure it with half hitch or jam knot.

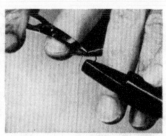
For tail use 6 or 8 hackle barbs. Hold with 3 or 4 turns, secure with jam knot. Now trim off waste butt ends of hackle.

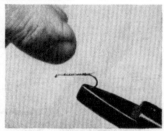
Few turns of thread under tail will set it up. Spiral thread up shank of hook to ⅛" of eye, and secure with jam knot.

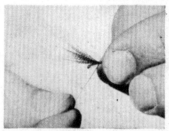
Strip down off wing feather. Tilt the feather toward you so it will be on top of hook when you pull the thread taut.

Tie feather with 3 or 4 turns silk. Divide barbs in half. Wrap sides figure-8 style. Turns in front set feathers up.

Select two hackle feathers with barbs ⅔ length of hook. Hackle should be stiff and glossy, without much fuzz.

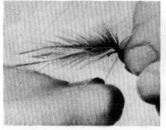
Rub hackle barbs so they stand out from the quills. Strip down from back. Tie hackles back-to-back between wings.

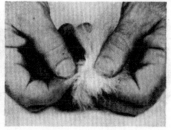
Body is creamy white fox belly fur. Pull some off, remove long guard hairs, and save downy part that grew next to hide.

Spread fur thinly on trouser leg. Taper it toward center. Now wax piece of tying silk with a tacky kind of wax.

Roll thread back and forth over fur until you have fuzzy thread. Tie this in front of tail. Wind silk behind wings.

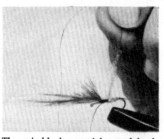
Then wind body material around shank, building up toward wings. Wind to wings. Be careful not to rub fur off.

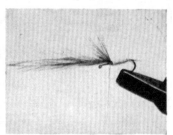
Now wind in the hackles. Start with hackle farthest away from you and wind so that shiny side is to back of hook.

By manipulating the hackle pliers you can leave the barbs free. Take about 2½ turns and then tie off with the silk.

Wind other hackle in same direction, shiny side toward hook eye. Pushing back hackles with fingernail sets 'em up.

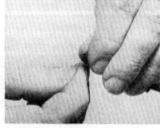
Finish by winding silk around the shank and making neat head. Leave room to tie in leader. Seal with lacquer.

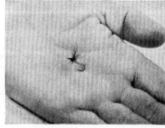
Here she is, all ready to go after that Big One. Drop fly in glass of water and check float and balance from all angles.

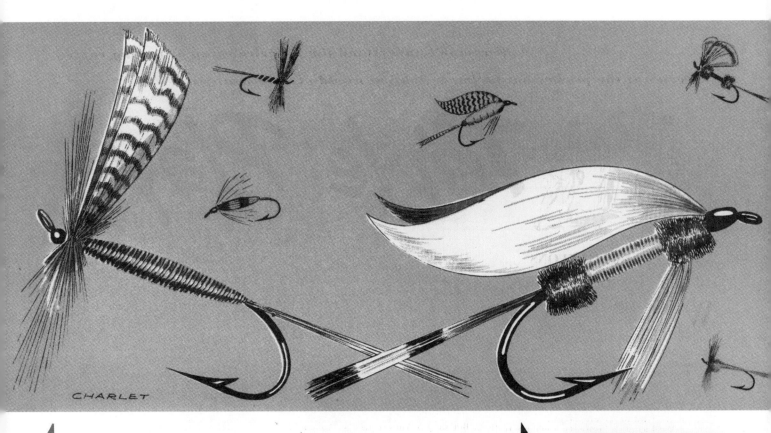

## Light Cahill

### A DRY FLY

Hook—#12 or #14, tapered eye, like wire shank
Tail—ginger colored hackle barbs
Wing—flank feathers of a Mandarin duck
Body—creamy-white fox belly fur
Hackle—ginger-colored, from a game cock or rooster

## Royal Coachman

### A WET FLY

Hook—#10 or #12, untapered eye, heavy shank
Tail—Golden Pheasant tipped feather
Wing—white duck quill (right and left feathers)
Body—peacock herl and red silk floss
Hackle—hackle feather from a Rhode Island red rooster

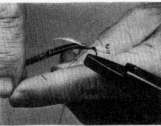

Start by tying in 6 to 8 barbs Golden Pheasant tippet, as for dry fly. Then trim off the waste butt ends afterwards.

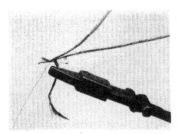

Tie in two bits of Peacock herl and a piece of red silk floss above tail barbs. Tie in pointing away. Wind clockwise.

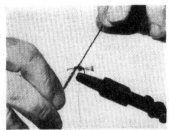

Make several turns of Peacock herl to build up butt end, then few turns ahead of that with floss. Bind down the herl.

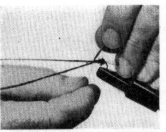

Tie off red floss with the silk. Next build up another herl section. Tie each section as you go. Stop ⅛" back of eye.

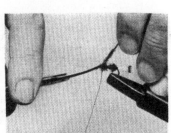

When you finish body, trim waste floss and herl. Avoid cutting too close to thread. No sense doing same job twice.

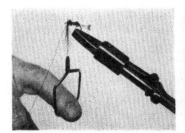

Just ahead of body, tie hackle feather. Wind on with 3 or 4 turns. Wind hackle, shiny side to eye. Tie a head on hook.

For wings cut two 3/16" wide sections from left and right duck quills. Match the two for exact size and for balance.

Line them up back to back, tie just behind with several turns of thread and jam knot. Wings must balance.

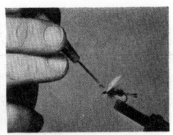

Clip off butts and wind raw ends. Finish with jam knots. A drop of lacquer over threads ends job. Look out, fish!

# Ice Fishing

TEXT AND PHOTOGRAPHS BY
SCOTT J. WITTE

**Fish or no fish,
it's a great way
to spend a cold
day this winter.**

WE WERE LOST in a fog white-out. Sky and earth melted into one and you could see no farther than 100 yards. Tire tracks crisscrossed the ice of Green Lake. They led everywhere but guided us nowhere. Now and then an ice shanty or pickup truck would materialize out of the mist and disappear again like a wandering ghost.

You can get lost when you go ice fishing, although a blizzard or sudden nightfall is the usual cause. You can end up wandering aimlessly over the feature-less ice—unless you use a compass. Eventually we came to a point on shore where we could get a compass fix. Following that floating needle led us dir-ectly to our spot—just over a gravel bar. In no time, the Scouts of Troop 30, Green Lake, Wis., were chopping and drilling holes through the ice and setting fishing lines.

It was March, late for ice fishing, but the deepest snow in Wisconsin history had made it all but impossible to fish during the early winter months.

The troop, which is chartered to American Legion Post 306, could wait no longer. Even if fishing was poor, they wanted some outdoor adventure.

They set to work with ice chisels and ice augurs to cut through several feet of ice. Once the hole was finished, they scooped out any remaining ice chips with a skimmer that looked like a soup ladle full of holes.

Scoutmaster Bob Francour explained how ice fishermen often "primed" a new hole by tossing in crumbled egg shells. The bits of shells catch the dim light and attract minnows that, in turn, bring larger fish.

"You can't cast when the hole is only 12 inches across," said Scout Don Weinkauf, "so we use jigging rods about two feet long." The short rods were limber enough to detect even the gentlest nibble.

The Scouts kept the lures in motion with short upward flicks of the rods.

In addition to the ice fishing rods, they used "tip-ups." These simple, effective devices consisted of two pieces of wood fastened at right angles. One piece spanned the hole in the ice while the other stood vertically.

The vertical bar had a reel fixed to its lower end. The reel was held below the water so it could not freeze and jam.

The top end of the vertical bar had a spring and a small flag attached.

When the tip-up was baited, the spring holding the flag was bent over and set on a trigger so that any fish nibbling at the bait would make the flag suddenly pop into the air.

Any time this happened, it was the signal for a mad scramble across the ice to grab the tip-up and reel before the fish could escape.

Arlin Bloch, father of Scout Peter Bloch and resident ice-fishing expert, was showing the boys how to set their lines. "Setting the depth is most important," he said.

To do so he let the weighted line sink until it touched bottom and went slack. Then he took back about 15 inches for the leader and about a foot for the depth of the reel under water and marked that point with a button threaded on the line. That showed how much line to feed out after baiting the hook.

The boys baited their hooks with two- or three-inch minnows since they were after the northerns, walleyes and trout that Green Lake is famous for. They were careful to plant the hook shallow enough in the minnow's back so as not to injure the spine. That way the minnow would swim in the pattern of a sphere around the sinker.

Since they were allowed three lines apiece, the boys could do some "prospecting." They would set tip-ups at different depths until they found where the fish were. Trouble was, none of those flags were springing up any more.

"Usually those flags pop up all over," said Greg Bryant.

In fact, few fish were being caught anywhere on the lake that day, which is unusual. "Normally you catch more fish in winter than in summer," Robby Fischer insisted.

Mr. Bloch agreed. "It's because you can control your fishing depth so well," he said. "Using three lines at a time probably helps too."

"Ice fishing is as much fun as summer fishing," Scott Schleicher said, "as long as you dress especially warm, and stay dry. You have to watch out for thin ice too, but if you follow the rules and stay off ice that's less than three inches thick, you'll be okay."

Of course the fish have to be there to get caught.

For the Scouts of Troop 30, a truly successful fishing trip would have to wait until the next season. They vowed to get out on the ice early next time. Then they could share some of the fastest fishing northern waters offer. ♣

Before you yell "Timber,"
be sure you know real

# AXEMANSHIP

By WILLIAM HILLCOURT

**A**XEMANSHIP is a he-man skill. It takes muscle to swing a felling axe, and endurance to finish the job of "falling" a tree, "lopping" it, and "bucking" it.

Before you take up the felling axe, be an expert with the hand axe. Learn to use it correctly, and to follow the rules for axemanship in the *Scout Field Book*. Then get a good axeman to teach you how to use a felling axe.

Some years ago, the North Star Council of Duluth, Minnesota, set up certain standards for axemanship. Every Scout, fourteen years of age, who met these standards in front of a "Timber Foreman" became a "Paul Bunyan Axeman." The idea has spread across the country. If your local council has a Timber Foreman, tell him you want to become a Paul Bunyan Axeman. If it doesn't have a foreman, you may want to ask your Scoutmaster to check with your Scout council about the possibility of getting the Paul Bunyan idea underway locally.

To become a Paul Bunyan Axeman, you must be fourteen years of age and agree to: 1. Become skillful in handling an axe by consistent practice, and 2. Teach other Scouts and Explorers "Safety Through Skill" in the use of the axe.

To show your axemanship, you must:

1. Own an axe with a properly fitting head weighing at least 2 pounds, with a handle at least 24 inches long, and equipped with a sheath. All the following requirements are done with this axe.

2. Demonstrate ability to sharpen the axe.

3. Demonstrate safety rules in the use of the axe.

4. Select a tree at least 6 inches DBH (diameter at breast height) for harvest cutting or thinning; drop the tree; lop it ("swamp" it); and cut it into two or more logs. (For harvest cutting a tree must be mature and must be used for a definite purpose. For thinning, a tree is removed because of poor formation, disease, or competition with more desirable trees.)

The Peter McLaren Axemen, a program for Explorers over sixteen, established by the San Francisco Council, requires more skill. Details are available from BOYS' LIFE.

**1**

Plan to "fall" the tree—as a lumberman would say—in direction in which it leans. Determine lean by using axe as a plumb line. Before you start cutting, clear the surrounding area of obstructions.

**2**

Grasp axe handle with both hands close together near butt end. Touch the axe head to the tree to be felled to get the proper distance. Then face tree in a firm stance, with your feet a comfortable distance apart.

Rule is "Clear the ground—an axe length around!" Remove underbrush, overhanging branches which might catch hold of the axe and deflect it. Test distance by holding axe by head, swinging handle.

**5**

The felling is done with two box cuts. Top of a box cut slopes into the tree at a 45° angle, and the bottom of it is horizontal. Make the first of the two box cuts on leaning side of the tree, close to the ground.

**6**

Most popular felling axes among Scouts are the full-size Explorer axe and the ¾-size Super Scout axe. When not in use, keep your axes "masked" by sticking them into a log or by placing them in their leather sheaths.

Use flat mill file for sharpening axe. Place head of axe against a log. Hold handle in position with a wooden hook. Push file down over edge. When one side is filed, turn over axe, file other side.

When carrying an unsheathed felling axe, grasp the handle close to the head with edge away from you. When you pass an axe to someone else, give him the handle. Don't let go until you're sure that he has a firm grip.

3

Instead of using a log, you can rest head of axe to be sharpened against peg driven into ground. Between filings, keep edge keen with carborundum stone. Rub along edge circularly.

4

Make the second box cut on the opposite side of the tree from the first, an inch or so higher up. Keep eyes on spot you want axe to hit. Separate hands in bringing axe overhead; move them together as axe comes down.

"Lopping" or "swamping" is process of removing branches. Aim your cuts toward top of tree—if you strike down into crotch, your axe will very likely stick. Stand on the opposite side of the trunk.

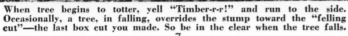

When tree begins to totter, yell "Timber-r-r!" and run to the side. Occasionally, a tree, in falling, overrides the stump toward the "felling cut"—the last box cut you made. So be in the clear when the tree falls.

7

"Bucking" is cutting tree into suitable lengths. Bucking is done with two "flying cuts." Make one cut as wide as the tree is thick, to the center of the tree, then another cut from the opposite side.

8

# On the Screen By CHICK COOMBS

THE WONDERFUL WORLD OF THE BROTHERS GRIMM (MGM) is not a fairy tale, but the true story of the two brothers who, back around 1812, searched the German countryside digging out the fairy tales and folk tales which had been handed down through the generations by word of mouth.

The two brothers, Jacob and Wilhelm Grimm (played by Karl Boehm and Laurence Harvey) wanted to preserve the tales by putting them down in writing. This involved a lot of eavesdropping, some of it under ticklish circumstances. Wilhelm, who was loaded with curiosity and imagination, did most of the exploration. Jacob was the serious, textbook writing type. Having to ride herd on his younger brother's enthusiasm was about as easy as picking up raw egg with a fork.

The movie is filmed in panoramic Cinerama.

Shot with three interlocking cameras, it projects its image on a curved screen from three separate lenses. This gives it a three-dimensional depth which makes you feel as though you are right in the middle of the action. In effect, the cameras' eyes become your eyes. You hang on tight while a carriage thunders along a mountain road, tottering precariously on the edge of a cliff. In "The Dancing Princess" sequence (one of three fairy tales which are filtered into the three-hour film) when Russ Tamblyn falls through a rickety bridge (they actually dropped the cameras on springs) you feel the jar. When Russ goes cartwheeling down a hill—the cameras were mounted on a giant rolling contraption—you get dizzy.

The Cinerama scenery on a boat and air trip along the Rhine River is something to remember. You get that I-was-there feeling.

There is also an eerie floating trip into the star-studded universe which will give you an idea of what John Glenn and Scott Carpenter experienced. There are other amazing Cinerama feats which we'd rather not divulge right now.

There are plenty of frightening moments, and lots of fun, too—such as in "The Singing Bone" episode which involves the slaying of a mighty fire-breathing dragon by the bungling servant (Buddy Hackett) of a cowardly knight (Terry-Thomas).

Remember, though, that THE WONDERFUL WORLD OF THE BROTHERS GRIMM is primarily a true story about the two brothers, their problems and frustrations met while gathering the famous tales.

The movie will be around for a long long time, as it can only be shown in theaters equipped for Cinerama. The work is now underway to adapt many theaters to Cinerama features. Soon many large cities in the United States are scheduled to have at least one.

* * * A couple of good movies which were previewed too late to be commented on at length are worth watching for. BILLY BUDD, (Allied Artists) is a strong, realistic tale of a young man on a naval ship in the Napoleonic Wars, based on a Herman Melville story. THE PHANTOM OF THE OPERA (U.I.) a real thriller will give you goose bumps and heart thumps.

*A TV Note:* Check your local schedules on September 9. At nine p.m. Eastern Daylight Time, C.B.S. will broadcast a film story titled **BADGE OF HONOR** on the General Electric Theatre. Art Linkletter is the star and Boy Scouts are featured in this story based on a true happening in Los Angeles.

# TRACK 'EM WITH TALC

## By RALPH BARNES

FASTENED TO YOUR foot, this tracking gadget will leave a white trail over rock surfaces as well as the ground. As in tracking animals, moist ground or rain will eliminate the trail, adding to the sport. To make one you need 1¼" wide elastic, 1½ oz. can of talc. Practice this type of tracking, in addition to the regular trail signs when preparing for a rally.

Talc can is held close to shoe by elastic harness; flow of talc can be controlled by tape over holes.

Note that the harness is made in two pieces, sewn together under instep to form one unit.

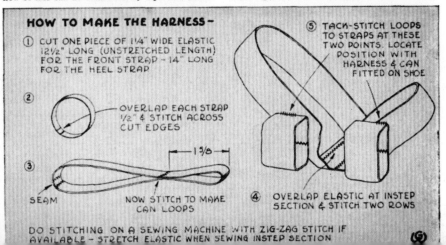

**HOW TO MAKE THE HARNESS—**

① CUT ONE PIECE OF 1¼" WIDE ELASTIC 12½" LONG (UNSTRETCHED LENGTH) FOR THE FRONT STRAP - 14" LONG FOR THE HEEL STRAP

② OVERLAP EACH STRAP ½" & STITCH ACROSS CUT EDGES

③ SEAM — NOW STITCH TO MAKE CAN LOOPS

④ OVERLAP ELASTIC AT INSTEP SECTION & STITCH TWO ROWS

⑤ TACK-STITCH LOOPS TO STRAPS AT THESE TWO POINTS. LOCATE POSITION WITH HARNESS & CAN FITTED ON SHOE

DO STITCHING ON A SEWING MACHINE WITH ZIG-ZAG STITCH IF AVAILABLE - STRETCH ELASTIC WHEN SEWING INSTEP SECTION

## SIT-UPS

| AIM | |
|---|---|
| DATE | RESULT |
| | |
| | |
| | |
| | |
| | |
| | |
| | |

## PULL-UPS

| AIM | |
|---|---|
| DATE | RESULT |
| | |
| | |
| | |
| | |
| | |
| | |

## BROAD JUMP

| AIM | |
|---|---|
| DATE | RESULT |
| | |
| | |
| | |
| | |
| | |

## 50-YARD DASH

| AIM | |
|---|---|
| DATE | RESULT |
| | |
| | |
| | |
| | |
| | |

## 600-YARD RUN (WALK)

| AIM | |
|---|---|
| DATE | RESULT |
| | |
| | |
| | |

*The exercises you do today will help make you*

# FIT FOR TOMORROW

*By WILLIAM HILLCOURT*

Posed by Boy Scouts of Troop 234, St. Petersburg, Florida

DO YOU WANT TO be fit? Of course you do! You know the importance of fitness, not just for today but even more for the future. The strength, agility, coordination, and endurance you build into your body today will benefit you the rest of your life.

There are three steps for making certain of this fitness. The first step is to try five simple tests and compare the results with the standards expected of a boy of your age. The next step is to go in for exercises that will improve your performance in the tests in which you are weak. The third step is to re-test yourself at regular intervals until you get up to par.

On the chart below, find the line for your age and check the standard you should be able to meet in each of the five tests. Decide whether you want to be GOOD or EXCELLENT. Write your aim for the five tests on each of the panels to the left. Then test yourself in the following manner and write down the date and the result underneath your aim for each test:

**SIT-UPS:** Lie on your back with a buddy holding your ankles. Clasp hands behind your neck. Sit up, touch right elbow to left knee and lie down again. Next time, sit up, touch left elbow to right knee, lie down. One complete sit-up is counted each time you return to starting position. Do as many sit-ups as you can.

**PULL-UPS:** Grasp an overhead bar with palms facing forward. Hang with arms and legs fully extended and feet off the ground. Pull body up with arms in a smooth movement, without kicking legs and without swinging, until you can place your chin over the bar, then lower yourself again. Do as many pull-ups as you can.

**STANDING BROAD JUMP:** Stand on a level surface with feet comfortably apart. Flex knees, swing arms back and forth, then take off and jump, swinging arms forcefully forward and upward. Measure distance from take-off line to nearest spot where heel or any part of body touches the ground.

**50-YARD DASH:** Measure out a 50-yard course. Place a buddy to act as starter at the finish line, with a stop watch. Starter raises one hand, then brings it down smartly. As he hits his thigh, you start running. As you cross the finish line, the starter notes the time in seconds to the nearest tenth.

**600-YARD RUN (WALK):** Measure out a 600-yard course. On the starter's signal, "Ready!—Go!" you run the distance. You are permitted to walk if you must, but the idea is to cover the distance as quickly as possible. Take time in minutes and seconds.

Now compare your performance with your aim in each of the five tests. Then set out to improve yourself through the exercises on the next page. Re-test yourself once a month and write down the new results. Keep it up until you have reached your aim!

(These exercises are based on pamphlet *Fit for Tomorrow*, prepared by Royal B. Stone and H. John Nelson, published by Boy Scouts of America. Available from your Scout distributor or local council office for 25 cents).

| Your Age | SIT-UPS | | PULL-UPS | | BROAD JUMP | | 50-YARD DASH | | 600-YARD RUN (WALK) | |
|---|---|---|---|---|---|---|---|---|---|---|
| | Good | Excellent | Good | Excellent | Good | Excellent | Good | Excellent | Good | Excellent |
| | number of times | | number of times | | Ft. In. | Ft. In. | Sec. | Sec. | Min. | Min. |
| 10 | 47 | 60 | 3 | 6 | 5 0 | 5 6 | 8.1 | 7.6 | 2:30 | 2:15 |
| 11 | 50 | 67 | 4 | 6 | 5 4 | 5 10 | 7.9 | 7.3 | 2:24 | 2:12 |
| 12 | 51 | 78 | 4 | 7 | 5 8 | 6 2 | 7.5 | 7.0 | 2:19 | 2:05 |
| 13 | 54 | 83 | 5 | 8 | 6 0 | 6 8 | 7.2 | 6.5 | 2:13 | 2:00 |
| 14 | 60 | 99 | 6 | 10 | 6 7 | 7 2 | 7.0 | 6.5 | 2:05 | 1:50 |
| 15 | 60 | 99 | 7 | 10 | 7 0 | 7 8 | 6.7 | 6.2 | 1:59 | 1:43 |
| 16 | 63 | 99 | 9 | 12 | 7 3 | 8 0 | 6.4 | 6.1 | 1:51 | 1:40 |
| 17 | 63 | 99 | 10 | 13 | 7 8 | 8 4 | 6.3 | 6.0 | 1:51 | 1:36 |

## INDIVIDUAL EXERCISES

Start at top right—at the 1 o'clock position—and follow the pictures clockwise around the page.

**1 o'clock—*ALL THE WAY:*** *Lie flat on your back, with your hands above your head. Raise your body and touch your toes with your fingertips. Return to starting position. Repeat this and all exercises several times.*

**2—*STRETCHER:*** *Lie with your back on the floor. Curl up your body slowly until your knees touch your chin. Return slowly to starting position.*

**3—*BRIDGE:*** *Lie on your back with your feet flat on the ground. Press your head down. Raise your whole body slowly. Lower your body again slowly.*

**4—*SQUAT THRUST:*** *Squat down. Place your hands flat on the floor, your arms straight. Thrust legs backward until your body is straight from shoulders to toes. Return to squat position. Stand up.*

**5—*LEG EXTENSION:*** *Lie flat on your back, hands on hips. Raise your legs. Spread your legs wide apart and bring them together again slowly three times. Then lower the legs, rest and repeat.*

**6—*BUTTERFLY:*** *Lie down on your belly. Raise your arms, chest and legs. Spread your arms and legs ten times. Return to starting position.*

## DUAL CONTESTS

Start at bottom left—at the 7 o'clock position—and follow the pictures clockwise around the page.

**7 o'clock—*STICK PULL:*** *You and your buddy sit on the ground, facing each other, with the soles of your shoes braced. Each of you grasps a stick and attempts to pull the other fellow to his feet.*

**8—*INDIAN ARM WRESTLE:*** *Lie down flat in such a way that you can grasp hands with one raised forearm. Now force your buddy's hand to the ground without moving your own elbow.*

**9—*COCKFIGHT:*** *Get into a low squat position and grasp ankles. Butt your buddy with shoulders or head in an attempt to make him fall or to force him to let go of his ankles.*

**10—*CHEST PUSH:*** *Stand chest to chest, with your arms out to the sides, hands locked. Now force your buddy backward ten feet.*

**11—*BACK PULL:*** *Stand back to back. Lock hands over shoulders. Pull your buddy off his feet onto your back and carry him forward for ten feet.*

**12—*STICK FIGHT:*** *You and your buddy face each other and grip a stick firmly with both hands. Each of you tries to force the end of the stick that's to your left down to touch the ground.*

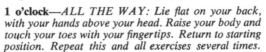

# RESCUE RULES

TOO MANY SWIMMING ACCIDENTS OCCUR WITHIN A SHORT DISTANCE OF SAFETY. PRACTICALLY EVERY ONE CAN BE AVOIDED IF THE SWIMMER DOES NOT BECOME PANICKY AND IF THE RESCUER KEEPS CALM AND USES HIS HEAD. "KNOW-HOW" CAN PREVENT AN ACCIDENT FROM BECOMING A TRAGEDY.

KNOW THESE SIMPLE RULES SO THAT IN AN EMERGENCY YOU'LL FOLLOW THEM AUTOMATICALLY!

## REACH

IF THE PERSON IN DISTRESS IS WITHIN REACH, EXTEND ANY OBJECT TOWARD HIM THAT HE CAN GRAB.

## THROW

TOSS A LINE, A RING BUOY, AN INNER TUBE OR ANY OBJECT THAT WILL FLOAT AND THAT YOU CAN GET HOLD OF IN A HURRY. THROW IT OVER AND BEYOND HIM!

## ROW

IF THERE'S A BOAT HANDY, ROW OR PADDLE OUT TO GIVE HELP.

## GO

IF YOU MUST SWIM OUT TO REACH THE PERSON IN DISTRESS, JUMP IN—DON'T DIVE. CARRY YOUR SHIRT OR TOWEL IN YOUR MOUTH. FLIP ONE END OF TOWEL OR SHIRT TO PERSON AND TOW HIM IN. KEEP YOUR EYES ON PERSON AT ALL TIMES.

## HANG ON

SHOULD YOUR BOAT OVERTURN, HANG ON! A SWAMPED OR CAPSIZED CANOE OR ROWBOAT WILL SUPPORT MANY PEOPLE IF THEY JUST HOLD ON TO IT. IT'S BETTER TO WAIT FOR SOMEONE TO PICK YOU UP OR TO PADDLE THE CRAFT SLOWLY TO SHORE THAN TO LEAVE IT AND BECOME EXHAUSTED.

# BEACH CAMPING

By STEVE NORMAN

**A**LL AROUND THE tip of Cape Cod, where the Mayflower first touched our shores, lie miles of beautiful expanses of beach and sand. A local Explorer post, working under the guidance of advisor Don Westover, spent most of last summer testing and working out gimmicks to make camping on the sand more fun.

Securing tentage was their first problem because ordinary tent stakes would not hold. Finally, they found that deadman logs, crossed-board anchors, or three-foot stakes provided the needed anchorage. They tried all kinds of tents, running into no special difficulties with any type of shelter. For short term camping, their favorite was the tarp tent. Prevailing winds at their sites are usually off the water, so they pitched their tents facing in toward the dunes.

Sleep was no trouble, if you put a good ground cloth under you to keep out dampness from the sand. Blankets, or sleeping bags, with or without rubber air mattresses were fine. While the sand is not as soft as you might think, you don't have to bother digging out holes for hips and shoulders. The shifting sands will form a contour to fit you before morning.

Hiking on sand is hard work. Carry a pack, and you'd better plan to go easy. Walk around a dune, or climb it at a shallow angle, rather than straight up. You'll find it easier on your wind. Wear shoes and socks and keep covered with, at least, shorts and a tee shirt. The sun is especially strong off sand and water and it's easy to get a bad burn.

These Provincetown Explorers found that firewood was no problem. A short hike along shore provided all the driftwood they could carry. Shallow wells would furnish brackish water, but it had to be boiled, so they brought in a fresh supply each day by sand jeep.

A sturdy driftwood pole dug just about two feet deep into the sand is secure enough to hold your tent up in any blow. You can even climb it.

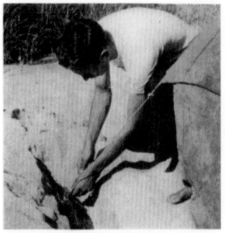

One method for securing side guy lines from a wall tent is to dig trench for a "deadman" log. Fasten lines to nails in the log or directly around log itself, then cover with sand.

A crossed-board anchor works very well, but the boards must be fairly wide and dug down a foot or more, then covered with sand. The normal crossed-sticks would simply pull out.

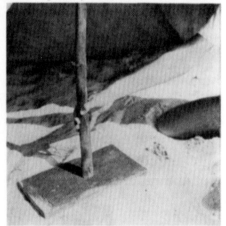

In the sand, tent poles quickly work down until the tent sags loosely. Simplest way to overcome this problem is to rest the bottom of your tent poles on wide sections of board.

The wind blows sand into everything. To keep it out of your tent, it helps if you pile up a bank of sand right against the side walls. Weight of sand serves to help anchor canvas.

The cold ocean keeps nearby sands cool, but you've got to dig down through sun-heated top layer. To keep sides of your "refrigerator" from caving in, line it with boards and cover.

Except in very heavy winds, your beach cooking fire will get enough protection from sand piled up around it, especially on the windward side. Dig down a bit before laying fire.

# CAMPCRAFT

## INSULATE YOUR SLEEPING BAG

WHEN SLEEPING OUTDOORS ON SNOW OR COLD GROUND—FIRST SPREAD A GROUND CLOTH...

THEN SPREAD LAYERS OF NEWSPAPER OR A LONG SHEET OF HEAVY BROWN WRAPPING PAPER OVER ALL OF GROUND CLOTH.

LAY YOUR SLEEPING BAG ON PAPER.

WEAR A WOOLEN CAP PULLED DOWN OVER YOUR EARS— OR A TOQUE (AVAILABLE AT GOV'T. SURPLUS STORES) OR WEAR A HOODED SWEATSHIRT.

## CHECK THE WIND

WHEN PITCHING YOUR TENT.

WIND
HEAPED-UP SNOW

ONE SIDE OF TENT SHOULD FACE PREVAILING WIND.
IF THERE'S SNOW ON THE GROUND, PACK SNOW AROUND SIDES OF TENT TO KEEP OUT DRAFTS.

## CHECK THE TREES

DON'T PITCH YOUR TENT UNDER TREES (FIRS, FOR EXAMPLE) WHICH MAY ACCUMULATE SNOW THAT WILL DROP ONTO YOUR TENT WHEN THE LOAD GETS TOO HEAVY.

## WHEN BOILING SNOW FOR WATER

KEEP STIRRING OR SNOW WILL SCORCH.

WHEN COMPLETELY MELTED, BOIL AT LEAST TEN MINUTES TO PURIFY WATER.

IT'S EASIER TO MELT ICE THAN SNOW—IF YOU CAN FIND ICE.

## ANCHOR

**YOUR** TENT SECURELY IN THE SNOW WITH "DEADMAN" ANCHORS.

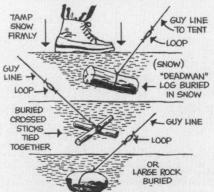

TAMP SNOW FIRMLY

GUY LINE TO TENT
LOOP

GUY LINE
LOOP

(SNOW)
"DEADMAN" LOG BURIED IN SNOW

BURIED CROSSED STICKS TIED TOGETHER

GUY LINE
LOOP

OR LARGE ROCK BURIED

WHICHEVER ANCHOR YOU USE, **DON'T** TIE TENT GUY LINES DIRECTLY TO DEADMAN. A HARD SURFACE FREEZE MAY PREVENT YOUR RELEASING TENT GUY LINE FROM DEADMAN.

# Back Yard Air Rifle Shooting

THE back yard air rifle range can be built at little cost, and will furnish many hours of amusement. In addition, the practice obtained on it will perfect one's marksmanship and teach how guns should be handled. If there were more boys who learned early how to shoot, what to do and what not to do, there would be fewer accidents when real firearms are used. And the air rifle gives that experience without question.

In laying out the back yard range, a few things should be borne in mind

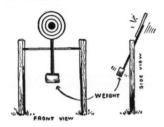

FRONT VIEW          WEIGHT          SIDE VIEW

and the principal one is safety. Under no condition should the line of fire be such as to endanger anyone and due consideration must be given to window lights. A back stop is advisable, although if a clear space of a hundred yards can be had, not absolutely necessary. A garage or other building made of brick, cement blocks, tile or stucco serves nicely to shoot against, but wood —especially painted white or a light color—will be defaced. An old piece of carpet, preferably of dark color, or a gunny sack, suspended at the top and weighted at the bottom, works out well. The targets should be placed about shoulder high for off hand shooting; lowered when kneeling or prone. A glance at the illustration will give an idea as to the arrangement.

Naturally, of course, one should, so far as possible, eliminate glare. Aiming against the sun, for instance, will produce poor results. Again, the exact distance should be marked off. Fifteen, twenty and twenty-five feet will be found best. Remember, to shoot well one must know what his gun will do and he can best find this out by tests over a known range. Surprising as it may seem, even the low priced air guns

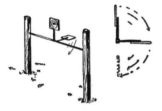

show accuracy in the hands of the marksman who understands where and how to hold.

A natural relaxed position is best when firing. The feet are not to be too close together, but rather spread out a bit. Aim with the cheek low on the stock, both eyes open. Theoretically, the front bead when lined with the rear sight ought to be held just below the center of the bull's eye. However, since guns shoot differently, there may be considerable variation. Distance, of course, plays an important part, for as this is increased, the sighting must be higher. Remember, bullets do not travel in a straight line, but in an arc. This is true not only with air guns but high-powered rifles as well. Therefore, considerable practice will be necessary before one may expect to hit the mark.

WHEN practicing, breathe naturally. Usually better results can be had when the aim is not too long. Never jerk the trigger but rather squeeze it. While some of these instructions may seem unnecessary to the beginner, while learning he may as well start out right as wrong.

For the outdoor range, some small portable targets are required. A simple one is made from a small box, with a hole in front. Back of the opening is suspended a piece of metal which will ring when struck by a bullet. Sliding fronts that may be changed, giving larger or small bulls, will be found good, considering the little extra labor involved.

Another good mark is made by attaching two round pieces of metal at right angles, on a heavy wire suspended between upright posts. The axis ought not to revolve too freely, but be so adjusted that the bulls will not turn except when struck. Hitting the top one will drive it flat, bringing the lower target into view. The impact of a shot on this makes the second disappear and the first to rise again.

A somewhat similar arrangement is as follows: On a metal rod of small diameter, twist a piece of wire, as shown in the drawing, so it will move freely. Weight the bottom and suspend on a frame. Note that the top of the wire is also coiled somewhat like a spring, and in the "loop" various sized

WRONG          SLIDE

and shaped metal objects may be placed, such as discs, birds, etc. When one scores by hitting the mark, whatever it is, that tips back but the weight swings it into position again. Incidently, for rapid fire shooting, this simple little target cannot be bettered, in the opinion of many, as it rights itself very quickly and may be shot at even when swinging.

A TIN can "game hunt" also is great fun. Get about a bushel of these old containers and number the labels. Then scatter them here and there in weeds, brush and grass, so as to hide as much as possible. Do not have the cans too close together, and it really is better if the actual shooters do not know where the "game" is. The first one who spies a mark shouts "rabbit" and fires. If he hits, the "bunny" is "dead" and the others dare not shoot at it. On the other hand, should he miss the one nearest to the can has the next shot and so on until all the players have had a chance. To increase interest the "hunters" ought not travel too closely together and of course they must be careful never to get in the line of fire of other boys. Score is kept; the one getting the largest total, wins.

A word about the care of air rifles. They should be given attention, the same as other guns. A few drops of oil down the barrels and into the actions, now and then, will make them work better. Wipe the stocks and outsides with a greasy cloth. Take pride in your air rifle and keep it in good shape, for otherwise you will not be able to do your best shooting.

—GEORGE J. THIESSEN

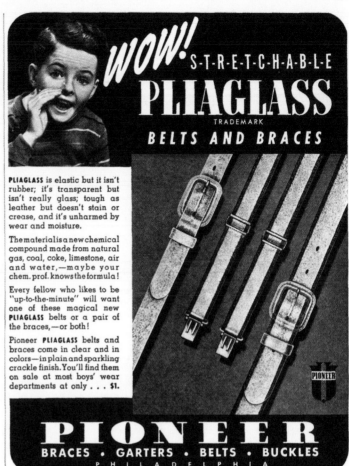

# LASHINGS

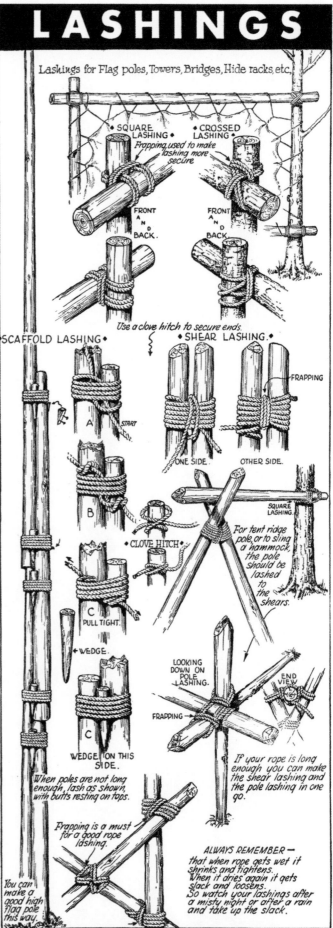

Lashings for Flag poles, Towers, Bridges, Hide racks, etc.

SQUARE LASHING • CROSSED LASHING
Frapping used to make lashing more secure
FRONT AND BACK.

Use a clove hitch to secure ends.

SCAFFOLD LASHING • • SHEAR LASHING •
FRAPPING
A  START
B
C  PULL TIGHT
WEDGE
C
WEDGE ON THIS SIDE.
ONE SIDE.  OTHER SIDE.

When poles are not long enough, lash as shown, with butts resting on tops.

• CLOVE HITCH •

SQUARE LASHING
For tent ridge pole, or to sling a hammock, the pole should be lashed to the shears.

LOOKING DOWN ON POLE LASHING.
END VIEW
FRAPPING

If your rope is long enough you can make the shear lashing and the pole lashing in one go.

You can make a good high flag pole this way.

Frapping is a must for a good rope lashing.

ALWAYS REMEMBER—
that when rope gets wet it shrinks and tightens. When it dries again it gets slack and loosens. So watch your lashings after a misty night or after a rain and take up the slack.

# Campin' in the Rain

## By ERNEST F. SCHMIDT

JUST YESTERDAY, the swift patter of rain on my tent woke me early in the morning. The sky over our campsite, 3,500 feet up in the mountains of Virginia's Shenandoah National Park had been beautifully clear when we went to bed. But it sure wasn't beautiful or clear now!

Years ago I guess that would have bothered me, but this morning, well, I just turned over and went back to sleep. More than half a hundred rainy mornings, and evenings, in camp over the years have shown me that camping is always fun—rain or shine! It just takes a little extra ingenuity to stay dry when the going is soggy. After you get that know-how, you'll have enough gumption to start off in the rain and go wet-weather camping, as these Scouts of Troop 39, Chapel Hill, N. C., did when BOYS' LIFE went along.

The most important rule for a rainy-day camper is this: Go equipped to stay dry. And the next rule, if you do get wet, is to get dry by the fire as soon as possible. Don't let nightfall catch you with wet clothing. And for wet shoes, here's a good drying stunt I found up in the Adirondacks. Parch two cups of dry rice in your frying pan. While it's still hot, pour it into the wet shoes. The rice may get athlete's foot, but the shoes will dry in a hurry. This takes a lot of rice, so it naturally would not be too practical for a whole Patrol or Troop unless you re-use the rice from shoe to shoe. Another way of drying shoes is to stuff paper in them.

True, the camping ideas on these two pages may not keep you bone dry on your next rainy hike, but I guarantee you they'll at least keep you from developing any gills or webbed feet.

### PHOTOGRAPHS BY BOB BROOKS

**HAT**—The hood on an official Scout poncho, or a regular sou'wester hat is probably best for you. A broad-brimmed Stetson is good, too. So is Dad's old fishin' hat if you can get it!

**SHIRT**—This depends on climate and season, but anytime it's a smart idea to take a warm wool shirt as well as a cotton one. You may not wear it in the daytime, but you can use it as a jacket or sleeping garment at night.

**PANTS**—For most of the year, long cotton ones are best. Roll 'em boot-top high for warm wet weather, but tuck them into boots when bugs are bad. In brush or high grass you'll get wet in spite of a poncho, but pants dry fast.

**PONCHO**—Keeping dry is the big thing, and a poncho helps you do it. Under dry conditions you can use your poncho as a groundcloth, but when it's really wet you want a poncho and a groundcloth. You can wear a raincoat instead of a poncho if the coat it tough enough, but it'll seal you up like a box, giving little breathing space. In canoe country a waist-long rainshirt is fine.

**JACKET**—A balloon-cloth windbreaker worn over your wool shirt is best for summer. In cooler wet-weather use a wool jacket that's warm but not too heavy. Leather? Not so good in rain.

**UNDERWEAR**—In late fall, winter, or early spring you want wool, of course. But now a cotton T-shirt and shorts are enough. Two-piece underwear is best. It's easy to wash; you can take half of it off if you get half-wet.

**SOCKS**—Wool socks, brother, and no exceptions. Wear cotton ones inside if you want, but wet or dry, wool socks are tops. Have an extra pair in your pack. Dry wet ones near a fire but not so near they'll shrink or scorch.

**BOOTS**—The most important part of wet-weather clothing. Leather boots? No—they just don't keep out water. Galoshes? Okay, but watch out for snags and sharp stones. Rubber bottomed, leather topped boots? Excellent. Not too good for hiking, true, but for wet weather or snow—unbeatable. Wear them with inner soles and wool socks, and your feet will be dry and warm.

# AIMS FOR FIREARM SAFETY!

THE PEDRO PATROL

SOME OF THE GUYS ARE GOING TO WORK FOR THIS, THE RIFLE AND SHOTGUN SHOOTING MERIT BADGE, AT SUMMER CAMP.

SO WE'RE BRUSHING UP ON FIREARM SAFETY. THIS IS *JUST A START.* WE'LL HAVE READ THE "*RIFLE AND SHOTGUN SHOOTING*" MERIT BADGE PAMPHLET AND HAVE BEEN INSTRUCTED BY A FIREARMS COUNSELOR *BEFORE* HANDLING A GUN.

THERE'S LOTS TO REMEMBER. LIKE THIS:

FIREARM SAFETY

FIRST, LAST, ALWAYS.

AND THIS:

1. ALWAYS POINT MUZZLE IN A SAFE DIRECTION, USUALLY UPWARD AND DOWNRANGE.

2. KEEP FINGER OFF TRIGGER UNTIL READY TO SHOOT.

3. KEEP ACTION OPEN AND GUN UNLOADED UNTIL READY TO USE.

THOUGH THERE'S MORE— SUCH AS COMMON SENSE— IF YOU FOLLOW THIS CODE, YOU WILL BE A SAFE SHOOTER.

## SHOOTER'S SAFETY CODE

A SCOUT:

- ALWAYS FOLLOWS THE RULES FOR GUN SAFETY.

- ACCEPTS THE RESPONSIBILITY GOING WITH THE USE AND POSSESSION OF GUNS.

- OBEYS LAWS GOVERNING THE USE AND POSSESSION OF GUNS.

- PRACTICES WILDLIFE CONSERVATION.

- FOLLOWS THE SPIRIT AND LETTER OF THE GAME LAWS.

- IS ESPECIALLY CAREFUL TO BE A TRUE SPORTSMAN WHEN USING GUNS.

NEVER TOUCH A GUN UNLESS A KNOWLEDGEABLE ADULT SAYS YOU CAN. *ALWAYS* ASK— HE OR SHE PROBABLY WILL BE HAPPY TO TEACH YOU ABOUT FIREARMS.

A-87/28

# Scout Program:The Winning Spirit
# ACTION ARCHERY

**BY DICK PRYCE**
PHOTOGRAPHS BY GENE DANIELS
Featuring Scouts of Troop 75,
Chartered to First Christian Church,
Moore, Okla.

Have you ever wondered how Indian boys your age learned to shoot arrows from a bow? The short answer is that they practiced. They shot at bushes, at rocks and at tufts of grass. Day in and day out they practiced. Some became so skillful they could hit a small target time after time.

You and the other Scouts in your troop can learn archery if you are willing to practice. Why not try a game called Action Archery on the next troop campout? You won't become an expert the first time you try, but at least you'll find out if you want to go for the Archery merit badge.

Action Archery is based on the field-course idea developed by the National Field Archery Association. A field course is laid out in woods and meadows. Archers do not stand in one spot and shoot at targets. Instead, they walk down a path and shoot at targets both near and far away.

Action Archery is similar to the way that Indian boys practiced. All that is needed to set up an Action Archery course are bows and blunt-tip arrows, plastic bottles, cardboard boxes, some strong string, a little paint and a few bales of hay.

Depending on where the campout is, the hay may not be needed. It is used as a backstop to keep arrows from zooming off into the distance. The field course should, if possible, be laid along a path that goes through woods and fields. Some targets should be partly hidden; others should be completely in the open. Hang some targets from tree limbs. Place others on the ground.

The distances from archer to target should vary from seven yards to 23 yards. Some targets will be big and some will be small. The whole idea of setting up an Action Archery field course is to vary everything—the size and shape of targets, the shooting distances and the number of targets.

At each station, drive a number of stakes into the ground so Scouts will all stand in the same spot to shoot from. An adult should be at each station to make sure standard archery safety rules are observed (see page 5 of the Archery merit badge pamphlet) and to score the hits.

Probably the best way to score is to award five points if the first arrow pierces the target, three if the target is hit with a second arrow, and one if the third arrow strikes. If you miss with all three arrows, no points. Do not shoot the two other arrows if you hit with the first. The patrol with the highest score wins.

Read and discuss the Archery merit badge pamphlet before trying Action Archery. If you have never before shot an arrow, an experienced archer should show you how before you walk down the field-course trail. You'll probably never be as good as the Indian boys were. But if you practice, you may be amazed how often you'll hit the target. ♣

**TO BECOME A TOP-RATED ARCHER,
TRY THIS ANCIENT SECRET
THAT WAS DISCOVERED AND
TREASURED BY AMERICAN
INDIANS OF LONG AGO. TAKE
YOUR BOW AND ARROWS OUTSIDE.
PRACTICE A LOT.**

An Eagle Scout gives some instruction at the
start of the contest. An adult supervises.
Trail is well marked, but targets may be partly hidden.

If you're interested in training your eyes and your mind, there are few things that can beat

# Tracking

1

By WILLIAM HILLCOURT

NATIONAL DIRECTOR OF SCOUTCRAFT

**T**HERE ARE PEOPLE who travel through woods and over fields and never see a thing. And then there are those who see the stories in everything around them. If you're a fellow with eyes in your head, you can train yourself to see and observe, and then, from your observations, figure out what is going on.

That's where tracking comes in. There's nothing like it for learning to use your eyes. You may not have actual use for tracking in your everyday life, unless you're a hunter, or intend to become a criminal investigator, or join the FBI—but you'll have fun using your ability for studying wild animals, and for tracking down your own friends in exciting wide games.

To become an expert tracker, begin with trailing. Have someone lay a trail of the regular Scout trail signs, then follow it. Try a more difficult trail the next time, and still another. When you are good at trailing, you set out for tracking.

If you happen to live in snow country, you will find tracks all around you in the winter time, and you can follow the tracks of rabbit, deer, raccoon and other animals, and discover what they are up to. In other parts of the country, you'll find lots of tracks at the edges of rivers and lakes, and in the sand along ocean and gulf shores.

For identifying the animal and bird tracks you see, check your *Scout Field Book,* or get hold of a copy of the most complete book on tracking ever written and illustrated—Ellsworth Jaeger's *Tracks and Trailcraft.*

2

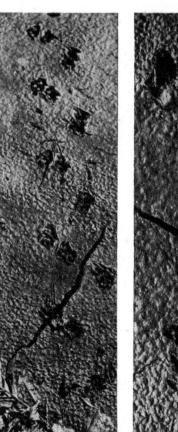
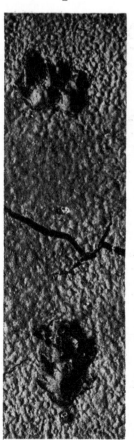
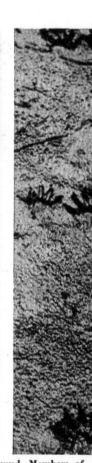

Tracking in snow is easiest kind of tracking. The most common tracks are probably of RABBIT (left). In running, the rabbit places its hind feet in front of the staggered forefeet tracks. SQUIRREL tracks (center) are quite similar, but forefeet are paired. At right, the squirrel had hard going in deep snow.

Of all places, tracks show up best in firm mud. Members of WEASEL family move in bounds or jumps, and show tiny tracks, usually in pairs (left). DOG and FOX tracks have nail marks (center). Dog tracks are round, fox tracks elongated. Fingered forefeet and flat-footed hind feet are of RACCOON (right).

Simple arrow shows road straight ahead; line crossed by arrow indicates new direction. Three stones on each other say "This is the road," one stone next to two others "Turn this way."

An "unnatural" trail is laid with two different kinds of materials, such as an oak leaf fastened to a birch branch, or a large leaf held down with a rock, or an acorn "growing" on a pine tree.

In laying a stick trail, the free end of the stick points in the correct direction. Another stick near tip of first says "Long way," at base "Short way." Tied grass tufts indicate trail.

The "whiffle-poof" is a nail-studded log with a rope attached to it. When you drag it over the ground, it behaves like a bucking bronco and leaves an interesting trail for the Patrol to follow.

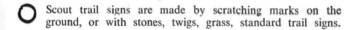

Scout trail signs are made by scratching marks on the ground, or with stones, twigs, grass, standard trail signs.

Instead of using ordinary signs, you can invent your own. For more difficult training, try the "Whiffle-poof" gimmick.

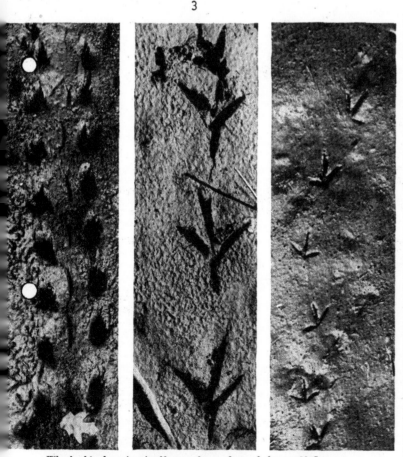
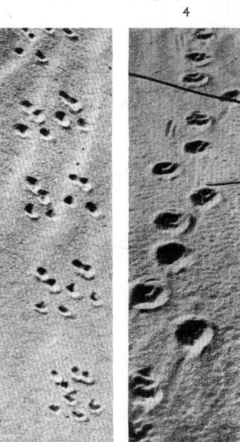

What's this dragging itself over the surface of the mud? Just a SNAPPING TURTLE (left) on its way back to the water. Tracks of the GREAT BLUE HERON (center) are almost unbelievable, so large they are. Note hind toe! KILLDEER and PLOVERS and other birds of their family leave tracks without hind toes (right).

Tracks in sand are seldom satisfactory; wind and rain blur the edges. Early in the morning, you may see a sand dune criss-crossed by the tracks of MICE (left). And where there are mice, there are usually CATS (center). And then there are the tracks of the most interesting of all animals to follow—MAN (right).

# LET'S SKI

SKIING IS A GREAT SPORT THAT HELPS KEEP YOU PHYSICALLY FIT THROUGH THE WINTER. IF YOU DON'T KNOW HOW TO SKI, NOW'S THE TIME TO LEARN—WHILE YOU'RE YOUNG.

GET SKIS THAT "FIT" YOU. A GENERAL RULE IS—ABOUT A FOOT LONGER THAN YOUR HEIGHT.

YOU'LL ALSO NEED SKI BOOTS, POLES AND BINDINGS.

YOU'LL SAVE MONEY IN THE LONG RUN BY GETTING AN EXPERT HELP YOU WITH YOUR EQUIPMENT.

**① START OFF**
BY "WALKING." THAT IS, SLIDING OVER THE SNOW WITHOUT LIFTING YOUR SKIS. PUSH YOURSELF ALONG WITH YOUR POLES—FIRST KEEPING BOTH SKIS SLIDING TOGETHER THEN, PUTTING YOUR WEIGHT ON ONE SKI, PUSH THE OTHER FORWARD, THEN PUT YOUR WEIGHT ON THE OTHER AND PUSH FORWARD, ETC.

THE "CAMBER." (BOW OR BEND THROUGH THE LENGTH OF THE SKI) SHOULD NOT BE OVER ONE INCH IN THE CENTER.

SKIS SHOULD HAVE STEEL EDGES, BE UNWARPED, STRAIGHT-GRAINED WITH A KNOT-FREE RUNNING SURFACE AND A STRAIGHT GROOVE DOWN THE CENTER.

THE "DOWNHILL" TYPE OF SKI IS BEST FOR GENERAL PURPOSE.

**② TRY "SKATING"**
ON YOUR SKIS. IT'S THE SAME AS ICE SKATING—JUST REMEMBER TO RAISE YOUR SKIS HIGHER THAN YOU DO ICE SKATES.

**③** NOW, ON AN EASY SLOPE, FREE FROM ROCKS AND TREES, TRY **DOWNHILL RUNNING**, LEAN THE WEIGHT OF YOUR BODY A LITTLE FORWARD, MUSCLES LOOSE AND RELAXED, KNEES AND ELBOWS SLIGHTLY BENT, HEELS FLAT ON SKIS.

GO SLOWLY UNTIL YOU GET THE FEEL OF PROPER BALANCE.

**④** THIS IS A **"SNOWPLOW CHRISTIE"** OR TURN. NOTE POSITION OF SKIS AND POLES.

**⑤** PRACTICE THIS BASIC **"SNOWPLOW"** FOR STOPPING AND MAKING SOME TURNS. NOTE POSITION OF SKIS AND POLES.

BUT **NOT** IF YOU'RE MOVING FAST. TO MAKE A FAST STOP, FALL TO ONE SIDE, HEAD UPHILL, SIDE TO A STOP.

*DON'T BE ASHAMED OF TAKING SOME SPILLS—EVERYONE DOES—EVEN THE PROS!*

**⑥** THIS IS HOW TO MAKE A **"KICK TURN"** OR TURN FROM A STANDING POSITION. STICK YOUR RIGHT POLE IN SNOW AHEAD OF YOU, YOUR LEFT POLE AT THE TAIL END OF YOUR RIGHT SKI. SWING YOUR LEFT SKI UP AND SET ITS TAIL END IN THE SNOW...

LET THE LEFT SKI DROP AWAY FROM YOU AND SET IT DOWN HARD IN THE SNOW. NOW IT'S EASY TO BRING THE OTHER SKI AROUND. USE POLES AS PROPS TO HELP KEEP YOUR BALANCE.

**⑦** THE **"HERRINGBONE"** IS ONE WAY TO CLIMB A HILL. KNEES BENT WELL FORWARD, STEP FROM ONE SKI TO ANOTHER.

**⑧** ANOTHER (AND EASIER, BUT SLOWER HILL CLIMBING METHOD) IS THE **"STAIRCASE"**. IT'S JUST A SERIES OF SIDESTEPS UP A HILL.

2480

# FIRST AID FOR SNAKEBITES

## By DICK PRYCE

**It's a wise patrol that's prepared with a plan of action to help a snakebite victim.**

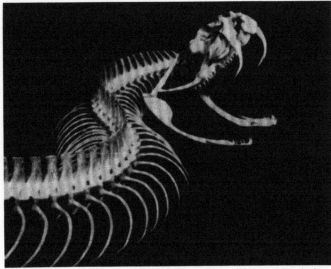

Skeleton shows spinal column, ribs, lower jaw and curving fangs of a pit viper.

Snakebite is not a major cause of death in the United States. Without any kind of treatment, experts estimate, 80 percent of the approximately 7,000 persons bitten annually by venomous snakes recover. Even so, it's a wise Boy Scout patrol that has an emergency plan of action to help a snakebite victim.

The first step in this plan is for members of a patrol to identify the poisonous snakes in their area. They should be familiar with the type of terrain in which these reptiles are most likely to congregate. Observing local snakes in a zoo—or studying colored pictures—will help the familiarization process.

There are more than two dozen species of rattlesnakes in the country. They and the other pit vipers—moccasins and copperheads—are dangerous. Generally, the bigger the poisonous snake, the more dangerous it is. A big snake has more venom and the larger fangs necessary to deliver a deadly dose.

OK. Your patrol has studied and learned to identify the snakes of your area. The next step is to learn what hospitals and doctors in the community have antivenin on hand. For the most effective snakebite treatment is *getting the victim and the antivenin together as soon as possible.* A patrol plan of action should be designed to accomplish this. First aid may be administered while speeding a victim toward antivenin.

Let's set up a hyphothetical case. The patrol is on a hike. Although it has avoided terrain where snakes may be, a member is bitten. And the snake is identified as one of the pit vipers. There

are fundamental steps to be taken. The plan might go something like this:

Someone should make sure that the victim lies down, with the wound lower than the rest of the body. He should talk quietly with the victim, assuring him that the other patrol members are working to bring help. He should try to control the excitement and panic that all too often follow a snakebite. Simultaneously, a second Scout should put a constriction band from two to four inches above the wound to keep the venom from spreading. The constriction band can be a neckerchief or handkerchief; keep it firm but loose enough to squeeze fingers between the band and the skin. Loosen the band for a few minutes every half hour—if it takes longer than that to get the victim to a doctor.

As the team of two soothes the victim and applies a constriction band, three other patrol members have sped from the site. One Scout's mission is to find the nearest phone and call a hospital or doctor where antivenin is available. The second finds transportation and the third looks for ice.

When he finds ice he returns quickly to the victim, puts the ice in a neckerchief and applies it directly to the bite. If there is nothing to put the ice in, he holds it directly on the bite. If practical—say if the bite is on a hand—he immerses the victim's hand in a pail or pan of iced water.

When a constriction band and ice-water treatment are used in combination, here is what happens. The band holds the venom at the injection site until the ice water lowers the temperature of the bite area. Lowering the temperature slows the rate at which the

venom can spread. In effect, the ice and constriction band both hold the venom—though not completely—at the point of injection. The chemical action of the venom is harmful only when the natural defenses of the body are overwhelmed. Because of the holding action, the venom spreads slowly in a diluted condition, so that the harmful effects are weakened.

With luck the patrol will have the victim in a car and heading toward antivenin in five or ten minutes. While transporting him, have him lie down and remain quiet. Keep the ice pack and constriction band in place. Don't forget to loosen it every half hour.

Only in very rare cases should Scouts and Scout leaders use the cut-and-suction method, for more harm than good may be done. Just what is a "rare case"? There are two factors to consider: How soon can you get the victim to medical help and antivenin treatment, and how serious is the swelling and discoloration? If you can't get the victim and antivenin together in from 60 to 90 minutes, and if the swelling and discoloration are spreading quickly, that is a rare case.

The best way to be prepared for those very rare cases is to have with you a regular snakebite kit—not an improvised one. Commercial kits have directions about how to use them. But generally, use the sharp, sterile blade to open the wound at the fang marks by making shallow cuts in the skin. Then apply the suction cup while you keep the constriction band in place.

In most instances, prompt first aid will keep the patient from undue suffering. But also remember that a patrol plan of action may save a life. ∎

—DICK PRYCE

# CAMOUFLAGE
## PROTECTIVE COLORATION

When you paint your hands and face, and fasten grass and leaves to your clothes in order to blend in with your local surroundings so as to be almost invisible, you're practicing one of the oldest tricks known in nature.

Many animals have developed mimicry to such a degree that, until they move, they are almost impossible to distinguish from their surroundings. Here are a few examples of protective coloration. See if you can identify the animal before looking at the key drawings in the bottom panel.

1 WALKING STICK
2 FAWN OF WHITE-TAILED DEER
3 PINE-TUFT CATERPILLAR
4 DIAMOND-BACK RATTLESNAKE
5 ROCK BASS
6 WALKING LEAF
7 TREE HOPPER
8 KALLIMA BUTTERFLY

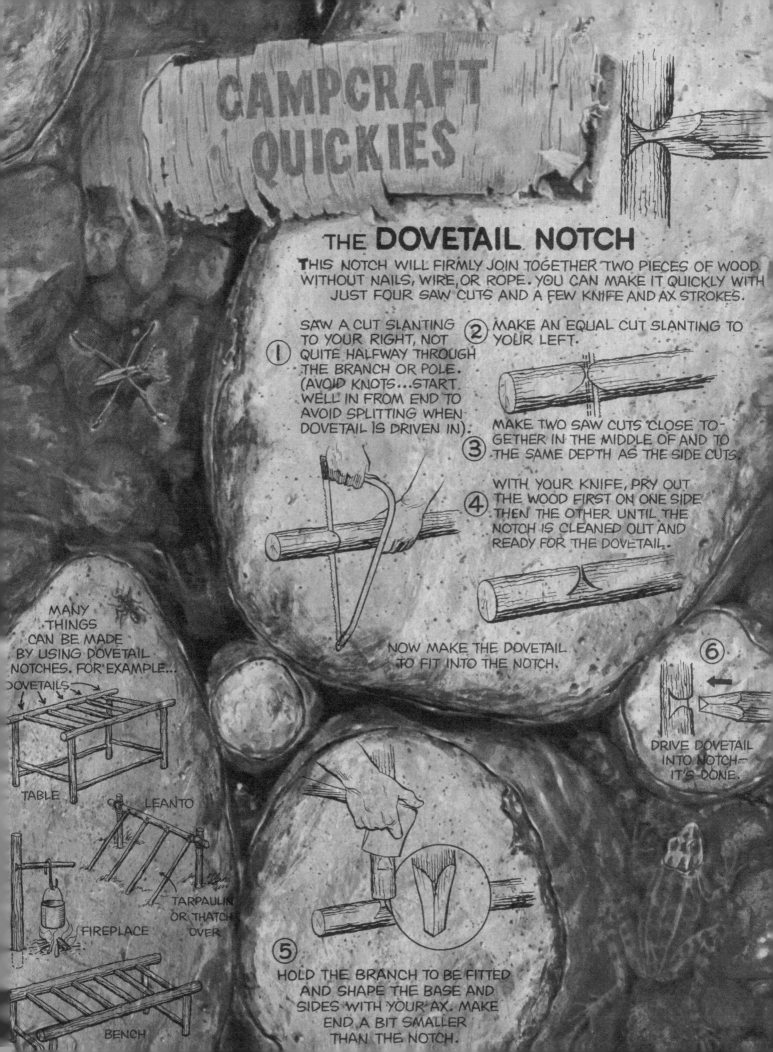

# CAMPCRAFT QUICKIES

## THE DOVETAIL NOTCH

THIS NOTCH WILL FIRMLY JOIN TOGETHER TWO PIECES OF WOOD WITHOUT NAILS, WIRE, OR ROPE. YOU CAN MAKE IT QUICKLY WITH JUST FOUR SAW CUTS AND A FEW KNIFE AND AX STROKES.

1. SAW A CUT SLANTING TO YOUR RIGHT, NOT QUITE HALFWAY THROUGH THE BRANCH OR POLE. (AVOID KNOTS...START WELL IN FROM END TO AVOID SPLITTING WHEN DOVETAIL IS DRIVEN IN).

2. MAKE AN EQUAL CUT SLANTING TO YOUR LEFT.

3. MAKE TWO SAW CUTS CLOSE TOGETHER IN THE MIDDLE OF AND TO THE SAME DEPTH AS THE SIDE CUTS.

4. WITH YOUR KNIFE, PRY OUT THE WOOD FIRST ON ONE SIDE THEN THE OTHER UNTIL THE NOTCH IS CLEANED OUT AND READY FOR THE DOVETAIL.

NOW MAKE THE DOVETAIL TO FIT INTO THE NOTCH.

MANY THINGS CAN BE MADE BY USING DOVETAIL NOTCHES. FOR EXAMPLE...

DOVETAILS →

TABLE

LEANTO

FIREPLACE

TARPAULIN OR THATCH OVER

BENCH

5. HOLD THE BRANCH TO BE FITTED AND SHAPE THE BASE AND SIDES WITH YOUR AX. MAKE END A BIT SMALLER THAN THE NOTCH.

6. DRIVE DOVETAIL INTO NOTCH— IT'S DONE.

# TRAILING BY DAN BEARD — The Why And the How of It

TRAILING, popularly speaking, means following footprints, but the term really implies much more than that and signifies following the trail by means of the many marks an animal leaves behind on its way—a displaced stone, a broken twig, a tuft of hair on a bush, a scratch on a stone—any of the things a roving creature must unintentionally leave to mark its path.

It is an axiom—that is a self-evident truth or a fact that does not need argument to uphold it—that it is impossible for one to travel on earth without leaving a trail of some kind. Even in a big city this is just as true as it is in the woods, the difference being that in a city there are so many thousands of trails that it is almost impossible to follow a given one. But when a man leaves home, the home is the beginning of his trail, he stops and buys a paper, thus leaving a second record of his trail, he takes the subway, street car, or other conveyance, and in each case he buys a ticket from some man and rubs up against others, thus leaving a trace of his travels; he arrives at or near his place of business, stops in at the drug store to buy a soda or the cigar store to get a smoke and at each place leaves more records, so that it is possible for someone to follow him all through his journey.

Trailing is essentially tracing by sight, or as the Dutch in Africa call it, following by the spoor when the quarry itself's hidden from view; and it is this use of the eyes alone in the pursuit of invisible game that distinguishes man, the hunter, from other animals. Other creatures follow a trail by scent as does the fox hound, or follow the game by direct sight of the thing itself, as does the greyhound.

There is no reason to think that any animal other than man employs eyesight for this purpose. Conspicuous tracks will not catch the eye of the stoat or the wolf in quest of prey, unless a recognizable odor draws attention to the fact that victim has passed that way.

There are no authentic cases on record of

*Only a trace in the long grass, but it tells the story.*

wolf, bear, dog, fox, or stoat following a trail unaided by its nose. The eyes of a bloodhound on the trail, for instance, are useful only to prevent the animal from bumping into trees and other obstacles in its path. There is nothing to cause one to believe that any of these animals, high though its intelligence be, in certain particulars, has the knowledge of the shape and structure of the feet such as is necessary to tell the nature of the species that has left the trace of the direction it has taken. The animal depends upon its nose. Smell will tell the fox whether the tracks are those of a chicken profitable to pursue, or those of a dog that had better not be molested, and the gradual waxing and waning of the scent in this or that direction will indicate the course of the trail made by the animal.

There is little doubt that to a dog, for instance, each stick, stone, leaf or tree trunk has an odor distinct and separate from all other similar objects, and that each individual creature has its own particular odor recognizable by a dog, which, by the aid of its nose alone, can pick its master's trail out from all those of others who have passed that way.

## MAN VS. OTHER ANIMALS

BUT to man alone is the power given to know these things by sight. The knowledge, however, is not instinctive any more than is the skill of a musician or a painter; on the contrary it must be acquired by strenuous application and long practice of Sherlock Holmes' methods applied to the outdoor world, and only the individual with keen visualizing power—that is with a healthy imagination, one who is able to picture to himself what he imagines—coupled with sound judgment, may hope to make a successful trailer and attain proficiency in the science in which our pioneer Americans were often even greater experts than the Indians from whom they learned the art.

For many years I have been telling the boys "How to Do Things" and "How to Make Things." But the most difficult thing to tell is "How to Follow a Trail," or "Track," as the English call it, or "Spoor," as the Dutch in Africa call it. Neither of these terms belong here in America. Trailing is the American word, and it means following the trace. Trace was the word used by the early Americans, and trace is a better word than spoor, track, or trail. Any chump could follow the spoor of an elephant, any small boy could follow tracks left in the mud or snow, a child could follow a well-beaten trail, but it takes an expert to follow a trace.

Some years ago when what is now Glacier Park was a raw wilderness uncontaminated by tourists, the writer, with

*The sign of a Scout.*

Mr. Frederick Vreeland and George Stanley, the trapper, took a trip across McDonald Lake to a wild meadow on the opposite side. The rich grass on this meadow, which grew over the bottom of an ancient beaver dam, was about waist deep, and it was evident that some animals had been walking through it. They had left a trace where they dragged their feet through the tall green plants, but there were no tracks, it was only a sort of an indentation in the surface of the grass (Figure 1) which could be seen better at a distance than at close quarters. Nevertheless, George Stanley stopped, looked over the surface of the grass with blazing eyes. "See!" he said, "There have been two moose here. They must have run away when they heard us land on the dam. And there was a big bear here, too, very

*"Who broke that stick?"*

near the same time."

Now that was trailing, the genuine real kind. An ordinary person would not have even noticed that anything had been there, though one could plainly see the trace when it was pointed out, and could also see, when attention was called to it, that two of the traces were made by large animals trotting through the grass and dragging their feet in long strides, while the other trace showed a sort of series of jumps, with no connecting link between one spot and the preceding spot, as there would have been if the animal had swung its legs along in a trot or any of the ordinary paces of a cow or a horse.

### THE INDISTINCT TRACK.

THIS is usually an old trail fallen into disuse. This sort of trail can be seen only by getting a perspective view of it, and is invisible when you are in the midst of it, for then it appears the same as all the surrounding field.

In the woods or in the brush an old trail may be traced by standing off at a distance. The trail may be overgrown and unused for years, yet there is a difference in the height of the bushes which from a distance plainly marks the trail. It was thus that the old war paths of the Indians were marked. They were not traveled frequently enough to be well beaten paths. With a few exceptions they were only used on occasions of raids and not for every day hunting.

### OLD WINTER TRAILS.

AN animal or a man walking in the snow, leaves distinct tracks, but a later storm will dim or wipe out these tracks. They may, however, often be traced (Figure 2) by getting a perspective or distant view. Then the slight hollows, unnoticeable at close quarters, make little blue shadows and a row of these little blue shadows makes quite a perceptible trace.

Another difficult place to follow a trace is over stony ground, but even here (Figure 3), a man or a large beast passing must necessarily dislodge or disturb some of the stones, consequently when one passes over such a bit of ground and sees the dark or damp side of the stones, one knows that something has been there recently, otherwise the stone would have dried out and been the color of the ones surrounding it.

Some years ago up in the Selkirk Mountains the writer discovered on a rocky place a well worn trail. Curiosity made him follow the trail to discover what crea-

tures had made it. He had not gone twenty yards before he found bunches of white woolly hair on the branches of a bush.

Now, then, white woolly hair doesn't grow on a bush. This was a wild place and it was very improbable that any person had placed the white woolly hair there; therefore it seemed reasonable to suppose that some wild animal had rubbed against the bush, some white animal, some good sized animal, because the hair was rather high from the ground; and putting all these things together it was evident that the writer was on the trail of a Rocky Mountain Goat; which proved to be the case.

### A BROKEN STICK.

THIS is not a thing that occurs without some outside force being used, so when a Scout finds a broken stick on the trail (Figure 5), it means that some creature has been there before him, probably a man who stepped on the stick. If the fracture looks fresh the break has occurred recently.

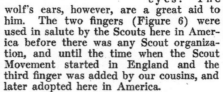

*The tell-tale tuft of hair.*

### THE SIGN OF A REAL SCOUT.

THE sign of a Scout is the two fingers (Figure 6), which represents the ears of a wolf, the wolf being considerably the best scout among the animals and best in tracing. But the wolf is guided by its nose and not by its eyes. The wolf's ears, however, are a great aid to him. The two fingers (Figure 6) were used in salute by the Scouts here in America before there was any Scout organization, and until the time when the Scout Movement started in England and the third finger was added by our cousins, and later adopted here in America.

### THE WATERHOLE.

IN the desert one wants always to find water. We know that the game or cattle trails all lead to water. Hence, if you strike the trail at (A) (Figure 7) and follow it down to where it joins (B), if you have any gumption at all you would know immediately that the animal did not go around that sharp angle and start back again, but went on to (D), and the nearer you come to the waterhole the more distinct and better beaten is the trail. Suppose, for instance, you struck the trail at (G) and went wandering off to the right, you would soon discover that the trail was becoming indistinct and branching, and would know that you were going in the wrong direction, therefore you would turn around and make your way towards (H) and thus reach the hole.

*The old winter trail.*

My good friend and expert outdoor man, Stewart Edward White, says in his novel called "The Leopard Woman": "Maji Hapana M'bale, Bwana (Water is not far, master). The white man, as well as Simba, had noticed the *gradual convergence* of the game trail." See (Figure 7).

A boy who is good in geometry should be good on the trail, because both require thought and reason. To be a good trailer you must be a backwoods Sherlock Holmes. In order to be a good backwoods Sherlock Holmes you must have a knowledge of the creatures, plants, and the things that are liable to happen in the woods. Had the writer been ignorant of the inhabitants of the mountains when he discovered the white hair on the bush he might have said, "Gee! I wonder whose white angora cat has been up here."

And in closing, let me caution you not to forget that we are Americans, that this is the United States of America. It is *not* Africa, Europe, or Asia. We have our own language and our own words for describing American things. We might as well go out West and call a butte a kopji as to call trailing, spooring, or even tracking. Or you might as well call your "outfit" a "safari." No, we are Boy Scouts of America and we are going to stick to American terms for American things.

*"Something has turned that stone over."*

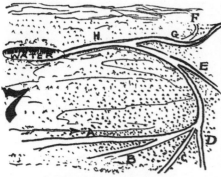

*The converging trails.*

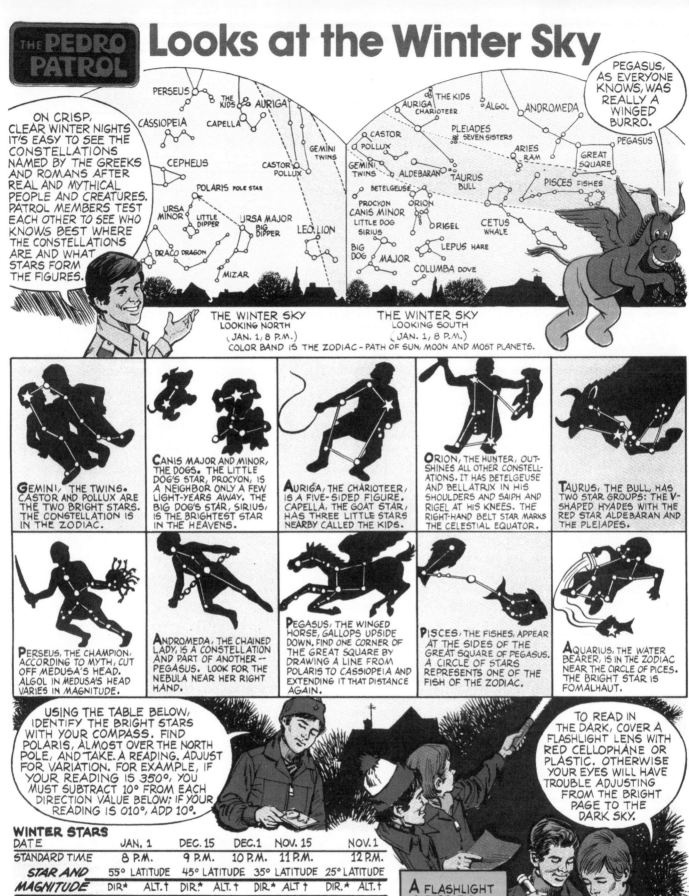

**THE PEDRO PATROL Looks at the Winter Sky**

THE WINTER SKY LOOKING NORTH (JAN. 1, 8 P.M.)
THE WINTER SKY LOOKING SOUTH (JAN. 1, 8 P.M.)
COLOR BAND IS THE ZODIAC – PATH OF SUN, MOON AND MOST PLANETS.

## WINTER STARS

| DATE | JAN. 1 | | DEC. 15 | | DEC. 1 | | NOV. 15 NOV. 1 | |
|---|---|---|---|---|---|---|---|---|
| STANDARD TIME | 8 P.M. | | 9 P.M. | | 10 P.M. | | 11 P.M. 12 P.M. | |
| STAR AND MAGNITUDE | 55° LATITUDE | | 45° LATITUDE | | 35° LATITUDE | | 25° LATITUDE | |
| | DIR* | ALT† | DIR* | ALT† | DIR.* | ALT† | DIR.* | ALT† |
| SIRIUS −1.6 | — | — | 122° | 08° | 120° | 14° | 118° | 18° |
| CAPELLA 0.2 | 095° | 65° | 075° | 63° | 058° | 60° | 045° | 54° |
| RIGEL 0.3 | 142° | 20° | 138° | 28° | 135° | 34° | 128° | 42° |
| BETELGEUSE 0.1–1.2 | 124° | 30° | 118° | 35° | 110° | 38° | 104° | 42° |
| PROCYON 0.5 | 102° | 14° | 098° | 15° | 095° | 18° | 092° | 18° |
| ALDEBARAN 1.1 | 142° | 48° | 132° | 54° | 120° | 60° | 104° | 64° |
| POLLUX 1.2 | 086° | 31° | 078° | 30° | 074° | 28° | 068° | 24° |
| FOMALHAUT 1.3 | — | | | | | | 230° | 12° |

*DIRECTION  †ALTITUDE

A8/370

# KEEPING PHYSICALLY FIT

## By Dr. C. Ward Crampton

## January

THE one best line for January is a bit of timely, well-worn advice that my father, who was also a doctor, used to give me on occasion: "Keep your feet warm and your head cool." It's good advice, any way you look at it, but especially good for January.

Feet get cold most often from getting wet or damp. Perhaps we don't like rubber over-shoes and we don't wear them, if we can get out of it. But when there is snow or wet, wear rubbers or arctics.

If the feet get wet, dry them, rub them, but do not heat them. A rapid change of temperature from cold to hot after exposure to cold injures the tissues. Wet cold is far worse than dry cold. Avoid it.

Wear double socks if you go out for long hikes, one silk or lisle next to the skin and one wool outside, or one very heavy pair of wool socks.

It is the air space surrounding the foot that acts like a blanket and keeps it warm.

Have your hiking shoes large enough. Give the feet plenty of room when out in the cold. The Laplanders wear large boots with room enough for a layer of dried grass around the feet. This makes an air blanket like the thick elastic air-space-containing woolen sock.

When Admiral Byrd took his first expedition down to the Antarctic he asked me to give a thorough physical and medical examination of the whole personnel. He made two requests, one of which was to give especial attention to the feet; for he said, "We expect them to use their heads in work and emergency, but they must use their feet all the time." And they did, except when they were sleeping or flying.

In sub-zero weather if the feet perspire easily, perspiration freezes so quickly that sharp ice crystals quickly form on the surface and cut into the skin. This tendency can be foreseen in the medical examination. It is associated with a tendency towards chilblains, which has more to do with the efficiency of the digestion than it has with the hands and feet.

## The Bridge Test

A WEAK neck makes a weak man. A strong neck is necessary for every kind of athletics and every field of human endeavor. A man with a strong neck can use his head better and he is less likely to lose it.

A well-muscled neck, with the blood circulating freely through it to and from the heart and head, is a great help to every part of the body.

There are nerves and nerve centers in the neck which control and direct respiration, heart action and digestion. In the neck is located the great power-control station, the thyroid glands, and the marvelous little chemical laboratories, the parathyroid glands.

There are great stories about these, but all point to the advantage of having strong muscles in the neck.

There are eighty-six muscles in the neck. Those at the sides and back of the neck are very important.

You have seen a wrestler on his hands and knees toss his head and throw the full weight of his opponent off his back. That is strength.

You have seen a wrestler thrown on his back, lift his shoulders off the mat so that his weight is resting entirely on his head and his feet. That is the "wrestlers' bridge." (See illus.) Try it.

If you can do it the first time you try it, you are good. If you can hold it for 30 seconds you are better. If you can rock your head from side to side or turn over so you rest on the brow and toes and then turn back to the "bridge" again, you are better than 99 out of 100. And if you can walk around your head without touching your hands to

AS I have repeatedly stated, it is the personal responsibility of every boy not only to know about his physical condition, but to know how he can make and keep himself physically fit. Scouts are obligated to do this by the Scout Oath. To help make this interesting and to enable the boy to better understand how he can keep himself physically fit, we have secured the services of Dr. C. Ward Crampton, for many years an active worker in Scouting and now a member of our Committee on Health and Safety, to conduct this page.

Dr. Crampton is a practicing family physician and one of the founders of the Public Schools Athletic League. He organized the New York State Medical campaign for health examinations, and the "Crampton test of physical condition" has just been adopted by the National Intercollegiate Athletic Association. He has been a Director of the National Congress of Parents and Teachers.

He is the author of The Daily Health Builder, and other books on health. Readers of BOYS' LIFE are invited to write personally to Dr. Crampton in care of BOYS' LIFE, asking any questions that they may choose relating to the subject of "KEEPING PHYSICALLY FIT."

James E. West
EDITOR

floor, you are wonderful and you have gone far enough.

But go at it easy; or you get a stiff neck. Train the muscles by daily exercise and you have a strong link where most people have a weak link.

Next month we will have an interesting and important test of athletic condition which you can do yourself. It requires you, first, to know how to take the pulse. Go to work and become expert

during this month, for now is the time to learn.

## How Long Is a Minute?

YOU would be surprised to learn what a difference of opinion may be found upon this point. Not more than one man out of three can tell the length of a minute within ten seconds. Two out of three will guess less than fifty seconds or more than seventy seconds. Test this out for yourself.

Get together a group of boys, or try it some evening with the family at home. This is the way to do it. Get your watch ready and then explain the test. Each one is to raise his right hand when he thinks that the minute is up. Now wait until the second hand reaches the even minute and give the word, "go!"

Mark down on paper the number of seconds that

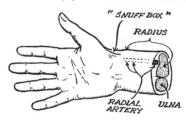

have passed as each one raises his hand. When all are finished read off your score.

There is one way that you can improve your score more quickly than any other. This is by counting the pulse. First you must learn how to take your pulse and then how many beats it runs to the minute. Some people have a pulse slower or quicker than others. The pulse will usually be faster when standing up than when sitting or lying down. Try out this test and develop some skill in it. Judgment of time is important as well as judgment of distance.

## How to Take the Pulse

The pulse may be found on the *inside* of the *thumb* side of the wrist, and this is the best way to find it, if you do not know how:

Stand in front of your "patient." He stretches out his right hand with the thumb up. Let it rest on the palm of your right hand, holding it steady. You will see two tendons running down from the thumb—one toward the back of the hand, which we disregard. The other one runs down the root of the thumb over the top and end of the bone on the thumb side of the forearm. This bone is called the radius. (Between these two tendons, by the way, is a little hollow which used to be called the "Snuff Box"; for when our Colonial ancestors took snuff they dropped a little in this hollow and snuffed it up the nostrils. This is quite out of fashion now, and a good thing at that.)

Run the three fingers of your right hand down the thumb along the tendon and along the radius. Now you will find the pulse just inside the edge of the radius where the radial artery lies. Let the fingers slip from the bone onto the artery and you feel the throb of the pulse. We use the pads of the fingers because they are the most sensitive. The thumb can be used almost as well, in spite of the old idea that it had a pulse of its own which interfered.

Practice finding the pulse and practice counting. Try first the right wrist and then the left. See that you can find it at any time, and quickly.

There are other places in the body where the pulse can be counted; any place, in fact, where an artery comes near the surface. For example, inside of the upper arm and behind the egg-shaped biceps muscle, in the neck under the angle of the jaw, in front of the ear, etc.

It is a good thing to know about these pulse-taking spots, for arteries in these positions are most likely to be injured, and a knowledge of their location will guide treatment in emergency.

*January*

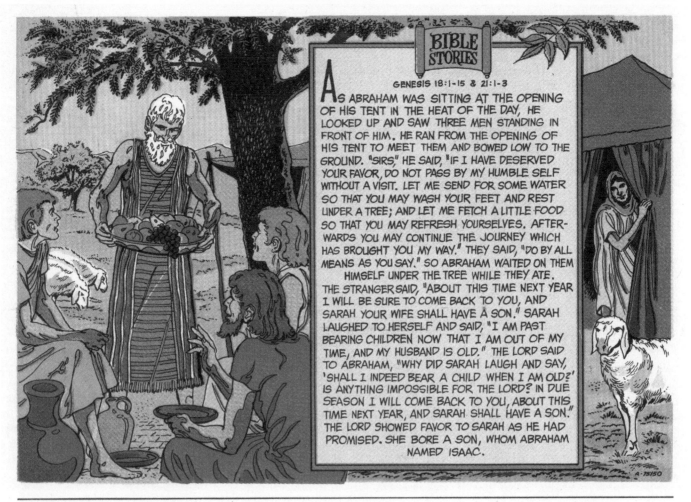

## BIBLE STORIES

### GENESIS 18:1-15 & 21:1-3

As Abraham was sitting at the opening of his tent in the heat of the day, he looked up and saw three men standing in front of him. He ran from the opening of his tent to meet them and bowed low to the ground. "Sirs," he said, "if I have deserved your favor, do not pass by my humble self without a visit. Let me send for some water so that you may wash your feet and rest under a tree; and let me fetch a little food so that you may refresh yourselves. Afterwards you may continue the journey which has brought you my way." They said, "Do by all means as you say." So Abraham waited on them himself under the tree while they ate. The stranger said, "About this time next year I will be sure to come back to you, and Sarah your wife shall have a son." Sarah laughed to herself and said, "I am past bearing children now that I am out of my time, and my husband is old." The Lord said to Abraham, "Why did Sarah laugh and say, 'Shall I indeed bear a child when I am old?' Is anything impossible for the Lord? In due season I will come back to you, about this time next year, and Sarah shall have a son." The Lord showed favor to Sarah as he had promised. She bore a son, whom Abraham named Isaac.

### SCOUTCRAFT

## FLAG SIGNALING

### SEMAPHORE CODE

MOST SCOUTS FIND SEMAPHORE EASIER TO LEARN THAN WIGWAG. WORDS CAN BE SENT FASTER BY THIS METHOD, BUT NUMERALS AND PUNCTUATION MARKS MUST BE SPELLED OUT.

### WIGWAG (INTERNATIONAL MORSE CODE)

WIGWAG'S BIG ADVANTAGE IS THAT IT USES INTERNATIONAL MORSE CODE, WHICH CAN BE USED IN SIGNALING BY LIGHT OR SOUND AS WELL. THOUGH SIGNALMEN CARRY TWO WIGWAG FLAGS, ONLY ONE AT A TIME —CONTRASTING WITH THE BRIGHTNESS OR DARKNESS OF THE BACKGROUND — IS USED FOR SIGNALING

FOR MORE INFORMATION, SEE SIGNALING MERIT BADGE PAMPHLET, BSA NO. 3237

A-75031

# KEEP HEALTHY AT CAMP!

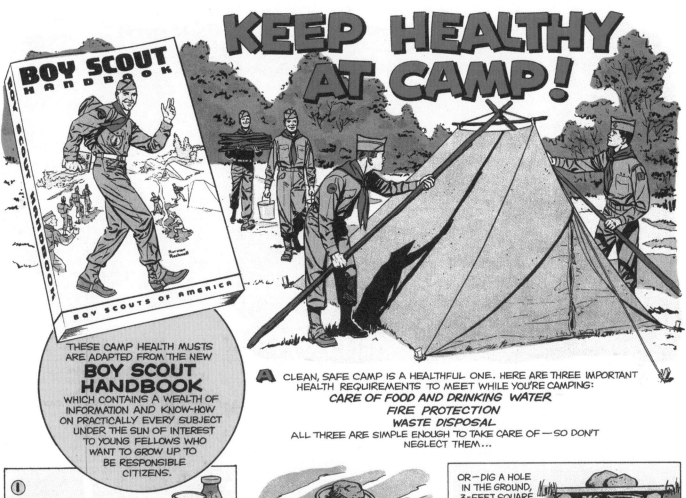

THESE CAMP HEALTH MUSTS ARE ADAPTED FROM THE NEW **BOY SCOUT HANDBOOK** WHICH CONTAINS A WEALTH OF INFORMATION AND KNOW-HOW ON PRACTICALLY EVERY SUBJECT UNDER THE SUN OF INTEREST TO YOUNG FELLOWS WHO WANT TO GROW UP TO BE RESPONSIBLE CITIZENS.

A CLEAN, SAFE CAMP IS A HEALTHFUL ONE. HERE ARE THREE IMPORTANT HEALTH REQUIREMENTS TO MEET WHILE YOU'RE CAMPING:

*CARE OF FOOD AND DRINKING WATER*
*FIRE PROTECTION*
*WASTE DISPOSAL*

ALL THREE ARE SIMPLE ENOUGH TO TAKE CARE OF — SO DON'T NEGLECT THEM...

① FOOD LIKE FRESH MILK AND FRESH MEAT MUST BE KEPT IN A REFRIGERATOR.

② FRESH VEGETABLES, FRUIT, BUTTER, SMOKED MEATS, SUCH AS BACON AND HAM, NEED TO BE KEPT COOL.

③ CANNED AND DRIED FOODS WILL KEEP AT AIR TEMPERATURE.

IF A BROOK RUNS BY YOUR CAMP, YOU CAN KEEP FOODS (IN GROUP 2 AT LEFT) COOL BY PLACING THEM IN A PAIL OR LARGE COOKING POT AND SETTING IT IN THE COOL, RUNNING WATER. PLACE A STONE ON THE COVER TO KEEP IT ON TIGHTLY.

OR — DIG A HOLE IN THE GROUND, 3-FEET SQUARE, 3-FEET DEEP AND LINE IT WITH STONES. COVER IT WITH A STURDY WOODEN COVER OR FLAT ROCK THAT NO PROWLING SKUNK CAN PUSH ASIDE.

THIS KIND OF CACHE WILL KEEP FOOD COOL BUT DO NOT TRY TO KEEP PERISHABLE FOODS WITHOUT AN ICE REFRIGERATOR. IF ICE IS NOT AVAILABLE, DON'T TAKE FRESH MILK OR FRESH MEAT TO CAMP...USE CANNED MEAT AND POWDERED MILK INSTEAD.

TO KEEP ANIMALS FROM GETTING AT DRY FOODS (BREAD, CEREAL, ETC.) HANG FOOD BAG FROM TREE.

KEEP COOKING AND DRINKING WATER IN A COVERED POT, PROTECTED AGAINST DUST, INSECTS AND ANIMALS...

...OR USE A DESERT WATER BAG. HANG IT WHERE IT IS EXPOSED TO THE BREEZE THIS KEEPS IT COOL BY EVAPORATION.

WASTE DISPOSAL IS JUST AS IMPORTANT AS FOOD PRESERVATION. DISPOSE OF GARBAGE BY BURNING TO KEEP FLIES AND ANIMALS FROM GETTING AT IT.

PUT SEVERAL FINGER-THICK STICKS ACROSS THE FIREPLACE. DUMP GARBAGE ON THEM. WHEN THE GARBAGE IS DRY, ADD A FEW STICKS TO FIRE AND IT WILL BURN UP.

BURN OUT EMPTY CANS, SMASH THEM FLAT AND BURY THEM. WASH OUT EMPTY BOTTLES AND BURY THEM.

MAKE A GREASE TRAP FOR DIRTY DISHWATER. DIG A HOLE ABOUT A FOOT DEEP. COVER IT WITH STICKS AND A LAYER OF DRY GRASS. POUR DIRTY WATER THROUGH GRASS WHICH WILL CATCH GREASE. BURN GRASS AFTER EACH USE...PUT ON NEW DRY GRASS.

MAKE A STRADDLE LATRINE. PILE UP DIRT AT ONE END. THROW IN DIRT AFTER EACH USE.

*FILL IN ALL PITS AND HOLES BEFORE YOU LEAVE FOR HOME!*

FIRE PROTECTION IS A HEALTH GUARD, TOO!

BUILD SAFE FIRES; KEEP THEM SAFE; PUT THEM OUT COMPLETELY WHEN FINISHED WITH THEM. HAVE A COUPLE OF LARGE POTS OR TINS FULL OF WATER HANDY AT ALL TIMES.

# Primitive Methods of Making Fire

## A Description of the Ways in which the Eskimos, American Indians, African Savages, Filipinos and Burmans Get Flames Without Matches

### By SCOUT EDWIN SMILEY

Troop 46, Philadelphia, Penn.

HOW many Scouts who make fire by "rubbing" sticks realize that they are using the good old-fashioned Eskimo method? Our American Indians never dreamed of a bow, simply whirling their fire drill between the palms of the hand. But our fat, slant-eyed Eskimo, with a brain made keener by the northern cold, saw the possibilities of a bow. So he took a curved walrus tusk, shaved down about half the ivory and strung it with a loose strip of walrus hide. The drill was inserted in the loop of the hide and held upright in a notch of the fire-board; and presto!—the Eskimo had fire with a few vigorous strokes of the bow, before the Indian could get his hand limbered up.

Ivory Eskimo Bow

walrus hide thong

Not only the bow, but the hand socket owes its origin to the Eskimo. In order to keep the drill upright in boring, he held the pointed, upper end in a hole gouged out of a slippery piece of serpentine or some other hard stone. In addition to the hand socket, the Eskimo developed a most, unique, socket mouthpiece. This was used mainly by the Eskimos of the coast, who relied on small pieces of drift wood to make fire upon. These fragments were often so small that the left hand had to be used to hold the fire board. To hold the drill upright they rigged up a mouthpiece instead of a hand socket. This was a crescent-shaped affair with a bit of hard stone inserted in the wood. No wonder the Eskimos have such powerful, square jaws after biting on this mouthpiece!

Eskimo mouthpiece

soapstone

Even the fire pan of the scout set can be traced back to an Eskimo device for saving his precious "coal" from falling on the snow. To this end he cut a "step" in the edge of his fire board to catch the coal. They even maintained a single coal for as long as two weeks by letting it slowly burn in a rope of woven cedar bark.

Step

But the truly artistic accessory of the Eskimo set, the Scouts have yet to adopt. This is the seal skin bag with its beautiful designs in bead work, which preserved the fire set from the damp snow.

The nearest approach to a bow among our North American Indian was the fire pump. "Pumping fire" sounds strange indeed, yet that is exactly what the Iroquois of New York did. Any epidemic of sickness they would blame on the "Old Fire," so they would get out their fire pump and go through the ceremony of the "New Fire." The principle of this set depends upon the winding and unwinding of a raw-

NOTE.—*The author wishes to thank Dr. Walter Hough, Mr. H. C. Mercer, of Douglastown, and Dr. P. Gordon, of the University of Pennsylvania museum, for their kindly suggestions in regard to this article.*—E. S.

CORRECT POSITION FOR BOWING, WITH ARM HELD TIGHT AGAINST KNEE.

Incidentally, this shows the author of this article who with his sticks has made fire in 21 seconds, as timed by Philadelphia Scout officials.

hide thong about a speared shaped drill. This is done by raising and lowering the "handle" of the pump. The circular disc just above the barb of the spear-like drill steadies it and acts as a flywheel.

Fire Pump
Handle
Disc
Drill

The other tribes of Indians had simply their rotary drill and fire board. The thin drill is spun around by the palms, while the hands exert a certain pressure as they slide down from the thin to the thick lower end of the drill. The trick here is to get the hand from the bottom to the top of the drill without stopping the motion of the drill. Obviously two men are needed for quick work. The longer the drill the better, for the Australian bushman has his drill long enough so that one man is standing, while his partner is kneeling.

There is one set which is cruder, however, than that of the American Indians. It is to be seen today in the Malay Islands, where the natives take a flat board and a pointed drill. They place the board on a tree stump, straddle it with legs apart and plow the drill back and forth in a groove. Strange to say they have acquired skill enough to produce fire in forty seconds.

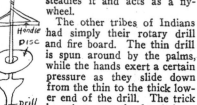
Drill
notch
Malay Set

Curiously, on the coast of East Africa one tribe preserves the trick of fire making as a man's right exclusively. Father secretly imparts the mystery to the son, for they fear that if the women learn the trick of fire making, they will want to run the government and be bosses in general. Evidently it is not the construction of the set that these Africans wish to hide from their women. But it is the art of cutting a notch in the side of the fire board and a particular form in drilling. As a matter of fact the author has found that the art of fire making can be learned only by close observation of an expert at work, rather than by any amount of explanation.

Yet for the few who may be bold enough to do it alone, I would say that the trick is briefly this:—A "V" shaped notch is cut

into the edge of a red cedar board three-quarters of an inch in thickness. To do this, start a hole three-quarters of an inch from the edge of the board with a penknife, then with a pointed drill bore into the hole until black dust appears. The notch is then cut right to the center of the hole. It should also be wider and deeper at the bottom. The drill should be about 16 inches long and three-quarters of an inch thick. When you drill, the punk peels forth and packs in the fire pan. Don't stop until you see the punk becoming black and smoking from the underneath. It is needless to say that unless you have held your drill steady so as not to have broken the coal in the punk you can attribute your first failures to either one of two things. The notch was not cut to the middle of the hole or you didn't bow hard and steady enough.

Let us turn our attention to some methods of fire making which are not drilling.

In the Philippines "strings" of bamboo cut in narrow strips are drawn crosswise over a very soft wood, but a more satisfactory method is good, hard sawing with two pieces of bamboo, as they still do in the Philippines to-day. Here they split a three-inch bamboo in half, cut a small groove across it, then with a sharp-edged bamboostick they saw away until enough punk collects to blow into a coal. Bamboo shavings are packed inside to serve as tinder.

Going back to Burmah we have the most baffling method known. Their fire piston has truly kept scientists guessing, even to-day if you were travelling in the windy jungles of Burmah, your coolie would light his cigarette with his little fire piston if the wind was high. He would get a little grease on the end of the piston to hold a wad of cotton in place, then with a quick snap the piston is forced into the air-tight cylinder, the compressed air becomes hot enough to ignite the cotton so that when the piston is quickly withdrawn the cotton is already aflame.

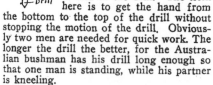
Burmah Fire Piston
Cylinder
string
Cotton

In conclusion, you might be interested to know how these various sets compare in speed. At the International Exposition at St. Louis in 1904 a primitive fire-making contest was held. An Igorote represented the Philippines, an Ainu, Japan, and the Indian stood for America. At the crack of the pistol they all started. The Ainu, with his flint and steel, very readily struck off sparks. But he became so completely bewildered before his audience that he failed to blow up the coal into a flame. The Filipino sawed at his bamboo set, but all in vain. Perhaps he lacked the inspiration of a rolling pin in the hands of his powerful wife, waiting for fire to cook breakfast. So the Indian quietly took his time and produced fire in two minutes.

Philippine Bamboo Saw
Tinder

# EXPLORING THE DESERT IN SUMMER

by E. LAURENCE PALMER

THE DESERT IS A FASCINATING PLACE ABOUNDING IN MUCH MORE LIFE THAN YOU WOULD BELIEVE WHEN YOU FIRST SEE IT. MANY SCOUTS AND EXPLORERS WILL TRAVEL ACROSS THE DESERT EN ROUTE TO AND FROM THE JUBILEE JAMBOREE IN JULY. THOSE WHO EXPLORE THE DESERT DURING THE DAY—THE NIGHT—AT DUSK AND AT DAWN WILL BE WELL REWARDED. FOR THE DESERT IS REALLY TWO WORLDS—ENLIVENED AT NIGHT BY ONE GROUP OF ANIMALS, AND IN THE DAYTIME BY ANOTHER GROUP—WITH A FEW, LIKE THE COYOTE AND JACK RABBIT ACTIVE BOTH DAY AND NIGHT.

SAGUARO OR GIANT CACTUS

OCTILLO

PRICKLY PEAR

BARREL CACTUS

ARGAVE

CHOLLA

ORGAN PIPE CACTUS

SPANISH BAYONET

ARGAVE

JOSHUA TREE

HEDGEHOG CACTUS

THESE ARE SOME OF THE PLANTS THAT GROW IN THE DESERT.

## DAYTIME ANIMALS

RED-TAILED HAWK

JACK RABBIT (AT NIGHT ALSO)

ROAD RUNNER

QUAIL

PRONGHORN

HORNED TOAD

SCORPION

CHUCKWALLA

## NOCTURNAL ANIMALS

ELF OWL

PACK RAT

KANGAROO RAT

KIT FOX

BADGER

## DAY AND NIGHT...

COYOTE

RATTLESNAKE

BILL WALSH

## DENS AND BURROWS

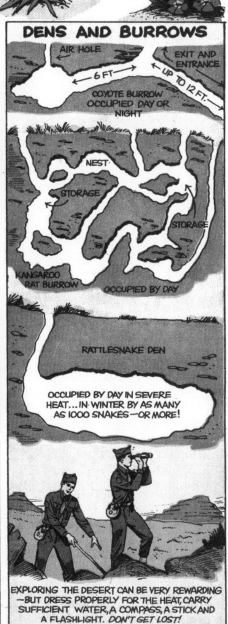

AIR HOLE

EXIT AND ENTRANCE

6 FT

UP TO 12 FT

COYOTE BURROW OCCUPIED DAY OR NIGHT

NEST

STORAGE

STORAGE

KANGAROO RAT BURROW

OCCUPIED BY DAY

RATTLESNAKE DEN

OCCUPIED BY DAY IN SEVERE HEAT...IN WINTER BY AS MANY AS 1000 SNAKES—OR MORE!

EXPLORING THE DESERT CAN BE VERY REWARDING—BUT DRESS PROPERLY FOR THE HEAT, CARRY SUFFICIENT WATER, A COMPASS, A STICK AND A FLASHLIGHT. DON'T GET LOST!

### To Break Large Sticks of Firewood

If you wish to break a large piece of firewood, and you have no hand ax, the following method may often be used,—place your stick in the crotch of a tree (X), B-C equalling the length you wish broken off. Then grasp the stick at A and pull backwards. The pressure at B is so great that the stick is broken there. The longer A-B the more pressure, and therefore the greater likelihood of the stick breaking.—*Paul H. Pfeiffer, California.*

### To Extract Salt from Salt Water

One who camps near a body of salt water can add more zest to the fun if the salt used in cooking is obtained in true huntsman fashion.

Procure a tin can and punch several small holes in the bottom. Nail the can to the limb of a tree and beneath the can fasten a piece of cloth so that it is inclined to the ground. Now fill the can with salt water. The water will fall in drops on the cloth, the capillary action of the cloth will cause it to spread and the wind will dry up the water, leaving a deposit of fine salt on the cloth.

Another method is to drop several pieces of cloth into salt water and then hang them up to dry.—*Jacob Jospe, N. Y.*

### How to Make a Sling Out of a Roller Bandage.

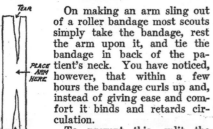

On making an arm sling out of a roller bandage most scouts simply take the bandage, rest the arm upon it, and tie the bandage in back of the patient's neck. You have noticed, however, that within a few hours the bandage curls up and, instead of giving ease and comfort it binds and retards circulation.

To prevent this, split the bandage in the same way that you would a "four tailed bandage," and tie the four ends in back of the injured person's neck.—*Scout Walter A. Kohn, N. Y.*

### A Handy Bicycle Kit.

When a scout goes out on a ride he generally takes along with him his first aid kit, and a sufficient amount of tools to repair a puncture. Some scouts are not

*T*HE Editor will be glad to receive from any reader of BOYS' LIFE, suggestions for this department. If you have discovered ways of doing things that you think might save other people time and trouble, let us hear from you. This department offers you a mighty good chance to do a good turn, don't you think? Address all letters to "Scout Discoveries," BOYS' LIFE, THE BOY SCOUTS' MAGAZINE, 200 Fifth Avenue, New York City.

so lucky as to have their "bikes" equipped with a tool box, while others with this "luck" cannot carry a very large quantity of tools in their tool boxes. But any boy who is handy at tools can readily make one that will be of two-fold service to him.

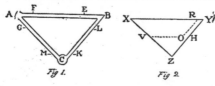

In Fig. 1 ABC represents the frame of a bicycle. To make this tool box, one should get the inside dimensions of this part of the bicycle frame, and get hard wood and measure it to fit the inside of the frame. The letters, F, E, L, K, M, G, are where the cleats should be fastened to the frame, to hold the box in place. Fig. 2 represents the inner section of the box. The upper part (XVHY) is reserved for the various tools. The section marked OR is for a battery, if the light requires any. The lower part marked ZHV is to carry the first aid kit. Both sections are separately opened. On the outside of the box, if the boy is clever with the brush, he can paint his own name and the number and name of his troop or patrol—*Scout Joseph B. Martin, N. Y.*

### How to Make a Drinking Cup.

Scouts in camp and on the hike often find a serious problem in the matter of a suitable drinking receptacle. I gave considerable thought to the subject and finally hit upon a plan for a collapsible cup which may be discarded after immediate use.

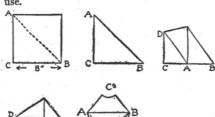

I use the clean part of the wax paper that comes around loaves of bread. A suitable piece of paper eight inches square will be found most satisfactory.

Fold on line A to B (see diagram), then fold A to half way between B and C, then B to D. Then fold the C No. 1 into slot made by the fold B. Then cut C No. 2 as shown in diagram to fit the mouth.—*A Tenderfoot, Conn.*

### To Prevent Losing Buttons and Badges.

Here is a safe way to hold small buttons and badges on a coat which I discovered with the assistance of a friend. About two years ago I joined the Health and Happiness League which an insurance company runs, and upon their sending me some badges I was afraid I might lose them off my coat, so I thought of this idea. Whether anyone else has ever done it I do not know. Directions: Cut off pin of button at X as shown in Fig. A. Then make notch at top of button as shown in Fig. B. Put pin through coat with notch at bottom, press in at notch and turn button around until notch is at top.—*Scout Fred Zener, N. Y.*

### To Keep Warm at Night.

Herewith is a small article that I think I have not seen in the "Scout Discoveries" Department of BOYS' LIFE yet, and one that I believe will be of at least a little value to those who are beginning their overnight hikes.

I went to a harness shop and bought six blanket pins. They are large safety pins, and are sold two for a nickle, but can only be gotten at harness stores at this price. They are willing to sell any number. I take the pins with me on my hikes and use them to pin the bedding down around the edges to prevent it from getting disarranged during the night. On these chilly evenings, it is not very pleasant to awake and find your foot out in the dew! If the pin is stuck through twice, or made to come out on the same side it went through first, there will be no danger of the bed clothes being torn. I have used less than six at a time, but six is a good number.

This is very simple, but is a great help to my scouts and myself. I always take several extra pins along to supply the "first nighters," and to sell to those wishing them.—*Scoutmaster Rollo C. Hester, Indiana.*

**Scout Program:**
## WHAT'S DOWN THERE?

# HOW TO FILLET FISH

**BY DICK PRYCE**

PHOTOGRAPHS BY GENE DANIELS

Featuring Scouts of Troop 95,
chartered to Kaycee Lions Club, Kaycee, Wyo.

Have you ever watched an expert cut fish away from the bones? It's called filleting. In what seems like seconds, the flashing blade has carved two pieces of boneless meat—called fillets—that are ready to cook.

The best part is that there is no messy cleaning job. The head, the entrails, the tail, and the skin are left intact in a single, easily disposable piece. Traditional fish-cleaning methods take a great deal more time. Eliminated are scaling and gutting.

The best tool for filleting is a knife with a thin, sharp, flexible blade. On the market are filleting knives made just for the purpose. Even an expert has trouble with a thick-bladed knife, for the knife needs to bend.

Work on a clean smooth surface. A cutting board is perfect. If you have none, try the blade of a canoe paddle if you're in the wilderness, or a boat paddle. For details of how to fillet, look at the pictures and read the captions.

Fillet and chill fish as quickly as possible. Don't soak the fillets in water. All that will do is remove the juices and the flavor. In most cases there is no need to wash the fillets. Dry with a clean cloth or paper towel, drop into a plastic sack, and put on ice if available.

On a camping trip, why not hand the fillets to a cook? He can dry them with towels, dip in milk or slightly beaten egg, and roll in a mixture of flour and cornmeal. Fry in about $\frac{1}{8}$ of an inch of cooking oil that is not hot enough to smoke. Most panfish require no more than five minutes cooking to a side. ♣

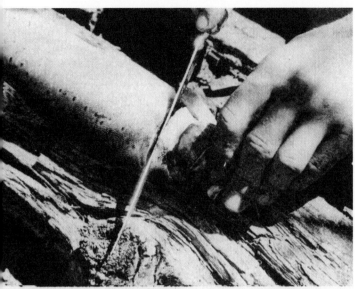

Cut behind the gills to the bone.

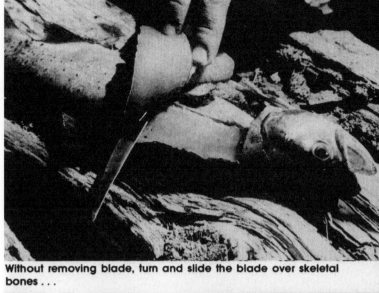

Without removing blade, turn and slide the blade over skeletal bones . . .

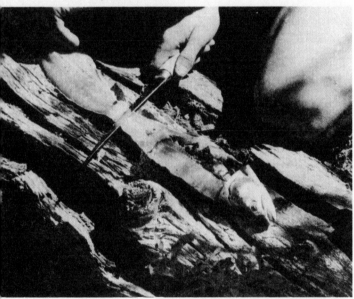

. . . to the tail. Stop. Do not cut through skin. Remove the knife from the fish.

Flop the attached side of the fish over and cut away the bony rib section, and . . .

. . . then insert the blade near the end of the tail and cut the meat away from the skin. Repeat for other side.

Steak for two—there's a hike meal that always goes over big!

# Your hike dish or camp meal is soon cooked when you follow these safe and easy steps of

# FIRE MAKING

## By WILLIAM HILLCOURT

IN RECENT YEARS more than nine million acres of woodland have been laid waste by fire *each year* and many people have been killed fighting these fires.

Just imagine: an area the size of Massachusetts and New Jersey together destroyed by a fire in a single year! You wouldn't want a Scout blamed for having caused any of such destruction! That's why it's important for all Scouts to know how to build a safe fire, and how to put it out correctly after use.

PREPARE YOUR FIRE SITE—A fire should be built only on a spot where you have complete control over it and from which it cannot spread. To be certain of this, clean the site down to mineral ground—sand, gravel, clay, or rock—and clear it for a diameter of ten feet of any material that may catch fire from a flying spark— dry grass, dry leaves and twigs, pine needles, and the like.

MAKING THE FIRE—Your fire should fit your pots or pans. That means a fire just big enough for the job—a tiny one for a quick hike dish, a larger one for a complete camp meal.

When you have used a match, break it in two—that's a Scout tradition. The breaking itself is not the point—the point is that you can't break a match without touching the burned part, and you'll then know quickly enough whether the match is OUT or not.

From the moment a fire is lit until it is extinguished, someone must watch it to be positive that it is under control. To be extra safe, have a container of water on hand near the fire.

EXTINGUISHING THE FIRE—When used, a fire is extinguished until it is not just out, but DEAD OUT! Dip your fingers in the water container and sprinkle water on the embers. Stir them up with a stick and sprinkle again. Turn over half-burned twigs and wet them down on all sides. Wet the ground around the fire.

If water is scarce, work mineral dirt into the ashes, then stir until the last ember is out. Test for this with your hand. A fire is not OUT until you are SURE that the last spark has been KILLED.

Some campers place two small sticks cross-wise over the dead ashes of their fire to show that it was out when they left. It is even better to bury the wet ashes and make the spot look so natural again that no one will know that you were there.

## HIKE FIRE

A hike fire is a small fire—not any bigger than absolutely necessary for cooking a simple dish. But even a small fire can spread unless you make certain that there's no flammable material around that'll catch a spark. So—as in all fire making—clean the fire site down to plain dirt or rock and clear away flammable material.

Place two stones on the ground a few inches apart. Lay a short stick across them from one to the other—this is your "draft stick." Place tinder under the draft stick, and lean small twigs and then larger twigs against the draft stick. Light the tinder—in a short while you have exactly the kind of fire you need: flames for boiling, coals for broiling. Move one more stone next to the other two to make a triangular support for your pot or pan.

When you've finished, put out the fire until every ember is dead.

## FIRE PLACES

When cooking in camp for the patrol, you'll want a fireplace. The kind you make depends on where you are.

If you are camping on a spot where there are plenty of rocks, you can build a simple *rock fireplace*. Arrange the rocks in two rows, close enough together to support your utensils.

In an open spot, a *trench fireplace* is good. Dig it just wide enough to fit your pots, about one foot deep, two to three feet long. Widen the windward end to catch the wind for good draft. The trench fireplace is especially good on a windy day.

In the woods, you may be able to make a *hunter's fireplace*. For this, you need two logs of hardwood, two to three feet long, six to nine inches thick. Roll them up on either side of your fire, about six inches apart. Build a crane for hanging your pots.

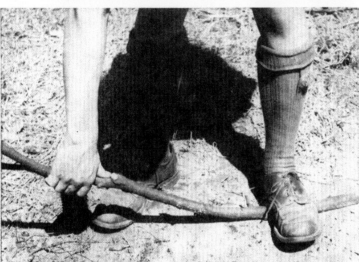

## FIREWOOD

You need three things for fire making: tinder, kindling, fuel.

*Tinder* is the kind of stuff that flares up when you touch it with the flame from a match. Outer bark of old grape vines and cedars is good. So are the "feathers" of white and yellow birches, and the bark from a DEAD gray birch. On the trunks of pines, firs, and spruces you'll find tiny twigs suitable for tinder.

*Kindling* catches the flame from the tinder and ignites the heavier fuel. In dry weather, you can use sticks you find on the ground. But far better is "squaw wood"—dead branches still on the trees. Take branches only that snap easily.

For *fuel*, break or chop heavier branches into pieces of suitable length for your fire—about a foot or so. Collect all the wood you need for your cooking fire before you start the fire.

# Wild Fruit: Yours for the Picking

### BY ESTER HAUSER LAURENCE

**Eat 'em off the vine, or try these tasty recipes.**

**W**ild fruits grow just about everywhere, even in large cities. Learn to identify them, and treat yourself to some of nature's goodies.

*Mulberry* trees spring up like weeds. Pick the berries while they are still red and firm. (When deep purple, they are too soft and too sweet.) If the berries take a little pull to get them loose, they are likely to be tart and tasty. Don't worry about the little green stem that comes off with the berry. You can eat the berry—stem and all. If you make a pie, maroon juice will cover the stems. Mulberry is found in the eastern one-third of the country.

*Elderberry* is another wonderful "weed." It grows all over the countryside (and fortunately, the cityside, too). In the late spring, look along roadsides and railroad tracks for tall bushes with high-standing clusters of white blossoms, to make elderberry blossom fritters. When the blossoms turn into purple berries, make elderberry-sumac jelly. Elderberries are found from Nova Scotia to Manitoba, and south to Georgia, Louisiana, and Texas.

*Sumac* is a beautiful bush with tall ferny leaves and high stalks of small, hard, red berries. Some people think sumac is a poisonous plant. There is a swamp variety with white berries that gives a skin rash. But many people plant harmless sumac in their yards because the leaves turn such a brilliant red in the fall.

To make sumacade, pick whole stems of berries. Harvest them in the early fall when the berries feel dry. Wash the berries outside with your garden hose. Then barely cover the stems with water and let them soak for several hours or overnight. As the berries soak, the water will darken and take on a lemony taste. When you think it's strong enough, strain the juice, using at least two thicknesses of cloth to eliminate fine hairs. Then sweeten your sumacade to taste. Sumac is found generally in the northeastern United States.

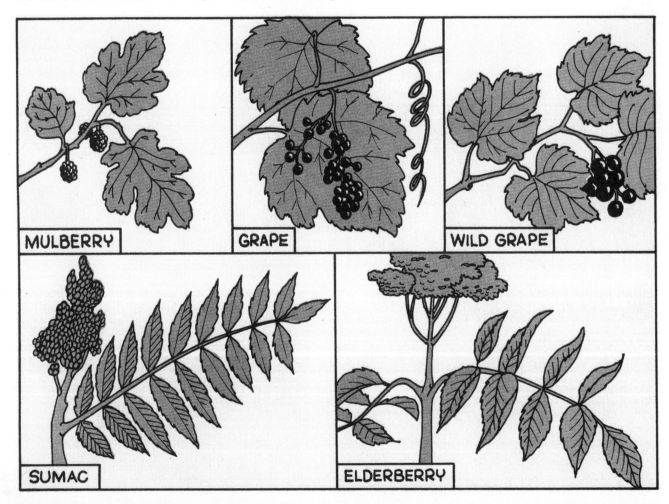

MULBERRY

GRAPE

WILD GRAPE

SUMAC

ELDERBERRY

*Wild cherries* come in two varieties. The native black cherry makes great jelly; the choke cherry will make your mouth pucker. Both grow on similar-looking trees, but you can learn to tell them apart without tasting. The good-tasting kind grow on either side of a stringer. The bitter ones grow in clusters, attached singly, close to the branch. Wild black cherries are found from the East Coast to the Great Plains.

You can find *wild grapes* growing along fences, up and around trees and bushes, or up the sides of buildings. The young leaves are delicious to eat! A Greek cookbook will tell you how to prepare them.

The bunches of grapes are deep purple when ripe in late summer or early fall. (You can continue to pick after frost.) They are not very good eaten off the vine because they are sour and mostly seed. But wild grape juice mixed one part grape to two parts sumac juice, and sweetened, is delicious. So is grape-sumac jelly. Wild grapes are found in the eastern half of the U.S. ♣

### RECIPES
### Elderberry Blossom Fritters

*Make a batter of: one cup flour, one tablespoon sugar, one teaspoon baking soda, two eggs, and ½ cup milk. Dip elderberry blossoms to coat with batter. Deep fry. Drain on paper towels, and roll in powdered sugar, or serve with butter and syrup.*

### Wild Fruit Jelly

*Soak sumac berries to make lemon-flavored juice. Strain juice through two or more thicknesses. Do not sweeten. Cover elderberries, wild grapes, or wild cherries with cold water in large pot. Heat to boiling, stir and mash berries. Allow to cool and strain the juice. Combine one pint (two cups) sumac juice and one pine other juice in large pot. Add one package powdered pectin. Stir to dissolve. Bring to boil. Add four cups of sugar all at once. Cook at full boil (a boil that cannot be stirred down) for one minute. Skim off foam and pour immediately into hot, sterile jars. Seal with paraffin or canning lids. Makes about 4 jars.*

### Mulberry Pie

*Prepare pie crust for eight-inch, two-crust pie. Line pan with bottom crust. Preheat oven to 425 degrees. Mix together in bowl: three cups mulberries (barely ripe, stems and all), ⅔ cups sugar, two tablespoons cornstarch, ¼ teaspoon allspice, one tablespoon lemon juice. Put berry mixture into crust. Dot top with one tablespoon butter or margarine. Cover with top crust. Make vents for steam. Sprinkle top of pie lightly with cinnamon sugar.*

*Bake for 35 minutes.*

# Secret signs of the hobo

## BY DONALD RUTHERFORD

There is a secret sign language in this country—not as common as it once was—written on sidewalks, fences, and walls. It's the private code of the hobos, those "knights of the road" who once roamed the nation in great numbers.

When hobos needed money, they looked for work, which—they proudly pointed out—distinguished them from "tramps" or "bums." Otherwise they enjoyed a life of freedom. They appeared here during the last half of the 19th century when the railroads were extending their tracks across the continent. When a job was finished, workers were given their pay and laid off on the spot. With bedrolls slung across shoulders and a few possessions clutched in their hands, they clambered aboard the first freight train headed toward civilization. These men became known as hobos.

They soon developed their own secret sign language. They left messages for others who would pass through after them. For instance, a fat cat told a hobo that the woman in the house was generous. If the cat was followed by several small triangles, she would fall for a hard-luck story.

A railroad locomotive followed by a circle with an arrow through it pointed to the nearest railroad, the hobos' main method of travel.

A hobo, seeing a large, block "T" on the sidewalk in front of a house, knew that he could get a meal there, in exchange for some work.

More than 40 secret signs were used by hobos to pass on information vital to survival. Nobody knows where the signs came from. Perhaps they originated in Europe, where the tradition of the wandering worker goes back to the time of Julius Caesar.

One hobo explained the crucial difference between himself, a tramp and a bum:

"A hobo is a migratory worker, a tramp is a migratory non-worker and a bum is a stationary non-worker."

A hobo who was ill usually could not afford to go to a doctor, so he looked for a house marked with a sign resembling a giant lowercase letter R. He knew that the people who lived there would care for him.

The signs at the bottom of the page are but a few of the many the hobos used. One told a wandering hobo that it was OK to sleep in the hayloft. Another assured him of a safe camp, where he could rest, wash, and mend his clothes.

In towns that didn't want hobos around, the police would often throw the wanderers in jail. Hobos warned their compatriots with an appropriate sign. They even had a sign that urged immediate departure.

Other symbols warned of a fierce dog, a policeman, a man with a gun, a good guy, and a dishonest man. A series of symbols showed the character of a resident in a house.

The hobo population in the U.S. reached a peak during the Great Depression of the 1930's. One man in five was unable to find a job. Then came World War II, and with plenty of jobs available, the hobo population began to get smaller. After the war, the railroads lost freight business to motor trucks and reduced the number of trains. The remaining hobos found it much more difficult to travel.

The hobos still have their own organization—Tourist Union No. 63. It had almost two million members at one time. Since 1900 the hobos have held an annual convention in Britt, Iowa. Each year their numbers are fewer, for the hobos are a truly vanishing breed. ◆

*Typical hobo signs: generous housewife; railroad this way; get meal for work; people care for sick; OK to sleep in loft; a safe camp; danger.*

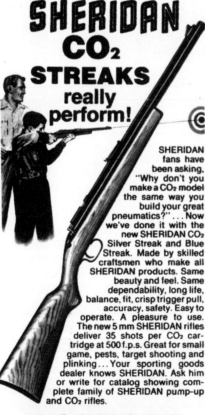

*You're not welcome here; get out quickly; fierce dog; policeman; a man with a gun lives here; a fine man lives here; a dishonest man lives here.*

# HUNTING SAFETY RULES

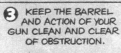

# BOYS' LIFE
# SCOUTS IN ACTION

"**A** True Story of Scouts in Action" is the most popular feature in *Boys' Life,* and it first appeared in cartoon form in January 1947. Originally titled "Scouts in Action" (and still used casually), the cartoon appeared occasionally until 1950, when it became a regular feature. The cartoon received its current title in 1952, along with a full color treatment.

Actions of Scouts appearing in the feature are based on medals awarded by the BSA's National Court of Honor. The court awards four medals in two categories: lifesaving and meritorious action. Three medals are lifesaving awards: Heroism Award (saving or attempting to save a life at minimum or no risk to self), Honor Medal (unusual heroism while saving or attempting to save a life at considerable risk to self), and Honor Medal with Crossed Palms (unusual and extraordinary skill or resourcefulness in saving or attempting to save a life at extreme risk to self). The fourth award, for meritorious action, is the Medal of Merit, earned for outstanding use of Scout skills and ideals but it does not have to be a rescue or involve personal risk.

The cartoon originally featured Scouts who had been awarded one of the four medals by the BSA. In 1953 the format changed, and Scouts were encouraged to send in stories of their own heroism (verified by their Scout leader) to receive $10 if chosen. In November 1958, the feature reverted to medal winners and has remained with that format ever since. "Scouts in Action" began appearing monthly in 1954 and has continued to this day, with an occasional interruption for such special features as "Scouters in Action," in which a medal was awarded to a Scoutmaster.

Since its inception in 1911, *Boys' Life* has recorded the heroic deeds of Scouts, sometimes under the headings of "News and Notes" or "Roll Call." Since membership was growing and space was limited, the magazine developed the representative "Scouts in Action" idea. The Heroism Award and Honor Medal were instituted in 1923, and the Honor Medal with Crossed Palms in 1938. The Medal of Merit was instituted in 1946. (A National Certificate of Merit has been awarded for a significant act of service deserving special national recognition since 1989.) Any youth or adult member of the Boy Scouts of America may receive each of these awards.

Several hundred medals are awarded annually, and *Boys' Life* editors pick a cross section of rescues, locations, medals, Scouts, and ranks to highlight in the cartoon. The feature is so popular (readers overwhelmingly say that it is their favorite part of the magazine—edging out jokes and cartoons) that an additional page, "More S.I.A." was added in September 2007, featuring two more stories.

Dozens of heroic and meritorious actions are displayed in the magazine each year, but hundreds are not. "Scouts in Action" exists to remind readers that these young men represent all boys who use skills learned in Scouting, boys who may never get a medal for saving a life or risking their own but are rewarded in a different way—with the satisfaction that comes from being prepared for a brave act.

### A TRUE STORY OF SCOUTS IN ACTION

**He Pulled His Dad And Uncle From Icy Waters!**

Alex Trollop, 13, his dad and his uncle were careful to test the ice before a day of fishing at Twin Valley Lake in Wisconsin. But before Alex's uncle could begin drilling a hole, he fell through.

Alex's dad attempted a rescue but fell through as well. Alex carefully made his way back to the pier.

Alex threw seat cushions to his dad and uncle to use as flotation devices, then ran to their truck and found a rope.

Alex looped the rope around a pole on the dock and pulled his dad from the water. Alex and his dad then pulled his uncle out.

The three warmed themselves with the truck's heater before driving back to the park entrance.

The Trollops alerted park rangers to the dangerous ice conditions. No one was hurt during the incident.

Star Scout Alex P. Trollop, a member of Troop 337, chartered to Hope Lutheran Church, Mineral Point, Wis., received a Heroism Award for his actions.

"Scouts In Action" subjects come from the National BSA Court of Honor. If you know of an act of heroism that should be recognized, contact your local BSA council office for a lifesaving or meritorious award application. Note: Consult approved safety guidelines as actions depicted here may not precisely follow standard procedures.

SIA ON THE WEB www.boyslife.org
Audio, Photos & More!

### A TRUE STORY OF SCOUTS IN ACTION
by ALSTEN

Explorer "Sonny" (Houston) Sansome and a few other explorers were working on various projects in his back yard. They were all members of Sea Explorer Ship 194, B.S.A., sponsored by Columbus Lodge III, B2OE, Columbus, Georgia.

One of the explorers had been removing pitch from his clothing with gasoline... Be careful with that gas...don't get too close to the fire!

But in a moment of carelessness, he walked too close to the flames... Suddenly...

He became panicky and started to run about wildly...

Sonny dashed after him, downing him with a flying tackle...

Having no other means of extinguishing the flames, Sonny covered the boy with his own body, beating out the flames and disregarding his own burns.

For his quick thinking and heroic action at considerable risk to himself, Explorer Sonny Sansome was presented with a gold wrist watch by the members of Columbus Lodge No. III.

Another brave example of Scout training and know-how in handling emergencies properly!

### HE LOST CONTROL OF THE CHAIN SAW
A TRUE STORY OF SCOUTS IN ACTION

On Jan. 21, 1983, Edward D. Eklof was cutting wood when he lost control of his chain saw, which cut his chin and neck. The out-of-control saw struck Mr. Eklof's jugular vein and vagus nerve, and he began bleeding heavily.

When he collapsed in the yard of his home, his son Jeff, 12, quickly ran inside to call an ambulance.

Then he returned to his father with towels to pack the wound. A friend, First Class Scout John Richart, 13, ran to get his mother, a registered nurse. Jeff continued to apply direct pressure until Mrs. Richart arrived. Then John assisted her until the ambulance came.

Jeff, a Second Class Scout in Troop 132, chartered to the Messiah Lutheran Church, Cottage Grove, Wis., saved his father's life and demonstrated the value of his Boy Scout training. He earned a Heroism Award for his lifesaving action.

A83347

### Struck by Lightning!
A TRUE STORY OF SCOUTS IN ACTION

On Aug. 20, 1981, while camping in the Wind River Mountains, in Wyoming, Scouts Matt Gregson, 15, and Pat Dietch, 14, were struck by lightning when a thunderbolt hit a nearby tree and followed an underground root to their tent.

Stunned by the lightning bolt and able to move only one hand, Matt Gregson called for help. At first, Pat moaned, but then he was silent. With great effort, Matt placed the hand he could move over Pat's face and found Pat was not breathing.

Matt struggled to move his hand so he could apply pressure to Pat's lower ribcage.

Pat soon gasped for air and started breathing on his own.

Despite burns to his chest and leg and considerable pain, Matt responded alertly and aided his friend. For his selfless service, Matt Gregson, a Star Scout in Troop 308, chartered to the United Methodist Church, Pocatello, Idaho, was awarded the Medal of Merit.

A82363

**A TRUE STORY OF SCOUTS IN ACTION**

# GRIZZLY ATTACK!

ON SEPTEMBER 23, 1979, MICHAEL C. NIEDEREE, 25, WAS HUNTING IN THE NAVAJO CANYON NEAR ALAMOSA, COLO., WITH GUIDE ED WISEMAN. SOON AFTER THE TWO SEPARATED, NIEDEREE HEARD WISEMAN YELL AND A BEAR GROWL. OUT OF NIEDEREE'S SIGHT, A 350-POUND GRIZZLY WAS ATTACKING WISEMAN, WHO WAS ARMED ONLY WITH A HUNTING BOW.

THE BEAR MAULED WISEMAN, ITS CLAWS RAKING THE MAN FROM SHOULDER TO LEG, AND ITS JAWS CRUSHING ONE LEG BONE. IN DEFENSE, WISEMAN STABBED THE GRIZZLY IN THE JUGULAR VEIN WITH A HAND-HELD ARROW, KILLING HIM. WHEN NIEDEREE REACHED WISEMAN, HE QUICKLY CONTROLLED THE BLEEDING, DRESSED THE WOUNDS, AND TREATED FOR SHOCK. HE BUILT A FIRE AND USED HIS OWN CLOTHING TO COVER THE VICTIM.

IN DARKNESS, NIEDEREE RODE HIS HORSE BACK TO THE BASE CAMP, WHERE HE SENT A RIDER FOR HELP. HE THEN RETURNED TO GUARD THE VICTIM UNTIL DAYLIGHT, WHEN A HELICOPTER TOOK WISEMAN OUT.

A80379

BOY SCOUTS OF AMERICA

FOR SAVING LIFE

EAGLE SCOUT MICHAEL NIEDEREE IS A MEMBER AT-LARGE OF THE KANZA COUNCIL AND LIVES IN GREAT BEND, KANS. HIS COURAGE AND DETERMINATION EARNED HIM THE HONOR MEDAL.

A TRUE STORY OF **SCOUTS IN ACTION**
by ALSTEN

AROUND NOON ON JANUARY 20, 1963, FIFTEEN-YEAR-OLD THOMAS J. HAYES, HIS FATHER, LT. FRANK X. HAYES, U.S.N., HIS MOTHER AND HIS YOUNGER SISTER THELMA, WERE ON THEIR WAY TO CHURCH. SUDDENLY, AS THEY DROVE PAST THE WINCHESTER BOAT BASIN AT CHASE CREEK, MD., TOM CRIED OUT...

DAD! STOP THE CAR! I JUST SAW A MAN FALL THROUGH THE ICE.

THE VICTIM WAS JACK BASS, A 60-YEAR-OLD FISHERMAN FROM BALTIMORE.

TOM HOPPED OUT OF THE CAR, GRABBED A 15-FOOT BOARD LYING NEARBY AND CRAWLED OUT ON THE ICE PUSHING THE BOARD BEFORE HIM TOWARD BASS, WHO WAS FLOUNDERING IN THE ICY WATER ABOUT A HUNDRED FEET OFF SHORE.

TOM HAD CALLED TO THREE OTHER FISHERMEN WHO HAD BEEN TRYING UNSUCCESSFULLY, TO AID THE VICTIM BY CASTING FISHING LINES TO HIM. THE ICE WAS CRACKING AND THE MEN DIDN'T DARE GO FAR OUT FROM SHORE. IT WAS SO SLIPPERY THAT TOM HAD TO TAKE OFF HIS SHOES TO GET ENOUGH TRACTION TO PUSH THE BOARD AHEAD OF HIM.

WHEN TOM REACHED BASS, THE MAN'S HANDS WERE TOO NUMB TO GRAB THE BOARD. TOM WORKED IT UNDER BASS, GOT HOLD OF HIM AND DRAGGED HIM BACK TO SHORE.

ONE OF THE FISHERMEN DROVE BASS TO A DOCTOR. WHEN THE HAYES' VISITED HIM A FEW DAYS LATER THEY FOUND HIM WELL ON THE WAY TO RECOVERY.

I OWE MY LIFE TO YOU, TOM.

MY SCOUT TRAINING SURE PAID OFF THAT TIME!

HE DID A BRAVE DEED!

FOR HIS COURAGE AND QUICK RESPONSE IN THIS EMERGENCY SITUATION, SCOUT THOMAS J. HAYES WAS AWARDED THE CERTIFICATE OF MERIT BY THE NATIONAL COURT OF HONOR, BOY SCOUTS OF AMERICA.

TOM WAS ALSO PRESENTED WITH A RECOGNITION PLAQUE BY THOMAS W. TRICE, PRESIDENT OF THE BALTIMORE AREA COUNCIL, BOY SCOUTS OF AMERICA.

AT THE TIME OF THIS INCIDENT, SCOUT HAYES WAS A MEMBER OF TROOP 933, SPONSORED BY ST. ANNE'S EPISCOPAL CHURCH. HIS FAMILY HAS SINCE BEEN TRANSFERRED BY THE NAVY TO THE HAWAIIAN ISLANDS WHERE HE NOW LIVES.

THE BOY SCOUTS OF AMERICA
UPON RECOMMENDATION OF THE NATIONAL COURT OF HONOR HEREBY AWARDS TO
THOMAS J. HAYES
This Certificate of Merit
IN RECOGNITION OF MERITORIOUS ACTION AND EXTENDS CONGRATULATIONS ON HIS DEMONSTRATION OF SCOUT TRAINING, SCOUT CHARACTER, AND SCOUT IDEALS
ISSUED ON THIS DAY OF

**Ice Rescues...**

DURING WINTER, MANY PEOPLE LOSE THEIR LIVES BY FALLING THROUGH ICE. IF YOU WITNESS SUCH AN ACCIDENT, ACT QUICKLY, BUT THINK CLEARLY FIRST...OR YOU, TOO, MAY BE A VICTIM.

IF YOU MUST CROSS A FROZEN BODY OF WATER ALONE— CARRY A STRONG POLE WITH YOU. THEN IF YOU BREAK THROUGH, YOU'VE GOT A CHANCE TO SAVE YOURSELF.

**SELF RESCUE...**
IF YOU BREAK THROUGH ICE WHILE ALONE—DON'T PANIC! TRY TO REACH SOLID ICE AS QUICKLY AS YOU CAN!

EXTEND YOUR ARMS OUT OVER THE ICE TO DISTRIBUTE AND SUPPORT YOUR WEIGHT.

KICK YOUR FEET...GET YOUR HIPS TO EDGE OF ICE...ROLL SIDEWAYS AND AWAY FROM HOLE.

**SINGLE RESCUE...**
PUSH ANY STOUT OBJECT TO VICTIM. LIE FLAT, LEGS WIDE APART.

IF VICTIM IS TOO WEAK OR NUMB TO HOLD ON, AS A LAST RESORT, CRAWL OUT ON PLANK OR LADDER TO GRAB HIM.

USING A ROPE... SECURE ONE END TO TREE OR ROCK. DON'T GET PULLED IN YOURSELF.

**HUMAN CHAIN...**
SAFEST RESCUE METHOD. NO. 1 MAN GRASPS VICTIM, NO. 2 HOLDS ONTO FEET OF FIRST MAN WITH ONE HAND, HELPS PROGRESS WITH OTHER. NO. 3 HANGS ONTO NO. 2, DIGS IN WITH SKATES OR HEELS. WORKS BACK-WARD WHEN NO. 1 YELLS "PULL."

ALL MOVE BACKWARD TO PULL VICTIM OUT ON HIS STOMACH.

A TRUE STORY OF

SCOUTS IN ACTION

Life Scouts Tyler Moody and Chris Crowder, both 14, and assistant Scoutmaster Jeff Disler decided to turn in after a day of rock climbing in Lost Valley, Ark., on Oct. 10, 1998. Suddenly, a female climber burst into their camp.

THERE'S A BOY TRAPPED ON A CLIFF!!

Another climber, Matt Richardson, 14, had frozen with fright on a ledge 200 feet above the Buffalo River. The woman couldn't get anyone to help until she came across the Scouts and their adult leader.

The three hauled 100 pounds of climbing gear four miles and forded the river to reach the base of the cliff. Their helmet lanterns were their only light as they began to climb toward Matt.

Topside, Matt's father and other climbers had been holding the rope connected to the 210-pound teenager for hours.

Once the three reached the top, Tyler and Chris rigged pulleys to Matt's line. Then everyone began pulling.

We'll never be able to pull him up!

We have to!

Finally, they lifted Matt to safety. Park rangers, who were eventually alerted, arrived as the group began descending the mountain.

Tyler Moody and Chris Crowder—members of Troop 241, chartered to Kirk of the Hills Presbyterian Church, Tulsa, Okla.—each received an Honor Medal for saving Matt's life.

BOY SCOUTS OF AMERICA

Text and art by Grant Miehm

A TRUE STORY OF
SCOUTS
IN ACTION
BY ALSTEN

Suddenly the fire broke out in the dry forest!

ON MAY 15, 1975, SCOUTS RODNEY GAGNON (17), MARK GAGNON (15), AND LEON BARON (14), ASSISTANT SCOUTMASTER PAUL FLYNN, AND TROOP COMMITTEE MEMBER REGINALD BOYNTON WERE PITCHING TENTS IN A WILDERNESS CAMPSITE IN BAXTER STATE PARK, MAINE, FOR A TROOP CAMPOUT THE NEXT DAY.

RODNEY, CARRYING TENT POLES ALONG A TRAIL TO THE CAMPSITE, SAW SMOKE IN THE WOODS WHERE HE KNEW NONE SHOULD BE. HE YELLED TO THE OTHERS, AND THEY ALL HURRIED TO CHECK THE SOURCE OF THE SMOKE.

THE SCOUTS FOUND THAT THE FIRE, WHICH WAS GROWING RAPIDLY, THREATENED TO LEAP ACROSS A SMALL ROAD INTO A LARGE AREA OF EXTREMELY DRY FALLEN TIMBER AND BECOME A MAJOR FOREST FIRE.

MR. BOYNTON IMMEDIATELY DROVE TO A RANGER STATION A FEW MILES AWAY TO GET HELP. MEANWHILE, THE OTHER SCOUTS BATTLED THE BLAZE WITH CANVAS TENT BAGS, AND CUT DOWN BRUSH AND TREES IN THE PATH OF THE FIRE WITH AXES AND A CHAINSAW. ABOUT 45 MINUTES LATER, PARK RANGERS ARRIVED WITH FIRE-FIGHTING EQUIPMENT. THE SCOUTS WORKED SHOULDER-TO-SHOULDER WITH THE RANGERS UNTIL THE FIRE WAS BROUGHT UNDER CONTROL 2½ HOURS LATER.

RODNEY GAGNON

LEON BARON

MARK GAGNON

FOR THEIR PROMPT, COURAGEOUS, AND EFFICIENT ACTION THAT KEPT THE FIRE FROM FLARING INTO A MAJOR DISASTER, SCOUTS RODNEY J. GAGNON, MARK GAGNON, AND LEON L. BARON WERE AWARDED THE MEDAL OF MERIT BY THE NATIONAL COURT OF HONOR, BOY SCOUTS OF AMERICA.

A76227

RODNEY, MARK, AND LEON ARE MEMBERS OF TROOP 57, MILLINOCKET BAPTIST CHURCH, MILLINOCKET, MAINE.

**A TRUE STORY OF SCOUTS IN ACTION**

# Buried by an Avalanche!

TRACY TACKER AND DUANE MASONHEIMER, BOTH 14, WERE SKIING NEAR TRACY'S HOME IN WATERHALL TOWNSHIP, PA., ON JAN. 20, 1978, WHEN TRACY WAS BURIED UNDER AN AVALANCHE OF SNOW AT THE BOTTOM OF A 50-FOOT BLUFF!

DUANE, WHO WAS AT THE TOP OF THE HILL, RUSHED DOWN AND BEGAN SEARCHING WHERE HE THOUGHT TRACY WAS BURIED. NOT FINDING ANY SIGN, HE QUICKLY LOOKED AROUND AND SPOTTED TRACY'S FINGERS ABOVE THE SNOW. DUANE THEN RAPIDLY AND CALMLY DUG AWAY THE SNOW TILL TRACY'S HEAD WAS CLEAR.

UNABLE TO DIG ANY DEEPER WITH HIS BARE HANDS, AND CERTAIN THAT TRACY WAS ABLE TO BREATHE, DUANE RACED TO HIS FRIEND'S HOUSE AND RETURNED WITH HELP!

DUANE'S FAST, CLEARHEADED ACTION SAVED TRACY FROM POSSIBLE SUFFOCATION AND FROSTBITE, AND EARNED HIM THE MEDAL OF MERIT FROM THE NATIONAL COURT OF HONOR, BOY SCOUTS OF AMERICA. DUANE MASONHEIMER IS A FIRST CLASS SCOUT IN MINSI TRAILS COUNCIL TROOP 59, CHARTERED TO THE SHEPHERD OF THE HILLS LUTHERAN CHURCH, LEHIGH VALLEY, PA.

A79028

**A TRUE STORY OF SCOUTS IN ACTION**

# Fall from a 40~foot Cliff!

WHILE HIKING WITH OTHER SCOUTS IN THE RED ROCK CANYON AREA OF RED ROCK STATE PARK, NEV., ON JAN. 30, 1977, SCOUT CHRIS BURT FELL ABOUT 40 FEET DOWN A CLIFF, LANDING ON ROCKS.

HIS SENIOR PATROL LEADER, FIRST CLASS SCOUT SEBASTIAN SPINEDI, 13, QUICKLY TOOK CHARGE. HE SENT OTHER SCOUTS FOR ADULT HELP AND CLIMBED DOWN TO CHRIS.

SEBASTIAN CALMED CHRIS'S FEARS AND TREATED HIM FOR SHOCK. HE STOPPED THE BLEEDING FROM A HEAD CUT, AND SPLINTED CHRIS'S FRACTURED LEG WITH TREE BRANCHES BY USING A NECKERCHIEF AND BELT. THEN HE STAYED WITH HIM UNTIL ADULT LEADERS ARRIVED.

SEBASTIAN'S FAST, CLEARHEADED ACTION AVERTED A TRAGEDY, THANKS TO HIS SCOUT TRAINING. SEBASTIAN IS A FIRST CLASS SCOUT, TROOP 92, LOUIS E. ROWE P.T.A., LAS VEGAS, NEV. HE WAS AWARDED THE MEDAL OF MERIT BY THE NATIONAL COURT OF HONOR.

A79342

# Fire! Fire!—Then the Scouts!

Little Stories About Quick Thinking and Quick Action

### A FOREST FIRE AND A BLOCKED ROADWAY

All fires are the same size at the start, says ex-chief Croker, of the New York Fire Department. Three troops from Poughkeepsie, N. Y., were so fortunate as to discover a forest fire which was just getting under way. It was attacked vigorously and soon extinguished.

No sooner was the fire out than a large tree which had been weakened by it fell squarely across the road. Scouts were

then despatched to the nearest farmhouse for axes, and when they returned chopped in relays until the tree had been cut into sections and rolled to the side of the road.

The owner of the land appeared just as as the work was completed. His gratitude was warmly expressed.

### MOUNTAIN ABLAZE

Troop No. 5, of Montclair, N. J., had just adjourned after a talk on forestry and fighting fire when a near-by mountain was discovered to be covered with flames. The scouts were immediately reassembled. Some were sent for old brooms, others cut brush, and all were soon busy putting out the fire.

It is hard to understand how a water works could catch fire, but this happened in Mount Joy, Pa. Perhaps someone was making some of that cent-and-a-half per gallon substitute for gasoline. Troop No. 3 has charge of the hook and ladder wagon of the local fire company, and it is their duty to see that this apparatus gets to the scene of the fire in due time. They arrived, and after turning over the apparatus to the fire company, made coffee for the firemen.

Troop No. 32, of Cleveland, Ohio, while on its way home from a parade, responded to a fire alarm and helped the police in keeping the crowd back from a burning factory.

In Mansfield, Mo., Troop No. 1 was taking second class tests when a forest fire was discovered. This was promptly extinguished.

Staunton, Va., scouts assisted in a fire prevention campaign directed by experts from Richmond. They distributed literature and pushed the clean-up and paint-up idea.

### FIRE CALL FOR SCOUTS

The fire department of Bath, Me., has a special call "66" for the boy scouts, who are summoned whenever their services are needed.

Boy scouts were among the volunteers who helped to fight a spectacular blaze in upper Manhattan, New York. The structure was on a hill 200 feet above the

street. A short distance away is the House of Mercy with 200 children, the Magdalen Home with 200 girls, and the House of Rest with 30 inmates. All these buildings were emptied promptly and without panic. Only one piece of apparatus was able to get near the fire and the hose had to be run 3,500 feet.

Troops Nos. 1 and 5 of Scranton, Pa., saved several frame dwellings by putting out a forest fire.

At a fire at McAnally Flats, Knoxville, Tenn., the scouts were so badly needed that they were permitted to stay out of school all day long and carry pails of water to pour on threatened roofs.

A newly organized troop at Kulpmont, Pa., did its first public service by extinguishing a mountain fire which threatened to do much damage to timber lands.

Dwellings in Nashville, Tenn., which were threatened by fire in an adjoining building, were saved by the prompt work of the scouts.

### JITNEYS TO THE FIRE

The scoutmaster of Troop No. 15, of Atlantic City, N. J., judged from the reflection in the sky following a fire alarm that his boys would be needed. He loaded them into jitneys and took them to the scene of the fire. A few minutes later they took charge of street traffic and directed the steady stream of automobiles which had to be turned into the side streets. Two teams of scouts obtained buckets and cups and supplied the fire engineers and stokers with drinking water. Others helped the police in maintaining fire lines.

The mayor of Salamanca, New York, has approved the organization of the local scouts for the purpose of fighting forest fires. They will be ready whenever they are needed.

Co-operation between the fire department and the scouts in Leavenworth, Kansas, has helped to keep down the fire loss. With three buildings ablaze the fire department was pushed to its utmost, but with the help of the scouts was able to prevent the fire from spreading.

A $20,000 blaze in New Haven, Conn., was only prevented from doing more damage by the help which the scouts gave the firemen. While the firemen were working on the blazing buildings, details of the scouts with axes cut away burning timbers and saved sheds and barns. They also assisted in taking forty or more horses out of burning barns.

### BAKED EGGS FROM INCUBATOR

A chicken farmer in Newington, Conn., had an incubator. The heating apparatus got out of order and after baking the eggs, started to burn the house. The boy scouts interfered at this point and saved the situation.

Two scouts in Rochester, N. Y., heard an explosion and saw flames burst from a house near by. They seized a sprinkling can of water and hurried to the fire. They discovered that a man had set a pan of varnish on a gas stove and that it had exploded. A fire alarm was turned in and first aid was administered to the varnish boiler.

# A TRUE STORY OF SCOUTS IN ACTION

## He Pulled His Dad And Uncle From Icy Waters!

Alex Trollop, 13, his dad and his uncle were careful to test the ice before a day of fishing at Twin Valley Lake in Wisconsin. But before Alex's uncle could begin drilling a hole, he fell through.

Alex's dad attempted a rescue but fell through as well. Alex carefully made his way back to the pier.

Alex threw seat cushions to his dad and uncle to use as flotation devices, then ran to their truck and found a rope.

Alex looped the rope around a pole on the dock and pulled his dad from the water. Alex and his dad then pulled his uncle out.

The three warmed themselves with the truck's heater before driving back to the park entrance.

The Trollops alerted park rangers to the dangerous ice conditions. No one was hurt during the incident.

Star Scout Alex P. Trollop, a member of Troop 337, chartered to Hope Lutheran Church, Mineral Point, Wis., received a Heroism Award for his actions.

TEXT AND ART BY GRANT MIEHM

**SIA ON THE WEB**
www.boyslife.org
Audio, Photos & More!

**A TRUE STORY OF SCOUTS IN ACTION**

# HE LOST CONTROL OF THE CHAIN SAW

ON JAN. 21, 1983, EDWARD D. EKLOF WAS CUTTING WOOD WHEN HE LOST CONTROL OF HIS CHAIN SAW, WHICH CUT HIS CHIN AND NECK. THE OUT-OF-CONTROL SAW STRUCK MR. EKLOF'S JUGULAR VEIN AND VAGUS NERVE, AND HE BEGAN BLEEDING HEAVILY.

WHEN HE COLLAPSED IN THE YARD OF HIS HOME, HIS SON JEFF, 12, QUICKLY RAN INSIDE TO CALL AN AMBULANCE.

THEN HE RETURNED TO HIS FATHER WITH TOWELS TO PACK THE WOUND. A FRIEND, FIRST CLASS SCOUT JOHN RICHART, 13, RAN TO GET HIS MOTHER, A REGISTERED NURSE. JEFF CONTINUED TO APPLY DIRECT PRESSURE UNTIL MRS. RICHART ARRIVED. THEN HE AND JOHN ASSISTED HER UNTIL THE AMBULANCE CAME.

JEFF, A SECOND CLASS SCOUT IN TROOP 132, CHARTERED TO THE MESSIAH LUTHERAN CHURCH, COTTAGE GROVE, WIS., SAVED HIS FATHER'S LIFE AND DEMONSTRATED THE VALUE OF HIS BOY SCOUT TRAINING. HE EARNED A HEROISM AWARD FOR HIS LIFESAVING ACTION.

A83347

## A TRUE STORY OF SCOUTS IN ACTION
### BY ALSTEN

## TRAPPED...ON THE TOOTH OF TIME!

SCOUTS MARK KNOWLES AND BOB LOVE WERE NEAR THE TOP OF THE TOOTH OF TIME—A HIGH ROCK PEAK AT PHILMONT SCOUT RANCH ON THE OLD SANTA FE TRAIL NEAR CIMARRON, NEW MEXICO.

SUDDENLY BOB LOST HIS FOOTING ON THE BARE, WINDSWEPT ROCK!

MARK LUNGED AND MANAGED TO STOP HIM JUST BEFORE BOB TUMBLED OVER A LEDGE TO THE GORGE 40 FEET BELOW.

ACTING COURAGEOUSLY AND CAREFULLY CHOOSING SECURE HAND- AND FOOTHOLDS, MARK PULLED HIS FRIEND BOB TO SAFETY.

FOR MAKING THIS RESCUE, EAGLE SCOUT MARK W. KNOWLES WAS AWARDED THE HONOR MEDAL BY THE NATIONAL COURT OF HONOR, BOY SCOUTS OF AMERICA.

MARK IS A MEMBER OF TROOP 589, SPONSORED BY THE MOORE JUNIOR HIGH PTA, TYLER, TEX.

# A True Story of Scouts in Action
# He Floated Unconscious in the Lake!

ON JULY 2, 1993, KENNETH HOFFMAN, 12, OF TUCSON, ARIZ., JOINED A CANOE RACE AT CAMP RAYMOND NEAR FLAGSTAFF. EACH CANOE HELD ABOUT EIGHT SCOUTS, WHO PADDLED ONLY WITH THEIR HANDS. DURING THE RACE, KEN'S CANOE FILLED WITH WATER AND SANK, THEN FLOATED BACK TO THE SURFACE. THE BOAT STRUCK JAMES FROST, 12, IN THE HEAD AND BACK.

KEN FOUND JAMES FLOATING, UNCONSCIOUS. ANOTHER CANOEIST PULLED ON JAMES'S PANT LEG, CAUSING JAMES TO GO UNDERWATER AND CHOKE. KEN CALLED TO JAMES BUT GOT NO RESPONSE. SO KEN GRASPED THE BACK OF JAMES'S LIFE JACKET AND TOWED HIM TO SHORE, 60 FEET AWAY. JAMES WAS TAKEN BY AMBULANCE TO THE HOSPITAL AND WAS RELEASED THAT EVENING. HIS HEAD AND BACK WERE BRUISED, BUT THANKS TO KEN, TRAGEDY HAD BEEN AVOIDED.

TENDERFOOT SCOUT KENNETH D. HOFFMAN, OF TROOP 297 — OPERATED BY SANTA CATALINA CATHOLIC MISSION, CATALINA, ARIZ.— RECEIVED A HEROISM AWARD.

# A TRUE STORY OF SCOUTS IN ACTION
### BY ALSTEN

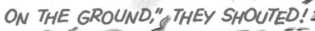
"STOP RUNNING AND ROLL ON THE GROUND," THEY SHOUTED!

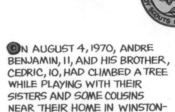

ON AUGUST 4, 1970, ANDRE BENJAMIN, 11, AND HIS BROTHER, CEDRIC, 10, HAD CLIMBED A TREE WHILE PLAYING WITH THEIR SISTERS AND SOME COUSINS NEAR THEIR HOME IN WINSTON-SALEM, N.C.

ANDRE CALLED DOWN TO HIS COUSIN, JEROME ROBINSON, TO STOP LIGHTING MATCHES. JEROME DID NOT LISTEN BUT RAN INTO THE HOUSE AND BROUGHT OUT SOME GASOLINE.

SOME OF THE GASOLINE SPILLED ON JEROME'S ARM AND LEG.

JEROME STRUCK ANOTHER MATCH AND IMMEDIATELY FLAMES LEAPED UP AND SET HIS ARM AND LEG ON FIRE.

HEARING JEROME'S SCREAMS, ANDRE AND CEDRIC LEAPED DOWN AND YELLED TO HIM TO STOP RUNNING AND ROLL ON THE GROUND.

JEROME DID, BUT THE FLAMES AND PAIN CAUSED HIM TO GET UP AND START RUNNING AGAIN. ANDRE TACKLED HIM AND ROLLED HIM OVER, PUTTING OUT THE FLAMES. THEN HE LAY ON HIM TO PREVENT HIM FROM RUNNING AGAIN.

A-71-991

MEANWHILE, CEDRIC DASHED TO THE HOUSE, GOT A HOSE AND SPRAYED JEROME WITH COOL WATER.

WHEN JEROME GOT TO THE HOSPITAL, HE HAD SECOND AND THIRD DEGREE BURNS OVER MOST OF HIS LEFT SIDE.

FOR THEIR QUICK THINKING, WEBELOS SCOUT ANDRE BENJAMIN AND CUB SCOUT CEDRIC R. BENJAMIN WERE AWARDED MEDALS OF MERIT BY THE NATIONAL COURT OF HONOR, BOY SCOUTS OF AMERICA.

BOTH ARE MEMBERS OF PACK 868, SPONSORED BY THE FIRST BAPTIST CHURCH, WINSTON-SALEM, N.C.

# A TRUE STORY OF
# SCOUTS
# IN ACTION
### BY ALSTEN

*HORRIFIED, THE SCOUTS SAW THE CLIMBER'S ROPE BREAK!*

ON JUNE 24, 1972, TODD FRYE, 25, AN EXPERIENCED MOUNTAIN CLIMBER, WAS CLIMBING ALONE IN ROCK CANYON NEAR PROVO, UTAH.
WHILE RAPPELING DOWN THE NORTH FACE OF "Y" MOUNTAIN HIS ROPE APPARENTLY BROKE AND HE FELL ABOUT FORTY FEET, SUFFERING SERIOUS INJURIES.

ACROSS THE CANYON FROM "Y" MOUNTAIN A GROUP OF SCOUTS, PRACTICING SECOND AND FIRST CLASS SCOUTING SKILLS UNDER THE DIRECTION OF SENIOR PATROL LEADER BOWMAN BARLOW, JR., 15, SAW HIM FALL.

SCOUT BARLOW DIRECTED ONE OF HIS SCOUTS TO STAY AND KEEP THE FALLEN MAN IN SIGHT, SENT OTHERS FOR HELP, AND WITH HIS FATHER, SCOUTMASTER BOWMAN BARLOW, SR., AND ANOTHER SCOUT, STARTED OFF TO HELP THE ACCIDENT VICTIM.

THEN YOUNG BARLOW SAW A CAR COMING UP THE CANYON ROAD AND SENT THE SCOUT TO ASK THE DRIVER TO GO FOR HELP. BOWMAN AND HIS FATHER CONTINUED TO CLIMB ON THEIR RESCUE MISSION.

LUCKILY, THE CAR WAS A POLICE PATROL. THE POLICE OFFICERS RADIOED THE COUNTY SHERIFF, WHO IMMEDIATELY DISPATCHED A TEAM OF EXPERIENCED MOUNTAIN RESCUERS. WITH THEIR SOPHISTICATED CLIMBING EQUIPMENT, THE TEAM REACHED MR. FRYE FIRST AND BROUGHT HIM DOWN.

ALTHOUGH HE DID NOT PHYSICALLY RESCUE THE BADLY INJURED MAN, HIS COOLNESS IN ORGANIZING THE STEPS THAT BROUGHT ABOUT THE RESCUE, PLUS HIS DETERMINATION TO REACH AND AID MR. FRYE, WERE OUTSTANDING ACTIONS; THEREFORE, EAGLE SCOUT BOWMAN O. BARLOW, JR., WAS AWARDED THE MEDAL OF MERIT BY THE NATIONAL COURT OF HONOR, BOY SCOUTS OF AMERICA.

BOWMAN IS A MEMBER OF TROOP 51, SPONSORED BY THE PROVO COMMUNITY CHURCH, PROVO, UTAH.

A-73/64

# Struck by Lightning!

ON AUG. 20, 1981, WHILE CAMPING IN THE WIND RIVER MOUNTAINS, IN WYOMING, SCOUTS MATT GREGSON, 15, AND PAT DIETCH, 14, WERE STRUCK BY LIGHTNING WHEN A THUNDERBOLT HIT A NEARBY TREE AND FOLLOWED AN UNDERGROUND ROOT TO THEIR TENT.

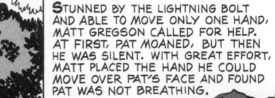

STUNNED BY THE LIGHTNING BOLT AND ABLE TO MOVE ONLY ONE HAND, MATT GREGSON CALLED FOR HELP. AT FIRST, PAT MOANED, BUT THEN HE WAS SILENT. WITH GREAT EFFORT, MATT PLACED THE HAND HE COULD MOVE OVER PAT'S FACE AND FOUND PAT WAS NOT BREATHING.

MATT STRUGGLED TO MOVE HIS HAND SO HE COULD APPLY PRESSURE TO PAT'S LOWER RIBCAGE.

PAT SOON GASPED FOR AIR AND STARTED BREATHING ON HIS OWN.

DESPITE BURNS TO HIS CHEST AND LEG AND CONSIDERABLE PAIN, MATT RESPONDED ALERTLY AND AIDED HIS FRIEND. FOR HIS SELFLESS SERVICE, MATT GREGSON, A STAR SCOUT IN TROOP 308, CHARTERED TO THE UNITED METHODIST CHURCH, POCATELLO, IDAHO, WAS AWARDED THE MEDAL OF MERIT.

A8226.3

# A TRUE STORY OF SCOUTS IN ACTION

## He Saved His Friend After An Electric Shock!

Peter Wysocki, 14, and Jimmie Stevens, 13, were walking near Peter's home in Detroit, Mich., when Jimmie brushed against a fallen power line and received a severe electric shock.

Jimmie was knocked unconscious, and his clothing burst into flames. Peter smothered the fire as the power line swung away.

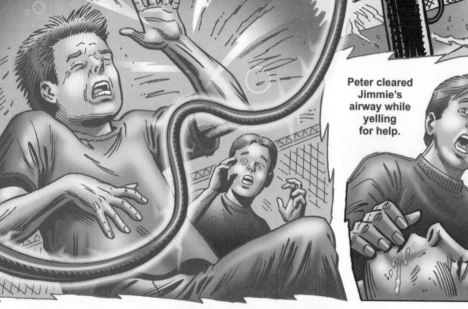

Peter cleared Jimmie's airway while yelling for help.

As a nearby resident called 9-1-1, Peter dragged Jimmie away from the power line and flagged down a passing motorist …

… then ran home to get his father.

Peter returned with his dad as the police and fire department arrived. An ambulance took Jimmie to a hospital. He underwent several surgeries on his hand over the next few months.

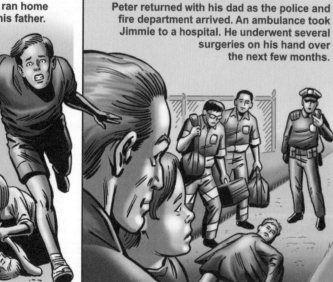

First Class Scout Peter Wysocki, a member of Troop 401, chartered to St. James of Redford Church, Redford, Mich., received an Honor Medal for his actions.

TEXT AND ART BY GRANT MIEHM

*"Scouts In Action" subjects come from the National BSA Court of Honor. If you know of an act of heroism that should be recognized, contact your local BSA council office for a lifesaving or meritorious award application. Note: Consult approved safety guidelines as actions depicted here may not precisely follow standard procedures.*

## S.I.A. ON THE WEB
www.boyslife.org
**Audio, Photos & More!**

A TRUE STORY of SCOUTS IN ACTION

by ALSTEN

EXPLORER "SONNY" (HOUSTON) SANSOME AND A FEW OTHER EXPLORERS WERE WORKING ON VARIOUS PROJECTS IN HIS BACK YARD. THEY WERE ALL MEMBERS OF SEA EXPLORER SHIP 194, B.S.A., SPONSORED BY COLUMBUS LODGE III, B.P.O.E., COLUMBUS, GEORGIA.

ONE OF THE EXPLORERS HAD BEEN REMOVING PITCH FROM HIS CLOTHING WITH GASOLINE...

BE CAREFUL WITH THAT GAS...DON'T GET TOO CLOSE TO THE FIRE!

BUT, IN A MOMENT OF CARELESSNESS, HE WALKED TOO CLOSE TO THE FLAMES... SUDDENLY...

HE BECAME PANICKY AND STARTED TO RUN ABOUT WILDLY...

SONNY DASHED AFTER HIM, DOWNING HIM WITH A FLYING TACKLE...

HAVING NO OTHER MEANS OF EXTINGUISHING THE FLAMES, SONNY COVERED THE BOY WITH HIS OWN BODY, BEATING OUT THE FLAMES AND DISREGARDING HIS OWN BURNS.

FOR HIS QUICK THINKING AND HEROIC ACTION AT CONSIDERABLE RISK TO HIMSELF, EXPLORER SONNY SANSOME WAS PRESENTED WITH A A GOLD WRIST WATCH BY THE MEMBERS OF COLUMBUS LODGE NO. III.

ANOTHER BRAVE EXAMPLE OF SCOUT TRAINING AND KNOW-HOW IN HANDLING EMERGENCIES PROPERLY!

A TRUE STORY OF SCOUTS IN ACTION
by ALSTEN

ONE DAY LAST MARCH, ELEVEN-YEAR-OLD STEPHEN SURASKY WAS SLEDDING ON WALLS' POND, AT LAKEVIEW, LONG ISLAND. SUDDENLY, THE THIN ICE GAVE WAY AND STEPHEN PLUNGED INTO THE FREEZING WATER...

TWO THIRTEEN-YEAR OLD SCOUTS, DAVID McAULEY AND GARY LEEDS, WERE ALSO SLEDDING ON THE POND...

GARY, LOOK! THAT BOY JUST BUSTED THROUGH THE ICE!

WE'D BETTER HAUL HIM OUT IN A HURRY, DAVE. THAT WATER LOOKS COLD!

ONE OF YOU GO CALL THE FIRE DEPARTMENT!

I'LL DO IT!

IT'S STEVE! TAKE IT EASY, STEVE. WE'LL GET YOU OUT!

DAVE STRETCHED OUT ON THE ICE, PUSHING A SLED TOWARD STEPHEN, WHILE GARY PULLED ON A ROPE FASTENED TO THE SLED. AS GARY PULLED ON THE ROPE, THE STRAIN WAS TOO GREAT...

GRAB THE SLED, STEVE, AND HANG ON...

SUDDENLY, THE ROPE SNAPPED AND DAVE LOST HIS GRIP ON THE SLED. STEPHEN WAS SO FROZEN, HE COULDN'T LET GO.

DAVE MANAGED TO GRASP THE SLED AGAIN AND WITH GARY HOLDING ON TO HIS LEGS, SLOWLY PULLED STEPHEN ON TO THE SOLID ICE...

I'VE GOT YOU THIS TIME, STEVE. PULL, GARY... THAT'S IT...OUT YOU COME!

JUST AS THE TWO SCOUTS HAD PULLED STEPHEN TO SAFETY, THE LAKEVIEW FIRE DEPARTMENT ARRIVED AND TOOK THE NEARLY FROZEN BOY HOME, WHERE HE QUICKLY RECOVERED FROM HIS ICY ORDEAL.

DAVID McAULEY IS A MEMBER OF TROOP 269, OF LAKEVIEW, SPONSORED BY EAGLE AVENUE, P.T.A. GARY LEEDS IS A MEMBER OF TROOP 336, OF LYNBROOK, SPONSORED BY ST. JAMES METHODIST CHURCH.

YOU KNOW, GARY, WITHOUT OUR SCOUT RESCUE TRAINING, WE'D NEVER HAVE BEEN ABLE TO PULL STEVE OUT OF THERE.

YOU CAN SAY THAT AGAIN. WITHOUT THAT KNOW-HOW, WE'D PROBABLY HAVE BUSTED THROUGH THE ICE WITH HIM!

# A TRUE STORY OF
# SCOUTS IN ACTION

By ALSTEN

MICHAEL CHUDY WAS DELIVERING PAPERS ON DEC. 15, 1966, IN SALAMANCA, N.Y. JUST AS HE WAS PASSING THE RAILROAD YARDS, LOUD SCREAMS RANG OUT. HE LEAPED OFF HIS BIKE TO INVESTIGATE.

ONE LEG OF THE GIRL'S SLACKS HAD BEEN TORN OFF BY A VICIOUS DOG. MICHAEL GRABBED THE PIECE OF TORN CLOTH AND USED IT TO PULL THE DOG AWAY FROM THE GIRL.

A RAILROAD POLICEMAN RAN UP AND RADIOED THE MUNICIPAL POLICE FOR HELP.

THE SNARLING DOG TRIED REPEATEDLY TO ATTACK THE GIRL UNTIL SHE WAS SAFELY INSIDE THE POLICE CAR.

LATER, WHEN THE POLICE COMMENDED MICHAEL FOR HIS BRAVERY, THEY TOLD HIM THE DOG BELONGED TO THE OTHER GIRL. NO ONE COULD ACCOUNT FOR HIS SUDDEN FURY.

FOR HIS WILLINGNESS TO HELP A PERSON IN DISTRESS, SCOUT MICHAEL CHUDY WAS AWARDED THE MEDAL OF MERIT BY THE NATIONAL COURT OF HONOR, BOY SCOUTS OF AMERICA.

MICHAEL IS A MEMBER OF TROOP 98, SPONSORED BY SALAMANCA FORD MOTORS, SALAMANCA, N.Y.

69/97

**A TRUE STORY OF SCOUTS IN ACTION**
BY ALSTEN

*SUDDENLY THE EXPLOSION ROCKED THE PLAYGROUND!*

ON MARCH 27, 1973, DANIEL REAVER, 12, WAS PLAYING WITH A DYNAMITE BLASTING CAP DURING RECESS AT MOTHER SETON ELEMENTARY SCHOOL, EMMITSBURG, MD.

WITHOUT WARNING, THE CAP EXPLODED, BLOWING TWO FINGERS OFF DANIEL'S LEFT HAND AND SEVERELY BURNING HIS RIGHT HAND!

LARRY KEHNE, 12, WHO WAS PLAYING SOCCER NEARBY, RAN TO DANIEL AND SAW THE BOY'S HANDS WERE BLEEDING BADLY.

HE IMMEDIATELY REALIZED HE COULDN'T CONTROL THE BLEEDING FROM DANIEL'S LEFT HAND BY DIRECT PRESSURE, SO HE SQUEEZED ON THE PRESSURE POINT ON DANIEL'S UPPER ARM TO SLOW THE FLOW OF BLOOD.

AT THE SAME TIME, HE SHOUTED TO BYSTANDERS TO CALL FOR AN AMBULANCE, AND DIRECTED A CLASSMATE, LENNY ZENTZ, IN GIVING FIRST AID TO DANIEL'S BURNED AND BLEEDING RIGHT HAND.

FOR HIS COOLNESS AND SKILL IN PREVENTING AN UNFORTUNATE ACCIDENT FROM POSSIBLY BECOMING A FATAL TRAGEDY, SCOUT LARRY KEHNE WAS AWARDED THE MEDAL OF MERIT BY THE NATIONAL COURT OF HONOR, BOY SCOUTS OF AMERICA.

LARRY IS A MEMBER OF TROOP 284, AMERICAN LEGION POST 121, EMMITSBURG, MD.

A-74367

A TRUE STORY of SCOUTS IN ACTION
by ALSTEN

IT WAS JUST ABOUT 7 A.M. ON FRIDAY, JUNE 11, 1965. THE QUIET LITTLE TOWN OF SANDERSON IN THE SOUTHWEST PART OF TEXAS WAS BEGINNING TO STIR AS ITS PEOPLE BEGAN GOING ABOUT THEIR DAILY CHORES.

SUDDENLY, WITHOUT WARNING, A DEVASTATING WALL OF WATER SWEPT DOWN THE NORMALLY DRY SANDERSON CANYON CARRYING DEATH AND DESTRUCTION ON ITS FOAMING CREST!

WITHIN MINUTES BOY SCOUTS OF TROOP 166 AND EXPLORERS OF POST 160 GATHERED AT THE NEW ELEMENTARY SCHOOL WHICH WAS JUST OUTSIDE OF THE FLOOD AREA.

THERE THEY HELPED SET UP A TEMPORARY INFIRMARY AND SUPPLY CENTER FOR THE FLOOD VICTIMS THAT BEGAN POURING IN.

SINCE THE ENTIRE COMMUNICATION SYSTEM WITHIN AND OUT OF SANDERSON WAS DESTROYED, THE SCOUTS SERVED AS MESSENGERS—A DIFFICULT BUT MOST IMPORTANT OPERATION.

THE EXPLORERS WADED, EVEN SWAM IN SOME CASES, LOCATING INJURED AND TRAPPED PEOPLE, CARRYING AND HELPING THEM TO SAFETY.

AS THE INJURED WERE BROUGHT IN, THE SCOUTS GAVE THEM FIRST AID, HELPED SERVE FOOD AND PERFORMED ALL SORTS OF NECESSARY TASKS.

FOR SEVERAL DAYS THE SCOUTS WORKED FROM DAYLIGHT AND FAR INTO THE NIGHT, STOPPING ONLY TO GRAB A BITE TO EAT NOW AND THEN.

WHEN THE FLOOD WATERS RECEDED THE SCOUTS PITCHED IN TO HELP IN THE VAST CLEANUP JOB. AN ESTIMATED 54 HOMES HAD BEEN DESTROYED, 36 RECEIVED MAJOR DAMAGE, 133 MINOR DAMAGE, 18 HOUSE TRAILERS WERE DESTROYED AND 18 BUSINESSES DAMAGED. SEVENTEEN KNOWN DEAD WERE COUNTED, BUT SO MANY OTHERS WERE REPORTED MISSING THAT THE ACTUAL NUMBER OF LIVES LOST MAY NEVER BE KNOWN.

THE TOWNSPEOPLE HAD NOTHING BUT PRAISE FOR THE JOB THESE SCOUTS HAD ACCOMPLISHED...

I SERVED IN THE SUPPLY CENTER—IF I SENT WORD THAT I NEEDED 10 BOYS TO HELP...IN A FEW MINUTES I HAD 10 BOYS!

THEY SURE LIVED UP TO THEIR MOTTO—"BE PREPARED"—THEY DIDN'T HAVE TO WAIT TO GET ORGANIZED, THEY WERE READY TO GO IMMEDIATELY!

I'VE NEVER SEEN A HARDER WORKING CREW! THEY'D KEEP GOING UNTIL WE HAD TO CALL A HALT TO THE OPERATION!

SCOUTING CERTAINLY HELPED OUR TOWN IN THIS DISASTER. THOSE BOYS REALLY WORKED! THEY SAVED 20-25 CHILDREN ALONE BESIDES MANY INJURED AND ELDERLY PEOPLE. WITHOUT THESE TRAINED AND WILLING SCOUTS THE DEATH TOLL WOULD HAVE BEEN TRAGICALLY HIGHER!

POST 160 AND TROOP 166, CONCHO VALLEY COUNCIL, SAN ANGELO, TEX.